RALLYING CRIES

Three Plays
by
Eric Bentley

Other Dramatic Works by Eric Bentley

Orpheus in the Underworld *(libretto, Program Publishing Company, 1956)*

A Time to Die *and* **A Time to Live** *(two plays, Grove Press, 1970)*

The Red White and Black *(a "political demonstration," Liberation, 1970)*

Expletive Deleted *(the drama of the White House tapes, Win, 1974)*

The two preceding titles were both published as a whole issue of a
magazine. **Roaring All Day Long** appeared as an item in the anthology
New Directions 16, 1957, and **Before the Un-American Committee**
appeared as an item in the anthology *Break Out!,* edited by James
Schevill, Swallow Press, 1973.

RALLYING CRIES

Three Plays by
Eric Bentley

Are You Now Or Have You Ever Been

The Recantation of Galileo Galilei

From the Memoirs of Pontius Pilate

THE NEW REPUBLIC BOOK COMPANY, INC.
Washington, D.C.

Published in the United States of America in 1977 by
THE NEW REPUBLIC BOOK COMPANY, INC.
1220 Nineteenth St., N.W.
Washington, D.C. 20036

Library of Congress Cataloging in Publication Data

Bentley, Eric Russell, 1916-
    Rallying cries : three plays

    CONTENTS: Are you now or have you ever been.—The recantation of Galileo
Gaililei.—From the memoirs of Pontius Pilate.
    1. Blacklisting of entertainers—United States—Drama. 2. Galilei, Galileo, 1564-
1642—Drama. 3. Pilate, Pontius, 1st. cent.—Drama. I. Bentley, Eric Russell, 1916-
    Are you now or have you ever been. 1977. II. Bentley, Eric Russell, 1916-
    The recantation of Galileo Galilei. 1977. III. Bentley, Eric Russell,
1916-   From   the   memoirs   of   Pontius   Pilate.   1977.   IV.   Title
PS3552.E548A19 1977   812'.5'4   77-1973
ISBN 0-915220-23-7
ISBN 0-915220-24-5 pbk.

Printed in the United States of America

Acknowledgments

Before each play is given a list of those who put on the first production: Let this serve as acknowledgment of their indispensable help. And let me add a word of thanks to those not listed here who staged subsequent productions.

Are You Now grew out of my book *Thirty Years of Treason* (Viking Press, 1971), which was the brainchild of my friend Ann Hancock. The play had been rejected by every New York management in sight when Robert Brustein picked it up for Yale Rep within hours of having received a copy in the mail. In the Yale production Allan Miller played Abe Burrows. He then not only played Burrows in the subsequent New York production (Theatre of Riverside Church under Arthur Bartow) but, along with Joe Stern and Kathleen Johnson, brought about a Hollywood production that ran for fourteen months and had an offshoot in a Washington, D.C., production at Ford's Theatre.

Galileo has been on my mind since I first had a script of Brecht's play in my hands in the forties. I sketched some scenes of my own about him in the fifties, and New Directions published one in their annual *New Directions* anthology. The world premiere of my play took place in Detroit in 1973 under the inspired direction of the late Don Blakely (Wayne State University Theatre).

My Galileo studies were guided (more than he realized, I am sure) by a leading Galileo authority, Stillman Drake. It was the idea of Cynthia Merman (Harper and Row) that my Galileo play, as well as *Are You Now*, should first be published as separate, lavishly illustrated editions, as they were.

Yale Rep offered a staged reading of the Pilate play in the spring of 1976. From there it went to full production by The Buffalo Project through the enthusiastic interest of Saul Elkin of SUNY-Buffalo—an institution that, incidentally, had let me offer a seminar in New Testament studies, as had Queen's College (CUNY) earlier. Financial help was provided by the New York State Council on the Arts and by the Office of Advanced Drama Research, Arthur Ballet, Director.

No one has read the whole literature of New Testament studies; a single lifetime would not suffice. I can only say I started as early as I could read, heard some of the "stories of Jesus" even earlier, and have never stopped reading about him, or thinking about him, since. The twentieth-century scholars from whom I have learned include Robert Eisler, Alfred Loisy, Charles Guignebert, Marcello Craveri, Hugh J. Schonfield, S.G.F. Brandon, and Joel Carmichael. One can learn as much, and perhaps I have, from artists like Bernard Shaw (Preface to *On the Rocks*), George Moore *(The Brook Kerith)*, Sholem Asch *(The Nazarene)*, and Robert Graves *(King Jesus)*.

Other debts are acknowledged in the separate dedications of the plays.

E.B.

Fall 1976

Contents

[*The Dreyfus Affair was*] *one of those moral crises that become starting points and high-water marks, and leave traditions and rallying cries and new forces behind them.*

—William James

The struggle is always between the individual and his sacred right to express himself on the one hand, and on the other hand the power structure that seeks conformity, suppression, and obedience. At some desperate moment in history, a great effort is made once more for the renewal of human dignity.

—William O. Douglas

Foreword

Among the many comments on my earliest plays, the one that caught my eye particularly came from a stranger on a greeting card and read: "Thank you for writing a play about honor, nobility, and love without mocking them." With friends like this, I asked myself, who needs enemies? Once the news gets around that I write about honor, nobility, and love without mocking them, I may be offered a job by the YMCA or perhaps by someone more up-to-the-minute, like Werner Erhard or a Swami. I may become a speechwriter for some politician who has not yet openly declared himself evangelical along with Charles Colson and Eldridge Cleaver, but, in my own gang, the little world of writers, I am through.

It has been said that the Dante of our day is Franz Kafka: The one expressed the faith of an age of faith, the other the lack of faith of an age of lack of faith.

> Things fall apart, the centre cannot hold,
> Mere anarchy is loosed upon the world.

This—by W. B. Yeats—is another of the classic formulations, and who can push it aside? What was already fairly apparent in the life of letters when I grew up (in the twenties) had become quite evident in dramatic literature* (ever a little behind the times) by the fifties: Pessimism was *de rigueur*. That despair which for John Bunyan in the seventeenth century had already been a giant was now the patron nonsaint, the infallible antipope.

You have guessed, reader, that I am talking about Samuel Beckett, Harold Pinter, and Edward Bond. One matches oneself with such playwrights at one's peril: They are good. They are probably the best we have. So much for talent. The second acknowledgment I hasten to make is that "talent" is not something racing away on its own, like a motor before the clutch has been slipped in. High talent of this caliber

---

*And of course in the European art film Politically, Ingmar Bergman's films may be summed up as anti-radical chic.

can only define itself *by* the slipping in of the clutch. These writers are not "being brilliant" about nothing: They give a rendering of the world we live in, and very pointedly. Everything, in realized art, is true. Can I fly in the face of truth itself?

No. While everything in realized art is true, nothing in a single work of art is ever the whole truth. Selectivity is something no artist can escape. One must avoid the claim that one has replaced some other writer's partial truth with one's own whole truth, but there is no obligation to be modest about asserting the importance of another side of the truth. If one takes art to be a spiritual (mental, emotional) need of human beings, and I do, then it is quite possible that, in attending to certain needs, the art of a whole period fails to meet certain others. When one comes forward protesting the inadequacy of the art that is in the ascendant, that may well have nothing to do with talent, it may well have to do with a dismayed sense that something has been neglected and to our great loss. Again, you will have guessed, I trust, what I have in mind, or rather at heart: that we have neglected the absolute necessity, humanly speaking, of hope.

What ever happened to dear old optimism? Has it been handed over, lock, stock, and barrel, to the hucksters and hustlers? Is it now the outright property of revivalists, politicians, and other con men?

The professional optimism of politicians perhaps deserves a special word from one who is attempting political theatre. Someone seeking electoral office cannot get elected by explaining—what may well be true—that after his election, things will go from bad to worse. Instead, he *has* to be—or seem to be—an optimist of the most offensive sort: one who asserts, not merely that things *can* get better, but that they must, shall, and will get better, which is too many types of future tense altogether.

If that were all there is to be said, one might reasonably commit oneself to pessimism forthwith, and many have. But there is a whole other dimension. Although it is not necessarily true, in this life, that "wishing will make it so," as the old song had it, there are many achievable ends that cannot be reached without a lot of wishing. Nor can one act from wishes alone. One cannot be propelled into action unless, to the wish, is added a conviction that success is possible. Does anything ever get better through human effort? If you say, "no," you are the Compleat Pessimist. If you are prepared to say "yes," then you require the courage of that conviction. If, after a while, it is not clear

that things *have* got better, you will simply manufacture the evidence—
make things get better. I am not concluding that politicians need to talk
all the optimism they do talk, but I *am* concluding that they must talk
optimism: They have no other reason for talking.

Are politicians—again, humanly speaking—in so unusual a situation? Isn't optimism—a degree of hope, anyway—a pragmatic necessity
for all of us? Not least for artists? For art, too, is action.

If only a sense of purpose, of possible success, can make us act, what
are we to make of art that is loaded with the sense of likely if not
inevitable failure, loaded with the sense of confusion and life's
purposelessness?

First, that if the art is indeed art, that *is* success for the artist; and his
pessimism, if any, is undercut right there. An envious writer said of
certain pessimists of our time: "By proving in their writings that
success is impossible, they achieve success. Preaching the emptiness of
all worldly rewards, they end up smiling for the cameras as they are
handed the Nobel Prize." I have noted the same contradiction at Yale
Repertory Theatre. The approved world-view is the cosmic pessimism
of Lowell's *Prometheus Bound* or Bond's *Lear** and *Bingo*, but woe betide
anyone who applies it to the Yale Repertory Theatre and its plans for
the current season! Well, for an optimist like myself, human
contradictions are often less loathsome than they are endearing.
Anyway, as the late Louis Jouvet said: The theatre has only one law,
success.

One of the people I'm thinking of told me he was temperamentally
an optimist but had to hand it to the pessimists as philosophers. "You,"
he added, pointing his finger right at me, "are temperamentally a
pessimist. You *need* optimism as some people need God."

Since I cannot wholly deny this, I will proceed to define it. My
memory goes back to the Yale of 1940 when I once sat listening to the
poet Robert Frost. As he talked, for all the bland Republican front he

---

*The attenuation of Shakespeare at the hands of modern nihilism is a topic to
itself: Further cases in point are Ionesco's *Macbett*, Roman Polanski's *Macbeth*
film, and Peter Brook's staging of *King Lear*, which was also made into a nihilistic
film. A tendency can be cited even in a footnote. Such plays and films,
originating no doubt in horror of violence, end up pandering to the public's love
of violence, and one can ask: Is the artist taking up arms against a sea of troubles
or merely drowning in it to general acclaim? The weaker brethren among the
artists are simply corrupt: they enjoy the violence which they pretend to
deplore.

put up, I realized what became clear to all the world in later years: that Frost was a disturbed personality. He would feel, sometimes, that he was *decomposing*. What he was telling us students that evening was that he had found the therapeutic formula his nature required. It was this: composition for composure. If one is an artist, the artistic work is precisely what one confronts one's, yes, natural pessimism with. The pessimism is overcome ("we *shall* overcome," and we do need to feel this) in the very sensations of the process of overcoming. The sculptor overcomes the stone, the writer the words. Optimally, one craves *recognition* for work done—the Nobel Prize. Next best is the satisfaction of at least having climbed the mountain, of having finished the work. And even for artists who don't finish, who leave fragments behind, there is a reward: the feeling, while the work is under way, of a thrust, amid the chaos, toward cosmos. One may not be winning the tennis game, but there is comfort in the existence of the game itself, of the net, of the white boundary lines painted on the court. Which is why Robert Frost felt such contempt for that "free verse" that he took to be "tennis without a net." No composure from composition that is only part of the general *de*composition!

One might even claim to find a deep and naive optimism within the cerebral and programmatic pessimism of Beckett and his followers. It is as though the house is on fire, and they, like children, continue to play in all innocence, confident that nothing can really go wrong. Play is "optimistic" in itself, and all art is play. Take that quality away and, at a certain stage, you destroy the art. One can do anything with an oil painting but put one's fist through it . . .

In tightlipped, Stoic fashion—or perhaps it is just the dominant Puritanism of modern Western history—some artists will allow no frivolity, no optimism, except the minimal frivolity and optimism inherent in artistic work itself. After this first flicker of a smile, the prescribed frown returns, freezes, and takes over the face—a cat from the county furthest from Cheshire. Others of us cannot survive without more hope than that.

How much more? And in how much more powerful a flood must it flow for us? Do we need a Salvation Army? Extrasensory perception? The Reverend Ike? Mother Church? Conversion to Communism? Before we laugh at any of these heady options, let us recognize that none of them has arisen arbitrarily but only out of dire human need— the need for hope.

One has to hope not to need *too much* hope. For, if one does, one will readily accept false prophets, who invariably turn out to be not only false but dangerous. They take advantage. And though a Swami may not be as dangerous as a Hitler, he takes advantage in fundamentally the same way. We, the victims, abdicate our responsibility, our very selves, in the same way. It is grimly amusing to find that the gurus encourage us to believe we don't have a self in the first place. Such is the art of self-fulfilling prophecy.

Jean Cocteau once spoke of the art of knowing how much *too far* to go, and the whole art of living, of survival, could be conceived as a calculation of *how hopeful to be*. The answer is not the same for all. One has to compute one's individual strength. It is the less strong who need the more optimism. But one simply cannot afford to be weak beyond a certain point. One's optimism then becomes overinflated, even supercolossal. What one dreams of is a thousand-year Reich, and what one gets is extermination camps and world wars. After which what is there to do, if one is still around, but return to one's natural pessimism?

If one is *not* weak beyond a certain point, one may, instead write plays about honor, nobility, and love without mocking them. What more can I say? Perhaps just this, that I often think of some words of a favorite philosopher of mine, Ernst Bloch. For Aristotle, Bloch says, it was pity and terror; for us, it is defiance and hope.

Are You Now
Or Have You
Ever Been

The investigation of show business by the Un-American
Activities Committee 1947-1956

A re-dedication. This play was dedicated to Philip and Daniel Berrigan from the beginning. Among those who wondered why were people working on productions of the play. Had they understood, their productions would have been better. In its 1977 edition the play is dedicated to the Berrigans once again.

Preface

The dialogue of *Are You Now Or Have You Ever Been* is taken from hearings before the Un-American Activities Committee. Hence no resemblance between the witness and the actual person is coincidental. These characters wrote their own lines into the pages of history. Though I did abridge and tidy up the record, I did not write in additional dialogue. Transpositions—of words within a sentence or of sentences within a sequence—I tried to hold down to a minimum lest there be any distortion of the sense.

No names have been changed, except that names of Committee members occur only as mentioned in the dialogue. Committee membership varied a good deal in the course of the nine years covered. Since these variations are unimportant to the action here presented, Committee members are designated in the text by number (CM 1, CM 2, etc.); the Chairman, also not the same man throughout the period, is called *the* Chairman; the Investigators are called Investigator, 2nd Investigator, etc. The image is of a single Committee in session throughout, presided over by a single Chairman, assisted by Investigators. Confronting them is a witness, usually accompanied by his attorney. All participants are equipped with microphones.*

The room was not always the same. It was not always even in Washington, D.C. But, for the imagination, a single room will suffice, looking like any courtroom, or better, like any larger room in a government building. Except as the text itself indicates that the room is cleared for an "executive" or closed session, there is an audience, and sometimes it fills the room to overflowing and the Chairman has to pound his gavel for attention. When the witness is a movie star, the Chairman may have to ask press photographers to be less obtrusive. Sometimes a witness may himself object to the use of TV lights and

---

*The *New York Times* described the Hollywood hearings of 1947 as follows: "Scores of correspondents covered the proceedings, which took place before 30 microphones, six newsreel cameras and blazing klieg lights. Fervent applause, boos, cheers, hisses and laughter punctuated the packed sessions, at which Mr. [J. Parnell] Thomas presided with a rapping gavel and flourishes of rhetoric."

cameras. Such is the transaction—the drama—known as Investigation. The investigation of show business is presented here in the testimony of a small minority of those actually investigated, and this testimony has been abridged, edited, and arranged. (By "arrangement" I refer chiefly to the order in which the "scenes" are presented. This order—with a couple of tiny exceptions—is chronological, and yet chronology did not do my work for me: Although after 1951 would come 1952, the question what to choose from the 1952 record was a matter of which 1952 items would follow upon the 1951 items with most "drama." It is by "arrangement" that the overall shape of the work is arrived at. It is by "arrangement" that the principal shock effect of this work—juxtaposition, collage—is produced.) All these processes—choice of witness, abridgment, editing, arrangement— bring into play the personal judgment, not to mention talent, of the writer responsible. To the extent that he is either a knave or a fool, the result will reflect his knavery or folly. I can only say I am aware of this, and I invite the skeptical or suspicious reader to check out his doubts and suspicions. Unlike many historians I am not using sources that the average person wouldn't have access to. On the contrary, I have used a record published by the United States government, and most of the testimony drawn upon can be found in its broader context in my own volume *Thirty Years of Treason*.

While I have my own opinions and commitments, I have tried to be fair, and my aim in employing a high degree of selectivity was not, lawyer-fashion, to make an overwhelming case for a client. The kind of client I represent would not be served by suppression of any relevant factors. Those who wish to study the investigation of show business in a more scholarly manner can do so by turning to my longer book or even the HUAC records as printed *in extenso* by the government. What I hope to have captured in this shorter treatment is a story, a newspaperman's "story," and a writer's, even perhaps a playwright's story: a dramatic Action. I have succeeded for you, the reader, if the reading of this script holds you from beginning to end and leaves with you an impression of wholeness, of a single tale told at the proper pace in proper sequence, without waste motion, without loose ends.

Like almost anyone who tells a story, I would like to believe that I have also presented credible and interesting human beings. Some of the characters in *Are You Now Or Have You Ever Been* pass too quickly across our line of vision to be portraits in any detail, but several of the witnesses whom the Committee held on to for hours (though here reduced to minutes) revealed themselves abundantly, more abundantly, in some instances, than they'd have wanted.

Lionel Stander's appearance before the Committee would repay study by dramatic critics. "Role playing!" said one of my friends who read the testimony, but Stander is by profession an actor, and what an actor does is play roles. An actor plays Georges Danton, let us say, making a speech when his life is at stake, when his every word and gesture is a matter of life and death. For Danton, not for the actor. Before the Committee, we find Lionel Stander *playing* with the idea of his life being at stake. It wasn't. No guillotine stood ready to cut off his head. The comic tone well expresses Stander's appreciation of this. Yet his life was, too, at stake: The Committee's target was a person's *livelihood,* his *living,* that without which he cannot live. Stander fought for his life like a tiger cat, yet it was less his own life he fought for— though blacklisted, he always maintained himself at a handsome level of income—than the lives of others and the principle of the thing. "Role playing!" then. "Just putting on an act." "Song and dance." Call this, in sum, a benefit performance, for the benefit of his profession, especially its most victimized members, carried off with brio, "for the hell of it." The histrionic element in Stander's testimony I see, not as falsifying it, but as giving it style and form and, ultimately, the exact emphasis and significance that it required.

Students of the theatre will note that, while some witnesses offered only *monologue,* and at that *read* from a piece of paper, Stander at every point related himself to his audience, to both his audiences, the one physically present and, beyond that, the American people at such a time as they would pay attention. He "bore witness" in constant interaction with Chairman and Investigator and Committee members, taunting them, shocking them, amusing them, dismaying them—and, finally, outplaying them. And although his prose is his own, as much as any monologue could be it is a prose of agile repartee, of fierce retort. Even what might strike his enemies as insincerity is part of the performance. Spontaneity is offset by control. Any apparent uncontrol is really controlled, as in all good theatre. Which again is only to say that Stander's encounter with the Committee is not mere experience but experience worked up into performance. And, if not a performance *for* his life, the performance, I would suspect, *of* his life.

Nor is Lionel Stander the only one whose nature, whose humanity, is revealed here, and this by the traditional means of the drama: a human crisis brought to a head by a conflict among a few persons on a "stage" before an audience and expressed in passionate words.

What is *Are You Now* about? Is it really about Communism, as has often been taken for granted? Is what it really communicates my desire to be soft on Communism, hard on anticommunism?

Oscar Wilde said "most people are other people," meaning thereby that they live as if they had no selves: they are completely identified with the others, with the mass. My play asks each spectator *Are You Now Or Have You Ever Been?* for, if you are *not*, and have *never* been, you are "other people," whether these be Middle Americans generally, or Hollywood Stars as you see them, or whatever. I believe that, except for hardened fanatics on both political sides, the Communist issue falls into the background, and what we see in the play is some people, faced with a challenge, settling for being other people, and others managing to be themselves. Surely it is not the Marxist philosophy of Paul Robeson that shines through the Robeson sequence but rather his firm identity as a Black American confronting the Others and those who choose to align themselves with the Others. People have described Lillian Hellman to me as a "fellow traveler" dominated by a lover who was a convinced Marxist, but is that what comes through in the play? Rather, a decidedly *in*dependent personality, strongly feminine—less Marxist than Christian, less proletarian than patrician. Lionel Stander *was* a Communist sympathizer, but again is that what is operative, dramatically? Hardly. What is coming through all the time is that he is a comedian, a Jewish comedian at that, a *New York* Jewish comedian emphatically, and that his Jewish humor expresses and asserts himself—and his cocky refusal to be assimilated in the Nixonian mass.

Such people, I hear it said, had it easier before the Committee than the average person. They were prepared, trained, for such encounters: no wonder that they were able to handle the occasion with skill. But, in my terms, this is only to say they had an identity that could not easily be shaken.

It is true that the role of a Kazan or a Robbins comes through with denunciatory force, which was bound to bring upon me the charge of being smug *(The New York Times)* and inquisitorial* *(Time* magazine). Mr. David Susskind, discussing a possible TV version with me, suggested I

---

*"Violent antipathies are always suspicious, and betray a secret affinity"—Hazlitt.

leave Kazan out because he is such a likable man. But how could I do that without implying that the men I leave in are not likable? Gadg Kazan, whom I knew fairly well at one time, is a great deal better than just likable. He abounds in good qualities. That makes any act of his that may *not* be good all the more important and significant. In the interests of fairness, I tried not to choose evidence that gives a worse impression than the evidence I have omitted. If the curious will look at the *full* testimony of Kazan, Robbins, and any of the others, they will, I think, be willing to confirm what I am saying here.

William F. Buckley, Jr., wrote in to *Time* magazine to find a scandal in the fact that my play underwrites courage, while I myself am, in his opinion, a coward. I don't know what parts of my life Buckley knows about or is ignorant of, or what specifically he had in mind in bringing this charge. I think, though, that *Are You Now Or Have You Ever Been* would be very acceptable as *a message from a coward*. For one assumes that cowards would like to overcome their cowardice and that, in cheering themselves along, they might cheer up some of the noncowards as well.

Actually, any good play will stand up without any author's name in the program at all. *Are You Now* is valid or invalid, no matter who wrote it, and whatever his courage or cowardice.

Are You Now had its first performances at Yale Repertory Theatre, November 8, 1972. Later it was done at the Theatre of Riverside Church, New York City; the Hollywood Center Theatre, Los Angeles; Ford's Theatre in Washington, D.C.; the Cleveland Playhouse . . . as well as in theatres in England and Australia.

Are You Now Or Have You Ever Been

Directed by	Michael Posnick
Scenery and Costumes by	Steven Rubin
Lighting by	Barb Harris

WITNESSES *(in order of appearance)*

Sam G. Wood	Tom Haas
Edward Dmytryk	Paul Schierhorn
Ring Lardner, Jr.	William Peters
Larry Parks	Stephen Joyce
Sterling Hayden	Nicholas Hormann
Abe Burrows	Allan Miller
Elia Kazan	William Peters
Tony Kraber	Michael Gross
Jerome Robbins	Michael Quigley
Elliott Sullivan	John McAndrew
Martin Berkeley	Joseph G. Grifasi
Lillian Hellman	Elizabeth Parrish
Marc Lawrence	Michael Gross
Lionel Stander	Leonard Frey
Zero Mostel	Jeremy Geidt
Paul Robeson	Al Freeman, Jr.
Stenographers	Marycharlotte Cummings
	Deborah Mayo

Understudies: *Edward Dmytryk* - Jeremy Geidt; *Larry Parks* - Alvin Epstein; *Lionel Stander* - William Peters; *Abe Burrows* - Paul Schierhorn; *Lillian Hellman* - Deborah Mayo; *Zero Mostel* - Joseph G. Grifasi.

Production Staff

Company Manager	John-Edward Hill
Assistant Technical Director	Bronislaw J. Sammler
Assistant to the Technical Director	Michael Kupferschmid
Sound Designer	Bronislaw J. Sammler
Lighting Assistant	Todd Jonz
Technical Building Crew	Daniel Koetting
	Frederick Penzel

Caiaphas was in his own mind
A benefactor to mankind . . .
The strongest poison ever known
Came from Caesar's laurel crown.

—William Blake

I don't want to be responsible for a whole stable of informers, stool
pigeons . . . who come in here beating their breasts and saying,
"I'm awfully sorry, I didn't know what I was doing! Please, I
want absolution! Get me back into pictures!" They will do
anything to get back into pictures! They will name names! They
will name anybody! , . . I resent the inference that anyone who
invokes the Fifth . . . is guilty of anything . . . The Puritans
used this right . . . The first instance was . . . when Jesus Christ
was asked by Pontius Pilate, "The judges have a lot of witnesses
against you?" And he said nothing.

—Lionel Stander before HUAC, 1953

There is one eternally true legend, that of Judas.

—Joseph Stalin

There was a comic peiod in the mid-Fifties when it was thought
that if people went down to Washington and said they wouldn't
name names but stated they believed in the Committee or some such
nonsense, then the Committee would clear them. The offer was
made to me, and I refused. I got a lot of calls from people begging
me to do it. I wondered why and then I realized, if I did it, the
others could do it without much shame. Judas-goat, me.

—Lillian Hellman, interviewed by Howard Kissell, 1976

9

Seventeen Witnesses

Sam G. Wood

Edward Dmytryk

Ring Lardner, Jr.

Larry Parks

Sterling Hayden

José Ferrer

Abe Burrows

Elia Kazan

Tony Kraber

Jerome Robbins

Elliott Sullivan

Martin Berkeley

Lillian Hellman

Marc Lawrence

Lionel Stander

Arthur Miller

Paul Robeson

Are you now, or have you ever been, a member of the Communist Party?

In 1947 the Un-American Activities Committee put this question to "the Hollywood Ten," a group of screen writers and screen directors who refused to testify, invoked the First Amendment, and, three years later, landed in jail for contempt of Congress. The Committee's adviser in this field was the Motion Picture Alliance for the Preservation of American Ideals.

Investigator. Will you state your name?

Mr. Wood. Sam G. Wood.

Investigator. What is your present occupation?

Mr. Wood. Motion picture producer and director.

Investigator. Would you name to the Committee some of the films you have produced and directed?

Mr. Wood. *Goodbye Mr. Chips, Kitty Foyle, For Whom the Bell Tolls.*

Investigator.Mr. Wood, are you a member of the Motion Picture Alliance for the Preservation of American Ideals?

Mr. Wood. I am. I was its first president.

Investigator. Will you tell the Committee why it was founded?

Mr. Wood. We felt that there was a definite effort by Communist Party members to take over the unions and guilds.

Investigator. Would you name individuals who were associated with you?

Mr. Wood. Yes, Gary Cooper, Clark Gable, Robert Taylor. Oh, Ginger Rogers.

Investigator. Will you tell the Committee of the efforts of the Communists to infiltrate the Screen Directors Guild?

Mr. Wood. Our most serious time was when George Stevens, who was president, went into the service, and the Guild was turned over to John Cromwell. With the assistance of three or four others, Cromwell tried to steer us into the Red River.

Investigator. Will you name the others?

Mr. Wood. Irving Pichel, Frank Tuttle, Edward Dmytryk.

Investigator. Mr. Wood, do the Communists maintain schools in Hollywood for the purpose of training actors or writers?

Mr. Wood. They have a Laboratory Theatre there.

Investigator. What is the function of this?

Mr. Wood. The youngsters go to these schools, they get parts, they study, and we see them in theatres. The Laboratory Theatre, I think, is definitely under the control of the Communist Party. Any kid that goes in there with American ideals hasn't a chance in the world. Then we have the Educational Center—

Investigator. Is that the *People's* Educational Center?

Mr. Wood. Yes. Eddie Dmytryk—I referred to him—is the instructor there.

Edward Dmytryk first appeared before the Committee on October 29, 1947.

Investigator. Mr. Dmytryk, are you a member of the Screen Directors Guild?

Mr. Dmytryk. Mr. Stripling, I feel these questions are designed to—

The Chairman. Just a minute. It is not up to you to "feel" what the design is. It is up to you to be responsive to the questions.

Mr. Dmytryk. Most other witnesses were given the right to answer as they pleased. Some went on at length—

Investigator. Pardon me, Mr. Dmytryk. About how long a time would you require to answer whether you were a member of the Screen Directors Guild? Would five minutes be enough?

Mr. Dmytryk. It would take a lot less than five minutes.

The Chairman. It would take five minutes to answer whether you were a member of the Screen Directors Guild?

Mr. Dmytryk. I said a lot *less* than five minutes, Mr. Chairman.

The Chairman. Go ahead.

Mr. Dmytryk. This kind of questioning is designed to bring about a split in the guilds at a time when we've just succeeded in getting unity between them. I was an officer of the Screen Directors Guild . . .

Investigator. Are you now, or have you ever been, a member of the Communist Party?

Mr. Dmytryk. Well, Mr. Stripling, there is a question of constitutional rights here.

The Chairman. When did you learn about the Constitution?

Mr. Dmytryk. I *first* learned about the Constitution in high school.

CM 1. Let's have the answer to the other question.

Mr. Dmytryk. I was asked when I learned about the Constitution.

Investigator. You haven't answered whether you are a member of the Communist Party.

Mr. Dmytryk. I answered by saying I do not think you have the right to ask—

Investigator. Mr. Chairman, it is apparent that the witness is pursuing the same line as—

The Chairman. The witness is excused.

Ring Lardner, Jr., came before the Committee the following day.

Mr. Lardner. Mr. Chairman, I have a short statement I would like to make.

The witness hands statement to the Chairman and to the Investigator.

The Chairman. The Committee is unanimous that, after you testify, you may read your statement.

Mr. Lardner. Thank you.

Investigator. Mr. Lardner, are you a member of the Screen Writers Guild?

Mr. Lardner. Mr. Stripling, I don't want to help you smash this particular guild or to infiltrate the motion-picture business in any way.

The Chairman. Now, Mr. Lardner, don't do like the others, or you will never read your statement.

Mr. Lardner. Mr. Chairman, let me—

The Chairman. Be responsive to the question.

Mr. Lardner. I am—

The Chairman. Are you a member of the Screen Writers Guild?

Mr. Lardner. I understood I *would* be permitted to read the statement.

The Chairman. Yes, after you've finished with the questions and answers.

Mr. Lardner. I don't think you qualified your statement that I'd be allowed to read this statement.

The Chairman. I will qualify it now. If you refuse to answer the question, you will not read your statement.

Mr. Lardner. That is an indirect way of saying you don't want me to read the statement.

The Chairman. You know right now you are not going to answer the question?

Mr. Lardner. I think I have to consider why the question is asked—

The Chairman. *We* will determine why the question was asked! We want to know whether you are a member of the Screen Writers Guild. That is a very simple question. You don't have to go into a long harangue.

Mr. Lardner. Well, I am not very good in haranguing, but, if you can make me answer this question, tomorrow, it seems to me you could ask somebody whether he believed in spiritualism.

The Chairman. There is no chance of our asking anyone whether they believe in spiritualism. That is just plain silly!

Mr. Lardner. If you asked somebody that, you might ask him—

The Chairman. Well, now, never mind what we *might* ask him. We are asking you now: Are you a member of the Screen Writers Guild? You are an American—

Mr. Lardner. But that is a question—

The Chairman. —and Americans should not be afraid to answer that.

Mr. Lardner. I am also concerned, as an American, with the question of whether this Committee has the right to ask me—

The Chairman. Well, we *have* got the right, and until you prove we *haven't* got the right, you have to answer that question.

Mr. Lardner. Mr. Chairman—

The Chairman. Aren't you a witness here?

Mr. Lardner. I am.

The Chairman. All right, then, a Congressional Committee is asking you: Are you a member of the Screen Writers Guild? Answer it yes or no.

14

Mr. Lardner. Well . . . .

The Chairman. All right, go to the sixty-four-dollar question.

Investigator. Are you now, or have you ever been, a member of the Communist Party?

Mr. Lardner. I would like to answer that.

Investigator. The charge has been made that the Screen Writers Guild which you are a member of, whether you admit it or not, has in it members of the Communist Party. Are you, or have you ever been, a member of the Communist Party?

Mr. Lardner. It seems to me you are trying to discredit the Screen Writers Guild through me, and the motion-picture industry through the Screen Writers Guild, and our whole practice of freedom of expression.

Investigator. If you and others are members of the Communist Party, you are the ones who are discrediting the Screen Writers Guild.

Mr. Lardner. I am trying to answer by stating, first, what I feel about the purpose of the question.

The Chairman. You won't say anything "first." You are refusing to answer this question.

Mr. Lardner. My understanding is . . .

The Chairman. Never mind your understanding!

Mr. Lardner. But I think that is a—

The Chairman. Any real American would be proud to answer the question, "Are you, or have you ever been, a member of the Communist Party?"—any *real* American!

Mr. Lardner. I could answer it, but if I did, I would hate myself in the morning.

The Chairman. Leave the witness chair!

Mr. Lardner. It was a question that would—

The Chairman. Leave the witness chair!

Mr. Lardner. Because it is a question—

The Chairman, *pounding his gavel.* Leave the witness chair!

Mr. Lardner. I think I am leaving by force!

The Chairman. Sergeant, take the witness away!

   A Sergeant takes him away.

The Chairman. Mr. Stripling, next witness.

Investigator. Mr. Russell, you were detailed to determine whether or not Ring Lardner, Jr., was ever a member of the Communist Party?

2nd Investigator. I was.

Investigator. Will you give the Committee the benefit of your investigation?

2nd Investigator. This Communist Party registration card bears the number 47180. It is made out in the name of Ring L., which, during the course of the investigation, developed to be the name of Ring Lardner, Jr.

Dmytryk and Lardner and their eight colleagues went to jail, and so, as it happened, did the chairman of the Committee, J. Parnell Thomas, who had been stealing the taxpayers' money. Before the grand jury Thomas invoked the Fifth Amendment. Eventually, he would receive a Presidential pardon from Truman, but before this happened he and Ring Lardner Jr., met again. In Lardner's words:

The blue prison fatigues hung loosely on the weary, perspiring man whose path across the quadrangle was about to meet mine. I felt I looked comparatively dapper in the same costume after a day of mild stenographic labor in the Office of Classification and Parole, but his job kept him in the August sun all day. He was custodian of the chicken yard at the Federal Correctional Institution, Danbury, Connecticut, and his name was J. Parnell Thomas. He had lost a good deal of weight, and his face, round and scarlet at our last encounter, was deeply lined and sallow. I recognized him, however, and he recognized me, but we did not speak. It would have been hard for either of us to pick up the thread.

On November 24, 1947, Helen Gahagan, whose husband was Melvin Douglas, asked on the floor of the House what films actually did contain Red propaganda. The next speaker was John Rankin of Mississippi who said:

Here is a petition condemning the Committee. I am going to read some of the names on that petition. One is June Havoc. Her real name is June Hovick. Another is Danny Kaye. We found his real name was David Daniel Kamisky. Another is Eddie Cantor, whose real name is Edward Iskowitz. There is one who calls himself Edward G. Robinson. His real name is Emanuel Goldenberg. There is another one here who calls himself Melvyn Douglas, whose real name is Melvyn Hesselberg.

The next speaker was Richard Milhous Nixon who said:

Ten witnesses refused to answer pertinent questions. These questions have to be answered. Our national security demands that we protect our free American institutions from being infiltrated and dominated by those who serve the Communist cause.

In 1950 Nixon said:

Helen Gahagan Douglas is pink right down to her underwear.

The first person in show business to testify to former party membership was Larry Parks, star of two then recent movies, *The Jolson Story* **and** *Jolson Sings Again.* **Parks spent a whole day with the Committee, March 21, 1951.**

MORNING

Investigator. The Committee has succeeded in exposing Communist infiltration into labor organizations, with the result that the Congress has been informed of important facts as the basis for legislative action. Many witnesses have told how they were duped into joining the Party, the activities they observed as members, and their reasons for breaking. They have performed a service of inestimable value to their country and should receive the plaudits of their fellow citizens. The hearing today is the first of a series designed to accomplish the same results in the entertainment field. It is hoped that any witness who made the mistake of associating himself with the Communist Party will have sufficient courage and loyalty to make an honest disclosure of all he knows. I would like to call, as the first witness, Mr. Larry Parks. Are you represented by counsel, Mr. Parks?

Mr. Parks. I am.

Investigator. Will counsel identify himself?

Mr. Mandel. Louis Mandel. Mr. Parks has prepared a statement. It will be enlightening to the Committee as his testimony unfolds. May he read it?

The Chairman. At the conclusion of the testimony.

Mr. Mandel. I would urge that he be permitted to read the statement now. There is a connecting link to what he will testify.

The Chairman. Proceed, Mr. Tavenner.

Investigator. Mr. Parks, when and where were you born?

Mr. Parks. I was born on a farm in Kansas. The closest town would be Olathe.

Investigator. Will you relate the details regarding your educational background?

Mr. Parks. I moved when quite small to Illinois, attending the high school in Joliet, graduated from the University of Illinois, where I majored in chemistry and minored in physics. I sometimes wonder how I got in my present line of work!

Investigator. Mr. Parks, there has been testimony regarding a number of organizations in Hollywood such as the Actors' Laboratory Theatre. Have you been connected with any of those?

Mr. Parks. I have.

Investigator. Will you state their names? I will hand you the list.

Mr. Parks, *looking at sheet of paper.* Well, I'm familiar with the Actors' Laboratory.

Investigator. Did you hold any position in that organization?

Mr. Parks. For a time I was sort of honorary treasurer. *He reads the list in silence.*

Investigator. Proceed.

Mr. Parks. I was a member of the Independent Citizens Committee of the Arts, Sciences, and Professions.

The Chairman. We will have to ask the photographers not to block the view.

Investigator. Now, referring back to the Actors' Laboratory, of which you were treasurer?

Mr. Parks. My job was to sign a batch of checks.

Investigator. Will you tell the Committee whether or not there were Communists in these various organizations?

Mr. Parks. There were Communists attached to the Lab.

Investigator. Did those Party members endeavor to obtain control?

Mr. Parks. No, the Lab was a school for acting and sort of a showcase for actors.

Investigator. Tell the Committee the circumstances under which you became a member of the Communist Party; and, if you left the Party, when you did and why.

18

Mr. Parks. I was a member in '41. Being a member of the Party fulfilled certain needs of a young man who was liberal in thought, idealistic, who was for the underprivileged, the underdog. I felt it fulfilled these needs. Being a Communist in '51, in *this* situation, is a different kettle of fish. A great power is trying to take over the world.

Investigator. You didn't realize that the purpose of the Communist Party was to take over other segments of the world in '41? You do realize that in '51?

Mr. Parks. This is in no way an apology for anything I've done, you see, because I feel I have done nothing wrong, ever. In '41 the purposes, as I knew them, simply fulfilled—at least I thought they would fulfill—a certain idealism, a certain feeling of being for the underdog, which I am today, this minute. This didn't work out . . . I attended very few meetings and petered out the same way I drifted in. I petered out in '44 or '45.

Investigator. Your Communist registration card for 1944 bore the number 46954 and for 1945 the number 47344. Does that refresh your recollection?

Mr. Parks. No, sir, it doesn't. Because I never had a Party card.
Pause.

Investigator. Now, do I infer that by '46 you had broken with the Party?

Mr. Parks. Correct.

Investigator. Will you state where you first became a member of the Party?

Mr. Parks. Hollywood, California.

Investigator. Who recruited you?

Mr. Parks. A man by the name of Davidson.

Investigator. What was Davidson's first name and position?

Mr. Parks. I don't remember. I haven't seen him for ten years.

Investigator. Where did he live?

Mr. Parks. I have no idea.

Investigator. What was his occupation?

Mr. Parks. I don't know.

Investigator. Give us some descriptive data.

Mr. Parks. Average-looking, young, dark hair.
Pause.

Investigator. Well, what were the circumstances under which you met?

Mr. Parks. This is hard to recall.

Investigator. Was it in your home or where?

Mr. Parks. I *really* don't remember. I'm being as honest as I know how!

Investigator. Did you seek this individual out or did he seek you out?

Mr. Parks. I certainly didn't seek *him* out. It's hard for me to say whether he sought *me* out.

Investigator. Were you assigned to a Party cell?

Mr. Parks. I was.

Investigator. What was the name of that cell?

Mr. Parks. Well, it had no name that I know of.

Investigator. Well now, you were a member of that group from '41 to '45?

Mr. Parks. That's correct.

Investigator. Tell us about the organization of the Communist Party during that time.

Mr. Parks. Well, I was a pretty bad member by their lights. Didn't attend too many meetings—maybe ten, twelve, fifteen.

Investigator. Who was the chairman of the group?

Mr. Parks. It had no chairman that I know of.

Investigator. Well, who was the secretary?

Mr. Parks. I don't know if there were any actual officers.

Investigator. Well, to whom did you pay your dues?

Mr. Parks. The few times I paid dues were to different people.

Investigator. What was the total membership of this cell?

Mr. Parks. I would say it went up to ten or twelve.

Investigator. Did Party organizers appear before your group from time to time—people from the East, let us say?

Mr. Parks. No, I don't recall ever seeing any big shot.

Investigator. Are you acquainted with Lionel Stander?

Mr. Parks. I've met him.

Investigator. Have you ever attended a meeting with him?

Mr. Parks. I don't recall attending a meeting with Lionel Stander.

Investigator. Do you know whether he's a Party member?

Mr. Parks. No.

Investigator. Are you acquainted with Karen Morley?

Mr. Parks. I am.

Investigator. Is she a member of the Communist Party?

Pause

Mr. Parks. Well, counsel, I would prefer not to mention names.

CM 1. Do you take the same position with respect to the leaders of the Communist movement?

Mr. Parks. I don't know the leaders of the Communist movement.

CM 1. Who directed the meetings you attended?

Mr. Parks. The meetings consisted mainly of discussions of how the war was going, current events, problems of actors in their work. Does that answer your question?

CM 1. It's an answer.

Mr. Parks. Hmm?

CM 1. It's an answer.

Mr. Parks. I'd like to answer your question . . .

CM 1. Who directed the activities this group were engaged in?

Mr. Parks. No one.

CM 2. Who would call the meetings together?

Mr. Parks. I really don't know.

CM2. Did you have a set, scheduled meeting once every week, or was it upon the call of some individual?

Mr. Parks. I don't believe there was any set—

CM 2. Certainly it wasn't run by mental telepathy!

Mr. Parks. No. Certain individuals would call.

CM 2. Somebody had to issue a call?

Mr. Parks. That's correct.

CM 2. Did *you* ever issue a call?

Mr. Parks. No.

CM 2. Then somebody would have to tell you when and where the meetings would take place.

Mr. Parks. I would get a call from a member of the group and they would say, "Let's have a meeting tonight, tomorrow night."

CM 3. Were the meetings always held at the same place?

Mr. Parks. No.

CM 3. Were they held in halls or in homes?

Mr. Parks. These were held at homes.

CM 3. Did you ever have meetings at *your* home?

Mr. Parks. Never.

CM 3. Where were some of the meetings held?
  Pause.

Mr. Parks. These were people like myself, small-type people, no different than you or I.

CM 3. Where were some of the meetings held?

Mr. Parks. In various homes.

CM 3. Can you name some?

Pause.

Mr. Parks. Well, if you will allow this, I would prefer not to mention names. These were people—like myself—who have done nothing wrong, ever.

The Chairman. Do you entertain the feeling that these parties you were associated with are guiltless of any wrong?

Mr. Parks. This is my opinion.

The Chairman. In what way would it be injurious to them to divulge their identities, when at no time did they do wrong?

Pause.

Mr. Parks. If you think it's easy—I've worked hard in my profession, climbed up the ladder a bit—if you think it's easy for me to appear before this committee, you're mistaken. This is difficult. One of the reasons is that, as an actor, my activity depends on the public. To be called before this Committee has a certain inference, a certain innuendo, that you're not loyal to this country. This is not true. I am speaking for myself. This is not true. But the inference, the innuendo, is there as far as the public is concerned. Also, as a representative of a great industry—as an actor who is fairly well known, in that respect I am a representative—This is a great industry! At this time it is being investigated for Communist influence—

The Chairman. Don't you think the public is entitled to know about it?

Mr. Parks. Hmm?

The Chairman. Don't you think the public is entitled to know about it?

Mr. Parks. I certainly do, and I'm opening myself wide to any question that you can ask me. I'll answer as honestly as I know how. And at this time, as I say, the industry is—it's like taking a pot shot at a wounded animal, because the industry is not in as good shape as it has been—economically, it's been pretty tough. This is a great industry! And I don't say this only because it has been kind to *me*. It has a very important job to do, to entertain people, in certain respects to call attention to certain evils, but mainly to entertain, and I feel they've done a great job. When our country has needed help, the industry has been in the forefront of that help!

Investigator. You are basing your reluctance to testify on the great job that the moving-picture industry is doing?

Pause.

Mr. Parks. On naming names, it is my opinion that the few people I could name, these names would not be of service to the Committee: I am sure you know who they are. These people are like myself, and I have done nothing wrong. I also feel that to be asked to name names like this is not American justice. We as Americans have all been brought up to believe it's a bad thing to force a man to do this.

The Chairman. I'm curious to understand what your reasons are for declining to answer the question.

Mr. Parks. I'm not declining. I'm asking if you would not press me.

CM 2. Are any of the members of your cell still active in the Communist Party?

Mr. Parks. I can't say. I divorced myself completely. I know what I *think*: that 99 percent of them are not.

CM 2. If you knew people in Hollywood that were identified with the Party *then*, would you be reluctant to cite their names if they were active members *at the present time*?

Mr. Parks. I don't think it's good for an American to be forced to do this. But I feel that the people I knew are *not* members of the Communist Party at the present time. If they are, they shouldn't be.

CM 2. If you had knowledge of a man who committed murder, you wouldn't be hesitant to give that information to the authorities?

Mr. Parks. That is correct.

CM 2. I assume you share our belief that a member of the Communist Party believes in overthrowing our government by force and violence. Now, if you would give information concerning a man you know has committed murder, wouldn't you give information of a man you knew to be working to overthrow our government by force and violence?

Mr. Parks. If I knew a man who committed murder, which is against the law of our land, I would name him immediately. The other thing—well, even now it is *not* against the law of our land.

CM 2. So when we are drafting men to fight Communist aggression, you feel it is not your duty to give the Committee the benefit of what knowledge you might have?

Mr. Parks. I think there is a difference, between people who would harm our country and people like myself, who, as I feel, did nothing wrong—

CM 2. You don't believe that anyone can be naive enough to be an active member of the Communist Party *today* and not know what he's doing?

Mr. Parks. That's correct.

CM 2. For that reason I can't see your consistency in saying you won't name someone you know, today, who is an active member of the Party.

Mr. Parks. But I don't know *anyone* today who is an active member of the Party.

CM 2. If you did know, you would tell?

Pause.

Mr. Parks. Yes, I think I would.

Pause.

Investigator. Mr. Parks, your argument is that this Committee should investigate Communism but should not find out who is a Communist.

Mr. Parks. No, this is not my argument!

Investigator. You are taking the position that it is not important to find out who may be in Communism in Hollywood—

Mr. Parks. No.

Investigator. —rather than for this Committee to determine what its obligations are under the statute which created it to investigate Communism?

Mr. Parks. No, counsel, I didn't say *this*!

Investigator. But isn't it the result of your argument?

Mr. Parks. No, counsel, what I say is that the few people I knew are as loyal to this country as you.

Investigator. And if every witness were permitted to take that position, the extent of the investigation would be *limited* by the attitude of the witness, wouldn't it?

Mr. Parks. These people were like me, and the most you can accuse them of is a lack of judgment. *Pause.* I say none of this in apology for what I did, because a young man at twenty-five, if he's not full of idealism he's not worth his salt. If you make a mistake in judgment like this, I don't believe it is serious!

Investigator. Yes, but if every witness would be the final judge of when a thing was serious and when it was not, how could the Committee carry out its statutory duty?

Mr. Parks. I'm asking that—

Investigator. And I'm asking that you see the other side.

Mr. Parks. I do see the other side.

Investigator. You understand the purposes of this organization. If you would be frank with regard to other people who are connected with this organization, the Committee would be permitted to function. And, therefore, I am going to ask you who acted as secretary of this group.

Mr. Parks. And I can honestly say I do not know.

Pause.

Investigator. Do you know Elizabeth Leech?

Mr. Parks. I don't recall.

Investigator. Do you know Elizabeth Glenn?

Mr. Parks. To the best of my knowledge, I do not.

Investigator. Do you know Marjorie Potts?

Mr. Parks. I do not.

Investigator. Now: Do you know Karen Morley?

Pause.

Mr. Parks. I do.

Investigator. Was Karen Morley a member of this group?

Mr. Parks. And I ask you again, counsel, to reconsider forcing me to name names, and I don't think this is American justice, to force me to do this, when I have come three thousand miles—

CM 1. Mr. Chairman, may I ask counsel a question? *To the Investigator:* By insisting that this man testify as to names, aren't we overlooking that we want to know what the *organization* did, how it attempted to influence the thinking of the American people through the arts?

Mr. Parks. May I answer your question?

CM 1. No.

Investigator. Some of these individuals have evaded service of process, so we cannot bring them here. That is one point. Another is that this Committee ought to receive *proof* of information which it has in its files.

CM 1. But isn't it more important to learn the purpose of the organization than to get a list of names of bleeding hearts and fools and suckers?

Investigator. As to organizations, that *was* the subject of much testimony.

CM 1. Mr. Parks, were you instructed to influence the thinking of the American people through stage or screen?

Mr. Parks. I was never instructed to do this. This was not done.

CM 1. Was it the purpose of the Communist organization to set up a hard core in Hollywood that would slant pictures and performances?

Mr. Parks. First of all, it's impossible to do this as an actor.

The Chairman. Wouldn't the *writer* be in a position to very decidedly slant—

Mr. Parks. A script passes through too many hands.

The Chairman. You're leaving an impression there was nothing off-color about your group. How then could it reflect against this group for the names to be known—any more than if they belonged to the YMCA?

Mr. Parks. I myself I am a good example. It is doubtful whether, after appearing before this Committee, my career will continue.

CM 4. Mr. Parks, have you any knowledge of the efforts of the movie industry to clean out subversive influence?

Mr. Parks. This is common knowledge.

CM 4. Is it *your* knowledge?

Mr. Parks. Mine, yours, everybody's.

CM 4. A few minutes ago, you said your duty was to sign a batch of checks. To whom were those checks written?

Mr. Parks. Well, these were to pay the office help, the clean-up man, the electric company—

CM 4. Was this cell limited to the actor's profession?

Mr. Parks. I believe it was.

CM 4. Did you have refreshments?

Mr. Parks. Yes. Coffee. *Laughter.* I'm serious! Coffee! Doughnuts!

CM 4. How much were the dues?

Mr. Parks. Well, I couldn't have contributed more than sixty dollars.

CM 4. You were connected with this cell from '41 to '45, yet you only paid a total of sixty dollars?

Mr. Parks. Well, the dues, when you weren't working, were about seventy-five cents a month. If you were working, you paid some percentage. I didn't.

CM 4. You were idealistic, liberal, progressive at the age of twenty-five, and that is one reason you joined the Communist Party—

Mr. Parks. That is *the* reason.

CM 4. Didn't the cell make efforts to increase its own membership?

Mr. Parks. I never made such an effort.

CM 4. You notice, Parks, at this time I'm avoiding asking you names.

Mr. Parks. Yes.

CM 4. I am assuming you want to be helpful to the Committee.

Mr. Parks. That's correct.

CM 4. Tell us what activities the cell participated in to increase its membership.

Mr. Parks. Well, I think certain members of the group approached people about becoming a member of the Communist Party.

CM 4. Was any difference in philosophy between Communism and our form of government ever discussed in the cell?

Silence.

What *did* you discuss besides drinking coffee?

Mr. Parks. We didn't discuss drinking coffee! The war was going on. This was the major topic. The discussion also had to do with actors, how we could get more money—

CM 4. You could get more money as a member of the Communist Party than as a plain Democrat or Republican? Why did you join? What was membership in this cell going to do for you in Hollywood?

Mr. Parks. As a man of twenty-five, with ideals and a feeling for the underdog, I felt this was the most *liberal* of the parties. I was a registered Democrat. From that time and before, I've voted the straight Democratic ticket! This was the practical thing to do. The other was an idealistic thing.

CM 4. How many years were you in that cell before you began to be disillusioned?

Mr. Parks. Well, "disillusioned" is not the word.

The Chairman. Do I understand, sir, that you are *not yet* disillusioned?

Mr. Parks. No, no. Don't bend it! It was a question of lack of interest, of not finding the things that I thought I would find.

CM 4. Did it come clearly to you that the Communist Party was part of an international conspiracy against our form of government?

Mr. Parks. No.

CM 4. Did you come to the conclusion that the Communist program was aimed at world domination?

Mr. Parks. Not at that time.

CM 4. When did you come to that conclusion, if at all?

Mr. Parks. With recent events in history.

CM 3. Were there members of the Communist Party who spoke to your group?

Mr. Parks. There was one instance.

CM 3. Can you give his name?

Pause.

Mr. Parks. Again I wish you would not press me.

Investigator. Mr. Parks, you are no doubt acquainted with Sam G. Wood, producer and director?

Parks nods.

Investigator. Sam G. Wood testified "The Laboratory Theatre is under the control of the Communist Party. Any kid that goes in there with American ideals hasn't a chance in the world." Do you agree?

Mr. Parks. I disagree.

Investigator. But, in light of that testimony, do you still feel *you* should be the judge?

Pause.

The Chairman. We are going to take a recess for lunch.

AFTERNOON

Mr. Mandel. Mr. Chairman, Mr. Parks would like to talk about naming names.

The Chairman. He expressed himself pretty fully this morning. Counsel has a few more questions. Maybe they will bring out what he wants to say.

Mr. Mandel. What he has to say is very pertinent *at this point.* I don't think we can judge it till he says it. It will take him three minutes.

The Chairman. Make it as brief as you can, Mr. Parks.

Mr. Parks. I will.

Pause.

Mr. Chairman, to be a good actor, you must experience from the top of your head to the tip of your toes what you are doing . . . . As I told you, this is probably the most difficult morning and afternoon I have ever spent, and I wish that, if it were at all possible . . . You see, it's a little different to sit *there* and to sit *here,* and if you could put yourself in my place . . . My people have a long heritage in this country. They fought in the Revolutionary War to make this country, to create the government of which this Committee is a part . . . I have two boys, one thirteen months, one two weeks. Is this the kind of heritage I must hand down to them? Is this the heritage you would hand down to your children? I don't think I would be here today if I weren't a star, because you know as well as I, even better, that I know *nothing* that would be of great service to this country. I think my career has been ruined because of this, and I would appreciate not having to—Don't present me with the choice of either being in contempt of this Committee and going to jail or being forced to crawl through the mud and be an informer! For what purpose? I don't think this is a choice. I don't think this is sportsmanlike. I don't think this is American justice for an innocent mistake in judgment, if it was that, with the intention of making this country a better place to live . . . This is probably the most difficult thing I have ever done, and it seems to me it would impair the usefulness of this Committee . . . . God knows it is difficult enough to come before this Committee . . . If you do this to me, it will make it almost impossible for a person to come to you and tell the truth. I beg you not to force me to do this!

Investigator. Mr. Parks, there was a statement you made this morning which interested me. You said: "This is a great industry. It has a job to do: to *call attention to certain evils,* but mainly to entertain." Now, do you believe that persons who "call attention to certain evils" ought to be dedicated to the principles of democracy?

Mr. Parks. I agree.

Investigator. Do you believe, on the other hand, that persons in those positions should be *antagonistic* to the principles of democracy, members of a conspiracy to *overthrow* our government?

Mr. Parks. Most assuredly I don't.

Investigator. Then what is your opinion as to whether members of the Communist Party should be in positions of power in the various unions which control the writing of scripts, the actors, and so on?

Mr. Parks. I do *not* believe those people should be in *any* position of power!

Investigator. Then we will ask your cooperation, before this hearing is over, in helping us ascertain those who are members of the Communist Party. *Pause.* Tell us of the methods by which money was raised for the Party.

Mr. Parks. I don't recall any.

Pause.

Investigator. I have no trick question here through which I am attempting to lead you into denial of something we know about!

Mr. Parks. I have been as aboveboard as I can! I am willing to help you, if you could be more specific! *Pause.* I have appeared at many benefits over many years—

Investigator. Were any of these for the benefit of the Communist Party?

Mr. Parks. I don't recall any.

Investigator. You have said you were subpoenaed because you were a star. You were subpoenaed because you had knowledge about Communist activities.

Mr. Parks. My point was that, if I were working in a drugstore, I doubt whether I would be here!

Investigator. I didn't understand your reference to the possible destruction of your career. You didn't mean to infer that this Committee was bringing you here *because* of any effect on your career?

Mr. Parks. No. What I said was that, because of this, I have no career left.

Investigator. Don't you think that question might be influenced by the fullness of the cooperation you give the Committee?

Mr. Parks. I think the damage has been done.

CM 5. Don't you think the damage occurred when you became a member of an organization which advocates the overthrow of every constitutional form of government in the world? Is the Committee more to blame than your own act in affiliating with that organization? This Committee is an expression of the will of the American people.

Mr. Parks. As I told you, Congressman, when I was younger, I felt a certain way about things. I felt strongly, and I still do, about the underdog, and it was for these reasons that . . . this organization appealed to me. I later found it would not fulfill my needs. At that time, I don't even believe this was a mistake in judgment. But my two boys, I would rather have them make the same mistake I did than not feel like making any mistake at all and be a cow in the pasture!

CM 5. Mr. Parks, upon what do you base the opinion that the people whose names you have in your possession have probably severed their relations with the Communist Party?

Mr. Parks. The few people I knew are people like myself and feel the way I do.

CM 5. Have you discussed Party affiliations with those with whom you were affiliated in the Party?

Mr. Parks. I have not. This is my honest opinion. And *you* know these people as well as I do.

Pause.

CM 5. In a recent case here in Washington, some of the highest officials in government testified that a man* with whom they had been associated had never been a member of the Communist Party and in no way constituted any threat to our institutions. Every man who reads the newspapers now knows how fallacious that opinion was!

Mr. Parks. You know who the people are.

CM 5. That is problematic, Mr. Parks. I "know who they are"—maybe. But it's within the province of the Committee to determine how far they will go.

Mr. Parks. I have told you of my activities to the best of my ability.

Pause.

The Chairman. We will make a break in the testimony. After we resume, the witness will be advised what the disposition of this Committee is with reference to his apparent disinclination to answer questions.

EVENING

The audience present during the morning and afternoon sessions is now absent. Present are only the Committee, the Investigator, Parks, and Parks' attorney.

The Chairman. Mr. Parks, we are going to seek your cooperation in a closed session for testimony that will not be publicized until such time, if at all, as the Committee itself may deem expedient. *Pause.* Counsel will now propound additional questions.

Mr. Mandel. Is is the intention of the Committee, unless he answers these questions in private, to cite him for contempt?

The Chairman. The Committee makes no threats.

Mr. Mandel. Just to clear his thinking, so he is fully informed of the consequences . . .

The Chairman. If Mr. Parks placed himself in the position of being in

---

*Alger Hiss.

contempt of Congress, it is possible that the Committee may request a citation. On the other hand, it may not. Does that answer your question?

Mr. Mandel. I would like to spend another minute on it. In view of Mr. Parks' cooperative attitude—and everyone here understands what is motivating him—he feels so bad about what he has to do, and if he thought there were any chance you would elicit information that was important, he would give it to you. It is only saving that little bit of something that you live with. You have to see and walk in Hollywood with that. You have to meet your children and your wife with it, your friends. It is that little bit that you want to save. Although I don't ask the Committee to commit itself, in fairness to Mr. Parks . . . he may have to sacrifice the arm with gangrene in order to save the body! He will walk around the rest of his life without an arm! I realize the purposes of this Committee, and our attitude has been one of cooperation: We want to go right through with that. Now, if this is the penalty he will have to pay, I have to urge him a different way . . . His opinion is that what he is going to give you will only eat up his insides and you will get nothing.

The Chairman. Mr. Attorney, the Committee is not responsible for the position he finds himself in. We are responsible for the position we find *ourselves* in.

Short pause.

Investigator. Mr. Parks, who were the members of the cell of the Communist Party to which you were assigned?

Pause.

Mr. Parks. This is what I've been talking about. This is the thing. I am no longer fighting for myself . . . I am probably the most completely ruined man you have ever seen.

Investigator. Mr. Chairman, if the witness refuses to answer the question, I see very little use in my asking him about *other* individuals.

The Chairman. The witness has got to make up his mind. It isn't sufficient, as far as this Committee is concerned, to say that, in your opinion, it is unfair. Or un-American. The question is: Will you answer?

Mr. Mandel. I would like to ask the Chairman whether he is directing the witness to answer?

The Chairman. The witness has been asked. He must answer or decline to answer.

Mr. Mandel. I think a little more is needed. He must be *directed* to answer, and if he refuses, merely asking him and not going beyond, under law, is not sufficient. I think he has to be told, "You've *got* to answer."

The Chairman. I don't understand any such rule, but, to avoid controversy, I direct the witness to answer the question.
Pause.

Mr. Parks. I do not refuse to answer the question but I feel that this Committee is doing a really dreadful thing! I don't believe the American people will look kindly on it!

CM 5. Mr. Parks, we are, each one of us, responsible to the American people. I, for one, resent having my duties pointed out to me!

The Chairman. The witness has said he doesn't *refuse* to answer. So I assume he is *ready* to answer.

Mr. Mandel. When the final gong goes down, he intends to respect the will of this Committee, but he reserves the right to talk to you gentlemen and possibly *persuade* you to think differently.

The Chairman. The Committee took the view, sir, that there might be some merit in your contention if we were still in an open hearing. But we are not.

Mr. Mandel. This is a private session, which is very considerate of the Committee, and I want to thank you . . . *Pause.* May I have a minute to talk to Mr. Parks?

The Chairman. Yes.

Mr. Mandel. I make this request of the Committee: I want no promise from you, just a sportsmanlike attitude, so what he gives you will not be used, if it can be helped, to embarrass people in the same position he finds himself in today.

The Chairman. Nobody on this Committee has any desire to smear anyone's name.

Mr. Mandel. In the internal struggle that Mr. Parks is going through, I think it would go a little lighter, having a statement from you.
Mandel and Parks confer inaudibly. When they stop conferring:

Investigator. If you will just answer the question, please. The question was: Who were the members of the Communist Party cell to which you were assigned?
A long silence.

Mr. Parks. Morris Carnovsky—

Investigator. Will you spell that name?

Mr. Parks. I couldn't possibly spell it. Morris Carnovsky, Joe Bromberg,

Sam Rossen, Anne Revere, Lee Cobb—

Investigator. What was that name?

Mr. Parks. Lee Cobb. Gale Sondergaard, Dorothy Tree—

Investigator. What was the name of Dorothy Tree's husband? Michael Uris?

Mr. Parks. Yes.

Investigator. Was he a member of the cell?

Mr. Parks. Not to my knowledge.

Investigator. Do you know whether Michael Uris was a member of the Communist Party?

Mr. Parks. I don't.

Investigator. Can you recall other members of that cell?

Mr. Parks. That's about all.

Investigator. Was Howard Da Silva a member?

Mr. Parks. I don't believe I ever attended a meeting with Howard Da Silva.

Investigator. Was Howard Da Silva a member of the Communist Party?

Mr. Parks. Not to my knowledge.

Investigator. Was James Cagney a member of the cell?

Mr. Parks. Not to my knowledge.

Investigator. Was he a member of the Communist Party?

Mr. Parks. I don't recall hearing that he was.

Investigator. Sam Jaffe?

Mr. Parks. I don't recall attending a meeting with Sam Jaffe.

Investigator. Was he a member of the Communist Party?

Mr. Parks. I don't recall that Sam Jaffe was a member of the Communist Party.

Investigator. John Garfield?

Mr. Parks. I don't recall a meeting with John Garfield.

Investigator. Do you recall whether John Garfield ever *addressed* a Communist Party meeting?

Mr. Parks. I don't recall any such occasion.

Investigator. Marc Lawrence, was he a member of that cell?

Mr. Parks. I believe he was.

Mr. Mandel. May I suggest to counsel, in view of the feeling of the witness—I don't mean to rush you, but this whole thing being so distasteful—I wonder if we can proceed a little faster so he doesn't suffer so much?

Investigator. I want him to be accurate. I don't want to rush him in matters as important as these.

Mr. Mandel. I am just trying to be considerate of the man's feeling, doing something that—

Investigator. I asked you this morning about Karen Morley. Was she a member of the Communist Party?

Mr. Parks. Yes.

Investigator. Was she in this particular cell?

Mr. Parks. Yes.

Investigator. Were lectures given in which persons outside of your cell took part?

Mr. Parks. I recall a talk by John Howard Lawson.

Investigator. Robert Rossen? Was he a member of this group?

Mr. Parks. No. I don't recall the gentleman.

Investigator. Sterling Hayden?

Mr. Parks. I don't recall a meeting with Sterling Hayden.

Investigator. Will Geer?

Mr. Parks. I don't recall a meeting with Will Geer.

Investigator. Lionel Stander?

Mr. Parks. I've met him. I don't recall a meeting with him.

Investigator. Andy Devine?

Mr. Parks. I don't recall a meeting with Andy Devine.

Investigator. Edward G. Robinson?

Mr. Parks. I don't recall a meeting with Edward G.Robinson.

Investigator. Madeleine Carroll?

Mr. Parks. I don't recall a meeting with Madeleine Carroll.

Investigator. Gregory Peck?

Mr. Parks. I have no remembrance of a meeting with Gregory Peck.

Investigator. Humphrey Bogart?

Mr. Parks. I don't recall a meeting with Humphrey Bogart.

CM 1. I think you could get some comfort out of the fact that the people mentioned have been subpoenaed. If they do appear here, it won't be as a result of anything you have testified to.

Mr. Parks. It is no comfort whatsoever.

Investigator. Do you know of any other person whose name comes to your recollection?

Mr. Parks. I don't recall anyone else.

Investigator. That is all, Mr. Chairman.

Pause.

CM 2. I'd like to say, Mr. Chairman, that Mr. Parks' testimony has certainly been refreshing!

On September 19, 1951, the Chairman stated:

There can be no odium attached to persons who have made a mistake and seek to rectify it. If there was, we would give the lie to the advent of Jesus Christ in this world, who came here for the purpose of making possible forgiveness upon repentance.

The Hollywood director Frank Tuttle testified:

There is a traditional dislike among Americans for informers, and I am an informer. The aggressors are ruthless, and I feel it is absolutely necessary for Americans to be ruthless.

The Hollywood director Robert Rossen testified:

I don't feel I'm being a stool pigeon or an informer. That is rather romantic like children playing at cops and robbers . . . I don't think any one individual can indulge himself in the luxury of individual morality or pit it against the security and safety of this nation.

The screenwriter Nicholas Bela told the Committee:

I want to humbly apologize for the grave error which I have committed, and beg of you to forgive me. I feel, if I am allowed, I would like to stand.

And he stood.

On April 10, 1951, Sterling Hayden came before the Committee.

Investigator. After your return to Hollywood in 1946, did you become associated with any organization?

Mr. Hayden. I joined the Communist Party.

Investigator. You joined the Communist Party?

Mr. Hayden. Yes.

Investigator. You have given a list of persons to the investigators of this Committee, have you not?

Mr. Hayden. I have.

Investigator. Are there any you can identify as members of the Communist Party?

Mr. Hayden. I wouldn't hesitate to say Karen Morley.

Investigator. Did Karen Morley meet with you?

Mr. Hayden. Yes.

Investigator. Where were these meetings held?

Mr. Hayden. Some at her house, some at a house owned by Morris Carnovsky.

Investigator. Have you taken any other action which would indicate good faith in the break you claim you have made?

Mr. Hayden. One month after South Korea was invaded, my attorney sent a letter to J. Edgar Hoover, in which—

Investigator. Suppose you read that letter.

Mr. Hayden, *reading.* Dear Sir, In June of 1946, in a moment of emotional disturbance, a young man became a member of the Communist Party. In November he decided he had made a mistake and terminated his membership. Ever since, this client of ours has had no connection with the Communist Party. He is an American-born citizen with a distinguished war record. He enlisted in the Marine Corps as a private and received his termination as a captain. He received the Silver Star medal. Since Korea, our client has felt that the time may come when his services might be of aid to the United States. He is concerned with the fact that his brief membership in the Communist Party may prevent the use of his services. He is married and has young children. If his services are not needed by the United States, conditions may require an answer, in connection with ordinary employment, to the query: 'Are you now, or have you ever been, a Communist?' Our client can answer that he is not now a member of the Communist Party. He could not answer the rest of the question without either lying, or, if he told the truth, finding himself unable to earn a living. Justice requires some method by which one mistake does not operate (a) to prevent the United States from making use of our client, (b) to prevent our client from earning a living. He is willing to submit to interrogation by the FBI. The purpose of this is to permit our client, if the question is asked, to say, 'Please inquire of the FBI.' The FBI could then notify the prospective employer that there was no reason for not employing our client.

Investigator. Was a reply received?

Mr. Hayden. Yes. *He reads.* Dear Sir: Contact Mr. R. B. Hood, special agent in charge of our Los Angeles office. Very truly yours, J. Edgar Hoover.

Investigator. Did you report as requested?

Mr. Hayden. Yes.

Investigator. Have you anything to add, Mr. Hayden?

Mr. Hayden. I would like to say I appreciate very much, very, *very* much, the opportunity to appear here today. I think there is a service to be rendered, not only to the country at large, but to those who find themselves in a similar position to mine. I have heard there are hundreds of thousands of ex-Communists who don't know what to do about it. The suggestion made by the Chairman of this Committee that people come up and speak is extremely fine, constructive. My appearance before this committee could serve a very useful purpose!

Twelve years afterward, Sterling Hayden changed his story:

I was a rat, a stoolie, and the names I listed—some of those, close friends—were blacklisted and deprived of their livelihood.

He had been talked into naming names by a psychiatrist whom, in his book *Wanderer,* **he addresses thus:**

If it hadn't been for you, I wouldn't have turned into a stoolie for J. Edgar Hoover! I don't think you have the foggiest notion of the contempt I have had for myself since the day I did that thing. Fuck it! And fuck you!

On April 25, 1951, Edward Dmytryk came before the Committee for the second time.

Mr. Dmytryk. The situation has changed.

Investigator. What do you mean by that?

Mr. Dmytryk. Before '47 I had never heard anybody say they would refuse to fight for this country in a war against Soviet Russia. Then I saw articles about Party members taking that position: I believe Paul Robeson was one. I signed the Stockholm Peace Petition along with other people. I hoped they were sincere. The Korean War made me realize they were not. The North Koreans would not have attacked the South Koreans unless they had the backing of very strong forces: Those forces are China and Russia. This made me realize there is a Communist menace and that the Communist Party in this country is a part of that menace. The next thing was the spy trials, the Hiss, Coplon and Rosenberg cases, the Klaus Fuchs case. This is treason.

Investigator. I would like to have you state what the real object of the Communist Party is in Hollywood.

Mr. Dmytryk. They had three purposes: to get money, to get prestige, and to control the content of pictures. The only way they could control the content of pictures was to take over the guilds and the unions.

Investigator. What guilds?

Mr. Dmytryk. The Communists were successful for a time in controlling the Screen Writers Guild. They were not successful in the Screen Directors Guild.

Investigator. How many people were there in the Screen Directors Guild?

Mr. Dmytryk. Two hundred and thirty.

Investigator. And of that number were there a few Communists?

Mr. Dmytryk. Seven.

Investigator. Will you give us the names?

Mr. Dmytryk. Frank Tuttle, Herbert Biberman, Jack Berry, he's the Berry who lives on King's Road, Bernard Vorhaus, Jules Dassin, myself . . .

Investigator. Then you were transferred to another group?

Mr. Dmytryk. A special group: John Howard Lawson, Adrian Scott, Francis Faragoh, his wife Elizabeth, and myself.
Pause.

Investigator. Mr. Dmytryk, I understand you learned a good deal about Communism through your association with the Hollywood Ten?

Mr. Dmytryk. We held affairs to collect money, functions, dinners, that sort of thing. Speeches were made. I made a couple myself. But I couldn't work in Hollywood: We were fired, those of us who were under contract, five out of the Ten. I went to England and came back when it was assumed our case would get up to the Supreme Court, and we would either go to jail or not. We had a great many meetings of the Ten. A change had taken place while I was gone. The group was now following the Party line all the way.

Investigator. When do you consider you withdrew from the Party?

Mr. Dmytryk. In the fall of '45. However, I was teaching at the Center till '47. I was a member of the Hollywood Ten. So I *didn't* break. I want to explain that. As a man who'd made his choice in his appearance before the Committee in '47, I felt I should follow this choice until the Supreme Court either decided we were right or we were wrong and went to jail. I felt, if I started crying uncle, I was doing it to avoid going to jail, although I'd already made up my mind, as soon as my sentence was over, I'd issue an affidavit and disclose that I'd been a member of the Party. Actually, I issued such an affidavit while in prison, the Korean War so bothered me.

Investigator. This was a statement dictated by your own conscience?

Mr. Dmytryk. Absolutely. *Pause.* I've heard rumors. One, that I'd been offered a job at MGM at five thousand a week if I would make such an affidavit. The other is, "They put the works to Dmytryk in jail, and *that's* why he made his affidavit." There was no pressure, nor have I ever been offered a bribe or a job—I wish I had!

CM 2. What would you call the final test of credibility of a witness purporting to be a former Communist? Primarily the willingness to name names?

Mr. Dmytryk. I believe so. That is why I am doing it. I know there have been comments that people who talk are informers. I went to the dictionary and looked up the word. An informer is a man who informs against colleagues who are engaged in criminal activity. By using this word, the Communists are admitting they are engaged in criminal activity!

The Chairman. Permit me, Mr. Dmytryk, to add my feeble expression of appreciation for the information you have given the American people, millions of whom haven't the vaguest conception what the Communist movement stands for!

On July 13, 1951, *Hollywood Life* carried the headline: Dore Schary and Dashiell Hammett, Communist Connections

Earlier that year they had run the headline: John Garfield   Lena Horne   Judy Holliday   José Ferrer   Howard Duff   Orson Welles Support Communist Party

In testifying before the Un-American Activities Committee, John Garfield said the Communist Party should be outlawed so that people like him would be protected from it. José Ferrer, who claimed that he had celebrated May Day without knowing what May Day celebrated and that he had helped elect Communist Councilman Ben Davis without knowing Davis' party, was propelled by the Committee on May 22, 1951, toward conclusions.

Investigator. Do you have any suggestions, Mr. Ferrer, about Communist-front organizations in your profession?

Mr. Ferrer. It is extremely important that the ability of this Committee rapidly to inform any member of the profession who wants instruction be highly publicized! There is nothing like dragging something out into the open and exposing it to air!

CM 1. That is what this Committee has been doing for years, and you didn't believe it until a few days ago!

CM 2. Mr. Ferrer, what course of action could this Committee take in advertising that May Day is an international Communist celebration?

Mr. Ferrer. I think that is no longer necessary.

CM 2. What course can we take, as far as artists are concerned, in instances where they support Communist candidates for public office?

Mr. Ferrer. We have all learned a lot in the last few months, sir. I certainly have. If the question ever comes up before me, I am going to very strongly advise people to find out, tell them this Committee exists and they should—

CM 1. Why wait until the question comes before you? Why not start now?

Mr. Ferrer. Mr. Kearney, if you tell me how, I will be glad to. I will. I'll ask you for a few suggestions!

CM 2. Do I understand, Mr. Ferrer, that you advocate the outlawing of the Communist Party?

Mr. Ferrer. Yes, sir, I do! Definitely! Emphatically!

CM 2. Would you assign a reason *why* it should be outlawed?

Mr. Ferrer. Because, through conversations, investigation, and research I have done, because of the subpoena and my appearance here, I have been convinced, and it has been pointed out to me irrefutably, that the Communist Party of America is the instrument, definitely, of a foreign government, that its aims are those of a foreign government, and have nothing to do with our own life or our own welfare. The mere fact that it is un-American seems to me to make it *ipso facto* illegal!

Before the end of 1951 Ronald Reagan proclaimed a victory:

For many years the Red propagandists and conspirators concentrated their big guns on Hollywood. They threatened to throw acid in the faces of myself and some other stars, so we would never appear on screen again. I packed a gun for some time. Policemen lived at my home to guard my kids. But that was more than five years ago. Those days are gone forever!

Less than two years later, July 15, 1953, Larry Parks addressed a letter to the Committee:

> In rereading my testimony, I am convinced that it improperly reflects my attitude. Some of the testimony can be explained by the fact that I was the first cooperative witness from Hollywood and under strain. Upon reflection I see that I did not adequately express my beliefs. If I were to testify today, I would not say, as I did in '51, that to give such testimony is to wallow in the mud. I would recognize that such cooperation would help the cause. Liberals must embrace the cause of anti-Communism with the zeal we once did that of anti-Nazism. Communists should be exposed. To assist your Committee in obtaining information about the Communist Party is the duty of all who possess such evidence. I completely support the objectives of the Un-American Activities Committee.

1952. *Guys and Dolls,* **already a Broadway hit, had been optioned for the movies by Paramount. They had paid $75,000 for their option when it turned out that one of the authors and owners of the work, Abe Burrows, had a past.**

Investigator. Mr. Burrows, you appeared in executive session in 1951. Your testimony was *vague* with regard to individuals who have been members of the Communist Party. The investigation has continued. There was a witness in 1952, Mr. Owen Vinson, who testified, "Abe Burrows attended meetings of the Communist Party which I attended, yes, sir." Upon taking this testimony, we heard that you desired to appear before the Committee.

Mr. Burrows. I wanted to come back and talk to you people again because I really want to get this thing cleared up. My Americanism being under suspicion is very painful to me, not just economically but painful to a guy who loves his country, his home, his people. I have no recollection of ever applying for Party membership, although I've been told that somebody had seen a card and I don't believe it. If someone testifies that he thought I was a Communist, I guess he's telling the truth as he sees it. However, kind of a stubborn pride on my part makes me happy in the belief that maybe I didn't take the final step.

Investigator. By "final step," what do you mean?

42

Mr. Burrows. I mean the actual going through the ritualistic stuff which you had to go through before you became a member.

CM 1. Did you attend Communist cell meetings?

Mr. Burrows. Back in '43 I met a fellow named Samuel Sillen. We met in the country or somewhere, and started to talk books. He introduced me to Joe North, who was managing editor of the *New Masses,* and another fellow named John Stewart, I think it was, and they would sit around and talk to me. At one time they said, "You ought to be much closer to us." When I came to California, about a week after I arrived, I was called by Albert Maltz, and Maltz said, "Samuel Sillen said for me to get in touch with you." He came with his wife and visited me at my home.

CM 2. Was Samuel Sillen a member of the Communist Party?

Mr. Burrows. Well, sir, he was literary editor of the *New Masses.*

CM 2. And Joe North, did you know *him* to be a member?

Mr. Burrows. He would say, "We Communists." *Pause.* They once invited me to a lecture under the auspices of the Communist Party in which Earl Browder had a debate with George Sokolsky! Everybody got along in those days! '43! A big crowd and stuff like that.

CM 2. How about John Stewart? Did you know him to be a member of the Communist Party?

Mr. Burrows. Well, he wrote a book with a fellow who used to give lectures in Hollywood on the Marxist approach to history or something. Everything was called things like that, you know. A fellow named Bruce Minton.

CM 2. Do you know whether Bruce Minton used any other name?

Mr. Burrows. His real name was Richard Bransten, I believe.

CM 2. How well did you know him?

Mr. Burrows. I was at his home a couple of times. His wife was Ruth McKenney. In those days, I was invited everywhere. Attended more parties than anyone. The *Saturday Evening Post* did an article about me and the fact that I played at parties all over Hollywood. It got a little out of hand. I used to go to too many, and, when I started to get asked by people I didn't know, I began to quit going. You know, people would say, "Come to the party," so I attended parties, with all kinds of people, right, left, middle. I never turned down an invitation to go to the piano. I played up these songs!

CM 2. Now, as to these study groups, you studied Communism?

Mr. Burrows. To orientate people on what they called a Marxist approach to show business. They used to have continual squabbles as to the role of a writer. If you recall, it was a tremendous controversy that Albert Maltz had, I think it was, where he said art is a weapon, and they said·art isn't a weapon. Or rather he said art *isn't* a weapon, and they said it *is* a weapon. I used to find myself in arguments. I'm a satirist, and one of my best-known satires is a satire of a kind of documentary radio program that was very common among the left-wing writers of the day. There was a big tendency to do these very pontifical radio programs with everybody talking very loud and introducing Thomas Jefferson and Abraham Lincoln. So I did a thing on that at the piano. The first time I did it was for some kind of a cause, and there was a pretty large left-wing crowd, I guess, and there was a kind of a quiet in the room, and then one of the fellows came over and said, "That is a very bad thing for you to do, Abe, you know." I said, "Why?" and he said, "Because I think it is wrong." These guys had no sense of humor about themselves. That's one of the reasons I wasn't too trusted.

CM 2. Do you recall any of these study groups?

Mr. Burrows. One of them was the group Bruce Minton ran. It was called a study group, but he just talked. Engaged in a terrific controversy with John Howard Lawson over how history was to be interpreted. I didn't know what either of them meant. That was one group. Then there was a book called *Literature and Art*, by Marx and Engels, or something. And a group gathered to discuss this. A lot of people were kind of faceless to me, and when I saw the list that Owen Vinson named as the group I was supposed to have been part of, I knew, maybe, two of them.

CM 2. Mr. Burrows, you are a fairly intelligent man. Couldn't you tell from the way their party line shifted that you were studying Marxist Communism?

Mr. Burrows. Oh, yes, I knew that.

CM 2. And if you were interested in Marxist Communism, don't you think it's reasonable to assume you were a member of the Communist Party?

Mr. Burrows. The study groups I mentioned were in '45 when there was no word of Marxist Communism as we know it. It was a case of the writer's role in the war, in establishing unity, how the writer should treat minorities, the war effort, he shouldn't make jokes about gas rationing, stuff like that. I attended no such study groups when the party switched back to a revolutionary role.

CM 2. But you know, don't you, that to get into those study groups you had to be considered for membership in the Communist Party?

Mr. Burrows. Well, because of my work, my humor, my satire, I wasn't very well trusted. I was called chi-chi because I did satires on folk songs in a period when the Communist Party had taken the folk song very dearly to its bosom.

The Chairman. During the period '43 to '45 what was your annual income?

Mr. Burrows. In '43 about $40,000, in '44 about $50,000, in '45 over $50,000.

The Chairman. Can you name organizations you contributed to?

Mr. Burrows. Hollywood Independent Citizens Committee. I once gave money to a *People's World* fund.

Investigator. And the *New Masses?*

Mr. Burrows. Yes, sir.

The Chairman. All right, then, categorically, did you pay dues to the Communist Party?

Mr. Burrows. Not to my knowledge, sir.

The Chairman. Categorically, were you ever requested to pay dues to the Communist Party as such?

Mr. Burrows. Not to my knowledge, sir.

The Chairman. Categorically, did you ever decline to pay dues because you didn't have the money with you?

Mr. Burrows. Well, categorically, no, sir, because it just doesn't sound like me.

The Chairman. I'm not asking what it sounds like. Did you or did you not?

Mr. Burrows. No, sir.

The Chairman. Did you ever give Owen Vinson any money for any purpose?

Mr. Burrows. I may have, sir.

The Chairman. Do you know whether you did or not?

Mr. Burrows. I couldn't answer that for sure, sir.

The Chairman. Now, categorically, when he said that you paid him money for Communist Party dues, was he telling the truth?

Mr. Burrows. He may have thought he was telling the truth.

The Chairman. I didn't ask you that.

Mr. Burrows. It is very difficult for me to say, because—

The Chairman. Did you pay Vinson Communist Party dues, as he swore before this committee?

Mr. Burrows. No, sir, not to my knowledge.

Pause.

Investigator. Mr. Vinson told us he was a member of that group of radio writers and named other persons. You stated you knew two of them. Who were the two?

Mr. Burrows. Sam Moore and Georgia Backus.

Investigator. Have you had any conversation with Sam Moore with regard to testifying?

Mr. Burrows. Yes, sir. I got the subpoena, got in touch with my lawyer, and we agreed to ask for an immediate hearing in Washington, well in advance of the date we were called. Sam called me up—I hadn't seen him for a number of years—and said he'd like to see me. We met at Moore's restaurant right next to the Forty-Eighth Street Theatre where I was rehearsing. Sam said, "I hear you got a subpoena." I said, "Yup," and he said, "I got one too." I hadn't known that. It wasn't in the paper. He said, "What are you going to do with it?" I said, "Well, I have to keep that to myself." He said, "Well, the only thing to do is to stick with the Fifth Amendment." I said, "Sam, it is something I don't agree with you on, but I can't argue with you." It got very cold in the restaurant and I got up. As a matter of fact, we ordered coffee and I didn't finish the coffee. I paid the bill and went to my rehearsal, and he left, and I haven't seen him since.

The Chairman. Why would he ask you to avail yourself of the Fifth Amendment?

Mr. Burrows. His theory was everybody ought to stick together.

The Chairman. Everybody?

Mr. Burrows. Everybody!

Investigator. Was Georgia Backus a member of the Communist Party?

Mr. Burrows. I kind of assumed it. She was very intense about everything.

Investigator. Do you recall meetings at which she was present?

Mr. Burrows. Yes. Georgia was at everything.

Investigator. Who acted as chairman?

Mr. Burrows. I don't recall.

Investigator. Were you acquainted with Hy Alexander?

Mr. Burrows. Slightly.

Investigator. Was he chairman?

Mr. Burrows. He wasn't the type. A very quiet fellow. I think he was married to Georgia Backus. He was married to somebody.

CM 2. Mr. Burrows, have you never signed an application for the Communist Party?

Mr. Burrows. Not to my knowledge, sir. I think I'd remember.

CM 2. Are you equally sure you never signed your name on a Party card?

Mr. Burrows. Yes, sir. As I said, somebody told me they saw a card with my name on it. I don't know how anybody would have a card that I signed.

The Chairman. Do you sign instruments without knowing what they are?

Mr. Burrows. No, sir.

The Chairman. You read what you sign?

Mr. Burrows. Yes, sir.

The Chairman. Then why are you indefinite about whether you signed it?

Mr. Burrows. I am not indefinite.

The Chairman. You say now, categorically, you did not do it?

Mr. Burrows. To my recollection, I never signed any such thing.

The Chairman. That is still indefinite. Will you tell us whether you signed?

Mr. Burrows. No, sir.

The Chairman. You did not do it?

Mr. Burrows. I have no recollection of doing such a thing.

The Chairman. I asked you, *did* you do it.

Mr. Burrows. Well, I say, sir—

The Chairman. Do you want to leave the Committee in doubt?

Mr. Burrows. No, sir.

The Chairman. Then did you?

Mr. Burrows. I didn't.

The Chairman. Proceed, Mr. Tavenner.

Pause.

Investigator. When did these discussions regarding literature take place?

Mr. Burrows. Somebody would say, "A group of us are getting together for a talkfest Monday night," or something.

Investigator. In whose home were these meetings held?

Mr. Burrows. A lot of them were held in places that didn't seem to be homes. They seemed to be houses but not homes. They were sparsely furnished. I remember one on the Crescent Heights Boulevard or something. Nobody seemd to live there. I remember Vinson's house because he was one who put up the chairs. You figure it's the host who's doing that.

Investigator. Were you acquainted with Elizabeth Glenn?

Mr. Burrows. I met her. She used to kind of wheel around at benefits and big functions.

Investigator. She was a functionary of the Communist Party?

Mr. Burrows. She was an exceptionally large lady. A lot of these people on the Left would show up at my place, and she was brought one night by Richard Bransten. Bruce Minton.

Investigator. What was the purpose of her visit?

Mr. Burrows. They dropped by after some kind of thing where everybody dropped by at somebody's house for a drink. After a rally or something. She said, "Did you read Albert Maltz's new book?" Maltz had just written *The Cross and the Arrow,* I think it was, a book about war in Germany, and I said, "No," and she said it was terrible.

Investigator. Did you know she was a functionary of the Communist Party?

Mr. Burrows. I assumed she was a wheel.

Investigator. Were you acquainted with Elaine Gonda?

Mr. Burrows. I remembered her when I read Charles Glenn's name because they were having a romance or something. They used to sit and hold hands.

Investigator. Well, they became married, didn't they?

Mr. Burrows. Really? Well, that's the end of the romance!
Pause.

Investigator. You met Samuel Sillen in New York. When *was* that?

Mr. Burrows. 1943. He introduced me to these other people from the *New Masses,* and they asked me to their houses. They said they hadn't had a humor column for a long time. You know there wasn't anything very humorous in the *New Masses.* So Joe North asked me would I consider doing a humor column. And I said no.

Investigator. Why?

Mr. Burrows. I never wrote for a Communist publication!

Investigator. But, if you would associate with all these Communists, if you would support the *People's World* and the *New Masses!*

Mr. Burrows. I never went all the way.

Investigator. You don't admit having been a member of the Communist Party, but you do admit—?

Mr. Burrows. When the Chairman questioned me today, I got a sharp insight. It hit me like a flash when he said, "Why did Sam Moore come to you?" I had never asked myself, *Why* did he come to me? Sam Moore thought I was a member, or he wouldn't have come to me.

Investigator. Sam Moore had a *right* to think you were a member?

Mr. Burrows. The people I was around with could have *thought* I was a member. My sloppiness or whatever it was gave them the right to think I was.

Investigator. Were you an instructor at the People's Educational Center, Mr. Burrows?

Mr. Burrows. I was.

Investigator. Who solicited you for that work?

Mr. Burrows. The executive director. Kenneth, I think. I don't know the whole name. Is there a name Kenneth something?
Pause.

Investigator. There may be a number of people by that name.
Pause.

Investigator. Were you affiliated with the Joint Anti-Fascist Refugee Committee?

Mr. Burrows. I don't know. Somebody called me and said, "Abe, would you do a benefit Saturday night?" I do thousands of things. But now I watch them.

Investigator. When did you begin *watching* them?

Mr. Burrows. Right after the war when the Communist Party was opposed to building up American defenses. I recruited soldiers and Marines, wrote the shows, prepared them, and put them on for the Army. I got a citation for it. And I have this letter from the Poor Richard Club of Philadelphia: "The directors are gratified to learn that you have consented to join the club honoring General Eisenhower at the Bellevue-Stratford Hotel, January 17." With General Eisenhower! I was thrilled! I went to the dinner. My stand on Communism itself never changed. I am kind of anti-authoritarian in my thinking. I hate their whole approach, that says any means to an end is ok.

CM 2. Were you conscious of the fact that the Party line was directed from Russia?

Mr. Burrows. I was, during the Pact, sir.

CM 2. Up to June 21, 1941, you were conscious that policy was directed by Russia?

Mr. Burrows. I was.

CM 2. After that you *weren't* conscious of it?

Mr. Burrows. To my eternal regret I got sucked back in by all the statements about unity.

CM 2. I must say, Mr. Burrows, you were pretty naive.

Mr. Burrows. I would say I was *stupid*. I could never go along with violence. I don't believe you kill people for their own good. All you do is make the world nonexistent. I want to fight Communism, prove how much I hate this whole thing! I can fight it best with my own weapons. An anti-Communist comedy—

Investigator. Our observation has been that ridicule is one of the most effective weapons against the Communist Party!

Mr. Burrows. They can't take it. I read somewhere they don't like jokes.

The Chairman. I'll ask you the question now: Are you a member of the Communist Party?

Mr. Burrows. No, Sir.

The Chairman. Have you ever been a member of the Communist Party?

Mr. Burrows. I've never applied for membership. If there's a Party card with my name on it, I know nothing about it.

The Chairman. Answer the question whether you have ever been, or considered yourself, a member of the Communist Party.

Mr. Burrows. I was *considered* a Communist.

The Chairman. You so considered youself?

Mr. Burrows. In my own heart I didn't, but I was considered a Communist, and that was the whole thing of my coming here.

The Chairman. You know whether or not you were, don't you?

Mr. Burrows. Well, you see, sir, I committed enough acts to be *called* a Communist.

The Chairman. Would you call *yourself* a Communist?

Mr. Burrows. Not in my own heart, sir. But I'm here to tell the truth, the whole truth, and nothing but the truth, and there's an element of truth in the statement that I was a Communist. *Pause.* There's also an element of untruth.

The Chairman. I can't understand how you can say you are not *now* a member of the Communist Party and not clearly express whether you have *ever* been.

Mr. Burrows. I was around with those fellows. I *was,* by association. I can't deny that.

The Chairman. Well. You're not necessarily a Communist by association.

Mr. Burrows. They *assumed* me to be one, and I'm not denying they had a right to.

The Chairman. You mean you participated in Communist activities with a reservation in your heart?

Mr. Burrows. Yes, sir. That is very well put.

CM 2. You did attend Communist Party meetings?

Mr. Burrows. Meetings at which Communists were present. *Silence.* Those were bad years for me. In personal trouble. My mother and father had both died. I had to seek help from a psychiatrist. That whole period is kind of painful, a very painful period to me. *Silence.*

The Chairman. They were *Communist Party* meetings?

Mr. Burrows. I imagine so. I really am vague on that. I am sorry if I sound overvague.

Abe Burrows did sound overvague to Paramount. They dropped their option on *Guys and Dolls* at once. The film was finally made by another company only when Burrows' case had been appealed to the unofficial chief justice of the United States in those years, the columnist George E. Sokolsky.

On April 11, 1952, *The New York Times* printed a paid ad signed "Elia Kazan":

Seventeen and a half years ago I was a twenty-four-year-old stage manager and bit actor making forty dollars a week when I worked. At that time nearly all of us felt menaced by the Depression and by Hitler. The streets were full of unemployed and shaken men. I joined the Communist Party in the summer of '34.

Investigator. Mr. Kazan, you testified in closed session on January 14, did you not?

Mr. Kazan. Correct.

Investigator. You declined at that time to identify others?

Mr. Kazan. Most of the others.

Investigator. Now you have requested the Committee to give you an opportunity to explain the participation of others?

Mr. Kazan. I want to tell you everything. *He reads from a paper.* "I was assigned to a unit composed of members of the Group Theatre. These were Lewis Leverett, J. Edward Bromberg, Phoebe Brand—later Mrs. Morris Carnovsky, I was instrumental in bringing her into the Party, Morris Carnovsky, Paula Miller, later Mrs. Lee Strasberg, Clifford Odets, Art Smith, Tony Kraber—he recruited me into the Party. The last straw came when I was invited to go through a typical scene of crawling and apologizing and admitting the error of my ways. The invitation came from a functionary from Detroit. I regret I cannot remember his name. He made a vituperative analysis of my conduct in refusing to fall in with the Party plan for the Group Theatre and invited my repentance. I had had enough. I had a taste of police-state living, and I didn't like it. That night I quit." *Glancing up from the paper:* There follows a list of the plays I have done and the films I have made. *Sing Out Sweet Land* by Jean and Walter Kerr. Full of American tradition and spirit. *The Strings My Lord Are False* by Paul Vincent Carroll. Shows courage in many kinds of people including, prominently, a priest. *Viva Zapata* is an anti-Communist picture: please see my article in *The Saturday Review,* which I have forwarded to your investigator. I have placed a copy of this affidavit with Spyros P. Skouras, president of 20th Century-Fox.

Investigator. Mr. Kazan, the Committee may desire to recall you for further explanations.

Mr. Kazan. I will be glad to do anything you consider necessary.

The Chairman. It is only through people such as you that we have been able to bring the attention of the American people to the Communist conspiracy for world domination.

Tony Kraber was summoned before the Committee three years later accompanied by his attorney Leonard B. Boudin.

Investigator. Mr. Kraber, were you a member of a Communist Party organization within the Group Theater in 1934 or '35?

Mr. Kraber. I believe this question to be an invasion of my rights, and I decline to answer on the ground of the First Amendment and the Fifth Amendment.

Investigator. Mr. Elia Kazan testified that he was recruited into a Communist Party organization within the Group Theatre by Tony Kraber.

Mr. Kraber. Is this the Kazan that signed the contract for $500,000 the day after he gave names to this Committee?

Investigator. Would it change the facts if he did?

CM 1. Do you say that Mr. Kazan committed perjury before this Committee?

Mr. Kraber. I will decline to answer this question.

Investigator. Did you recruit Mr. Kazan into the Communist Party?

Mr. Kraber. I decline to answer on the ground of the First Amendment and the Fifth Amendment.

On May 5, 1953, Jerome Robbins came before the Committee.

The Chairman. I understand you desire the lights be turned off, Mr. Robbins?

Mr. Robbins. Yes.

Investigator. You were at one time a member of the Communist Party, is that correct?

Mr. Robbins. Yes.

Investigator. For how long were you a member?

Mr. Robbins. I attended my first meetings in the spring of '44. At one of the earliest meetings, I was asked in what way did dialectical materialism help me to do my ballet *Fancy Free*!
Laughter.

Investigator. Will you tell the Committee what brought about the termination of your relationship with the Communist Party?

Mr. Robbins. The last meeting I attended was in '47. A fight broke out. Everyone began arguing and yelling. I suddenly realized I was in the midst of chaos, of an unorganized frantic group. It was too much. I didn't know what I was doing here. I had no interest in contributing.

Investigator. Who recruited you into the Party, Mr. Robbins?

Mr. Robbins. Miss Lettie Stever.

Investigator. Will you give us the names of other persons in this group?

Mr. Robbins. Lloyd Gough. Lionel Berman.

Investigator. A Party member asked you to what extent dialectical materialism influenced you in the production of *Fancy Free*?

Mr. Robbins. Yes.

Investigator. Who *was* that?

Mr. Robbins. Madeline Lee.

Investigator. Can you recall the names of other persons?

Mr. Robbins. Elliott Sullivan.

Investigator. Elliott Sullivan. Do you know how Elliott Sullivan was employed?

Mr. Robbins. I believe he was an actor. *Pause.* Edna Ocko. Jerome Chodorov.

Investigator. Jerome Chodorov?

Mr. Robbins. And Edward Chodorov.

Investigator. Edward Chodorov.

CM 1. Mr. Robbins, I want to compliment you on what you have done! We have had men before us who have referred to people who have named others as "stool pigeons," "informers." You realize, no doubt, that when you volunteered the names of Communists you would be put in that class?

Mr. Robbins. Yes, sir.

CM 1. You did it with your eyes open?

Mr. Robbins. I did it according to my conscience.

CM 1. Now, I have a very personal question—and I have never met you, I have never talked with you before, have I?

Mr. Robbins. No, sir.

CM 1. What is it in your conscience that makes *you*, certainly one of the top men in your profession, one who has reached the *pinnacle* in your art, willing to come here and testify as you have today, in spite of the fact that you knew some people would put you down as a "stool pigeon"?

Mr. Robbins. I've examined myself. I think I made a great mistake in entering the Communist Party. I feel I am now doing the right thing as an American.

CM 1. Again, I want to compliment you! You are in a wonderful place, through your art, your music, your talent which God blessed you with, to be vigorous and positive in promoting Americanism in contrast to Communism! Let me suggest that you use that great talent which God has blessed you with to put into ballets in some way, to put into music in some way, that interpretation!

Mr. Robbins. Sir, all my works have been acclaimed for their American quality particularly.

CM 1. But let me urge you to put even more of that in it!

The Chairman. Mr. Robbins, you have performed a patriotic service to the Committee. Congress and the American people are very thankful to you.

Elliott Sullivan was summoned before the Committee two years later accompanied by his attorney, Bella Abzug.

Investigator. Mr. Martin Berkeley described a fraction meeting of the Communist Party which he said Elliott Sullivan attended. Mr. Sullivan, are you acquainted with Martin Berkeley?

Mr. Sullivan. This Committee does not have the right to ask me about my associations. As for the long, tired list of men who have sold their honor and dignity for a mess of pottage, for a job, for a movie contract, I believe they will be judged by the decent people in this country.

Investigator. Are you acquainted with Jerome Robbins?

Mr. Sullivan. I know him. I used to know him. I will amend that definitely: I used to know him.

Investigator. When did you cease to know him? When he testified before this Committee?

Mr. Sullivan. Will you repeat the question?

Investigator. I am asking whether the time you ceased to know Jerome Robbins began when he testified before this Committee?

Mr. Sullivan. I would say that is the case. Yes.

Martin Berkeley was a screenwriter who, after initial hesitation, had come in to the Committee and named 162 names.

Mr. Berkeley. My name was mentioned by cooperative witness Richard Collins, and I sent a very silly telegram to the Committee. I charged Mr. Collins with perjury and said I had never been a member of the Communist Party, which was not true. I did it in a moment of panic and was a damn fool.

Investigator. Since that time you have determined that you will aid this Committee in every possible way?

Mr. Berkeley. Yes, sir.

Investigator. Tell the Committee what the Communist Party was attempting to accomplish and the methods by which they expected to accomplish it.

Mr. Berkeley. I am reminded of one day at Lionel Stander's house. He came in all excited. He says, "By golly, I got away with it." I said, "What did you get away with?" because—I don't want to refer to him again as a screwball, but the man was a screwball! He said, "Well, I was shooting this picture, and I had to wait for the elevator. I pressed the button, and there was a pause, and the director said, 'Whistle something and fill in, so I whistled four bars of the 'Internationale.'" That was about the extent of what the Communists were able to do!

Investigator. Tell the Committee when and where the Hollywood section of the Communist Party was organized.

Mr. Berkeley. By a strange coincidence, in my house. In June 1937. In my house out on Beverly Glen. We were honored by the presence of many functionaries. The spirit was swell.

CM 1. Is that "swell" or "smell"?

Mr. Berkeley. "Smell" I would say now!

Investigator. Give us the names of those in attendance who were members of the Communist Party.

Mr. Berkeley. Well, in addition to those I've mentioned, there was Donald Ogden Stewart, Dorothy Parker, her husband Allen Campbell, my old friend Dashiell Hammett, now in jail in New York for his activities, and that excellent playwright Lillian Hellman.

Summoned to Washington in May 1952 to answer Martin Berkeley's charges, Lillian Hellman wrote a letter to the Chairman.

Dear Mr. Wood,
I am willing to testify before the representatives of our Government as to my own opinions and action regardless of any risks to myself. But I am advised by counsel that if I answer questions about myself, I will have waived my rights under the Fifth Amendment and could be forced legally to answer questions about others. If I refuse to do so, I can be cited for contempt. This is very difficult for a layman to understand. But there is one principle that I do understand: I am not willing, now or in the

future, to bring bad trouble to people who, in my past association with them, were completely innocent of any talk or any action that was disloyal or subversive. To hurt innocent people in order to save myself, is, to me, inhuman and indecent and dishonorable. I cannot and will not cut my conscience to fit this year's fashions. I was raised in an old-fashioned American tradition and there were certain homely things that were taught to me: to try to tell the truth, not to bear false witness, not to harm my neighbor, to be loyal to my country. I respected these ideals of Christian honor and did as well with them as I knew how. It is my belief that you will agree with these simple rules of human decency and not expect me to violate the good American tradition from which they spring. I am prepared to waive the privilege against self-incrimination and tell you everything you wish to know about my views or actions if your Committee will refrain from asking me to name other people.

> Sincerely yours,
> Lillian Hellman.

The Chairman informed Miss Hellman that the Committee could "not be placed in the attitude of trading with the witness as to what they will testify to." Miss Hellman invoked the Fifth Amendment.

Almost as informative as the screenwriter Martin Berkeley was the actor Marc Lawrence.

Investigator. How long did you remain a member of the Communist Party, Mr. Lawrence?

Mr. Lawrence. I didn't believe myself to be a *member* in terms of participation. I merely investigated and wanted to hear what these people had to say. About 1946 I did one play for the Actors' Lab—

Investigator. What was the title of the play?

Mr. Lawrence. *Volpone.*

Investigator. Your primary interest was to investigate. What do you mean by that?

Mr. Lawrence. Well, I am a curious kind of schmoe. I am the kind of guy that listens to speeches. The guy comes over to me and says, "Listen, that sounds pretty good, why don't you defend this idea?" I got involved that way. I didn't defend the idea, I listened to the idea. It is a very destructive thing. It has been to me. Having been a member of the Communist Party has been a great error in my life. I have never voted the Communist ticket. I have been a registered Democrat. The Communist Party is very destructive. I will not, as a patriot, defend any of its interests. I feel that strongly about it! I will defend this country in case of war with Russia! I will defend it with my life!

Investigator. Give us the names of those who were members with you in this cell within the Actors' Lab.

Mr. Lawrence. J. Edward Bromberg, Karen Morley, Morris Carnovsky.

Investigator. You stated Lionel Stander was the one who introduced you into the Communist Party.

Mr. Lawrence. He said to me, "Get to know this stuff and you will make out more with the dames!" This is the guy, this is the introduction!

On May 6, 1953 Lionel Stander, accompanied by his attorney, Leonard B. Boudin, came before the Committee at his own request to deal with the charges of Marc Lawrence and Martin Berkeley.

Mr. Stander. Mr. Velde, I would like it very much if you turned off the lights and disconnected the television cameras as I am a professional performer and I only appear on TV for entertainment or for philanthropic organizations, and I consider this a matter that doesn't fall into either category.

The Chairman. You mean a man who has been before the cameras would have difficulty testifying?

Mr. Stander. Yes. When I am before a camera I am an entertainer, not a witness.

The Chairman. You are before the United States Government now!

Mr. Stander. Which is a very serious thing, sir!

The Chairman. A very serious thing.

Mr. Stander. If I were here as an entertainer, I wouldn't have any objection, but—

The Chairman. The Committee desires to give the public the information that comes before it in all shapes and forms and the *excuse* that you are an entertainer—

Mr. Stander. That isn't an *excuse*, it is a fact.

The Chairman. —has no bearing whatsoever.

Mr. Stander. I *am* an entertainer. And it is quite different to come before the camera in a carefully rehearsed script and, on the other hand, to come before the camera as a witness before a Committee.

The Chairman. Now, Mr. Stander—

Mr. Stander. I would appreciate it if you would turn the lights and cameras off.

Mr. Boudin. It's been done for other witnesses!

The Chairman. Because it would make them nervous and/or interfere with the testimony they had to give.

Mr. Stander. I am not exactly calm this morning. I am playing in another city, and haven't had any sleep. I was unable to get a room in a hotel.

The Chairman. Well, Mr. Stander, let me ask you—

Mr. Stander. I've been in Philadelphia, and—

The Chairman. If we do turn off the cameras, will you answer the questions put to you by counsel?

Mr. Stander. I intend to cooperate! I took an oath, and I believe in my oaths!

The Chairman. In that case, will the television and newsreel cameras please desist, and will the still photographers take their pictures and kindly retire during the witness' testimony?

Pause while this happens.

Investigator. The witness appeared before this Committee in 1940, denied having been a member of the Communist Party and stated that he never intended to be. In 1951 Marc Lawrence testified before the Committee and alluded to this witness. On the following day a telegram was received in which the witness denied the statements made by Mr. Lawrence and requested an opportunity to appear before the Committee.

The Chairman. This matter has been before the Committee for two years?

Investigator. Yes.

Mr. Stander. I tried to get an *immediate* hearing! I sent a letter to every member of the Committee! I went in person to Washington and saw Congressman Kearney, who assured me—

CM 1. Mr. Stander—

Mr. Stander. —I would have an immediate hearing. It was important. Merely receiving the subpoena caused me to be blacklisted in radio, television, and motion pictures. At the same time I sued the witness who perjured himself before this Committee, Mr. Marc Lawrence, in the State Supreme Court of New York, which ruled that he enjoyed congressional immunity. However, if he—

The Chairman. Mr. Stander, we are not interested in extraneous matters.

Mr. Stander. Extraneous? When a man comes directly from the psychopathic ward! I informed the Committee that this psychopath was used as a witness against me and, under advice of counsel, fled to Europe and is still a refugee from this court case.

CM 2. Do I understand, Mr. Stander, you are here to answer the sixty-four-dollar question?

Mr. Stander. I will answer *every* question! I have made an oath, and I'm not in the habit of violating my word, even when I *don't* swear an oath.

Investigator. Mr. Stander, will you tell the Committee, please, when and where were you born?

Mr. Stander. New York City, January 11, 1908.

Investigator. What is your occupation?

Mr. Stander. I'm basically an actor. I've been a newspaper reporter. I've been a director of stage entertainments for the Red Cross, the Air Force, the Kiwanis' junior and senior chambers of commerce, Elks, Moose, and other organizations with animal names. I've produced two Broadway plays—I've been a theatrical person for the last twenty-six years. With an occasional venture into journalism.

Investigator. Have you also done screen writing or acting?

Mr. Stander. I've done screen acting. I've written a script or two for the screen.

Investigator. How long were you a screen actor, and where?

Mr. Stander. Well, my first jobs were in the old silent days as a kid actor. I worked with Marion Davies at the old Hearst Cosmopolitan.

Investigator. How long did you remain in Hollywood?

Mr. Stander. Until I exposed the criminal records of Browne and Bioff, the racketeer gangster officials who later went to jail. Because I exposed them one week before Westbrook Pegler exposed them in the paper, I was blacklisted by the Motion Picture Producers Association!

Investigator. How long did you continue as an actor?

Mr. Stander. After the major studios blacklisted me, I worked for independent producers—

Investigator. Approximately—

Mr. Stander. —up until Marc Lawrence mentioned my name, or rather, until Larry Parks said he *didn't* know me as a Communist.

Investigator. Let me—

Mr. Stander. That appeared in the paper. Just to have my name appear in association with this Committee! It's like the Spanish Inquisition!

Investigator. Let me remind you—

Mr. Stander. You may not be burned but you can't help coming away a little singed.

Investigator. How long did you engage in screen acting?

Mr. Stander. '35 to '48 or '9, except for a period in the Air Force. *He looks at a paper.* And while I'm looking at it here I notice the Chief of Staff gave me letters and autographed pictures attesting to my excellent service record and character!

Investigator. What is the date of—

Mr. Stander. I see a citation from the Red Cross, the war bond drive, the Treasury Department, and here's a tribute from the Armed Forces Radio Service. "Dear Mr. Stander, may I extend my appreciation for your splendid . . ."

The Chairman. Mr. Stander, if there is some part of your career you are proud of—

Mr. Stander. I am proud of *everything.*

The Chairman. You have made some self-serving statements, and—

Mr. Stander. Does the Committee charge me with being a Communist?

The Chairman. Mr. Stander, will you let me tell you? Will you be quiet while I tell you what you are here for?

Mr. Stander. Yes, I'd like to hear!

The Chairman. You are here to give us information which will enable us to do the work assigned to us by the House of Representatives: to investigate reports regarding subversive activities in the United States.

Mr. Stander. Well, I am more than willing to cooperate—

The Chairman. Now, just a minute.

Mr. Stander. —because I know of subversive activities in the entertainment industry and elsewhere!

The Chairman. Mr. Stander, the Committee is interested—

Mr. Stander. If you're *interested,* I can tell you right now.

The Chairman. —primarily in any subversive knowledge you have—

Mr. Stander. I have knowledge of subversive action! I know of a group of fanatics who are trying to undermine the Constitution of the United States by depriving artists of life, liberty, and the pursuit of happiness without due process of law! I can cite instances! I can tell names. I am one of the first victims, if you are interested. A group of ex-Bundists, America Firsters, and anti-Semites, people who hate everybody, Negroes, minority groups, and most likely themselves—

The Chairman. Now, Mr. Stander, unless you begin to answer these questions and act like a witness in a reasonable, dignified manner, under the rules of the Committee, I will be forced to have you removed from this room!

Pause.

Mr. Stander. I am deeply shocked, Mr. Chairman!

CM 2. Mr. Stander, let me—

Mr. Stander. I don't mean to be contemptuous of this Committee at all!

The Chairman. Will you—

Mr. Stander. I want to cooperate with your attempt to unearth subversive activities. I began to tell you about them, and I'm shocked by your cutting me off. I am not a dupe, or a dope, or a moe, or a schmoe, and I'm not ashamed of anything I said in public or private!

Investigator. Do you recall whether you left Hollywood in '48 or in '49?

Mr. Stander. I'm not sure. I made a tour of the night-club circuit, which was the only thing left to me after being blacklisted by the major studios—

Investigator. Will you tell—

Mr. Stander. —by merely newspaper accusation, without anybody charging me with anything. In fact, the last time I appeared here the Chairman *said* this Committee didn't charge me with anything, and I swore under oath—I would like, if you want, to introduce the record of my testimony here in August 27, 1940.

The Chairman. Well, you are not charged with anything.

Mr. Stander. I am not charged with lying under oath? You are not charging me with being a Communist?

CM 2. Will you subside until the Chairman finishes?

The Chairman. You are brought here as a witness.

Mr. Stander. I am a witness—

The Chairman. Please don't—

Mr. Stander. —not a defendant. I haven't been accused of anything! I want that very straight, because through newspaper headlines people get peculiar attitudes. Mere appearance here is tantamount to being blacklisted, because people say, "What is an actor doing in front of the Un-American Activities Committee?"

CM 2. Why did you want to appear before the Committee so badly, then?

Mr. Stander. Because I was told by my agent, if the Committee allowed me to refute Marc Lawrence's testimony, I'd be able to get back in motion pictures. One of the biggest TV agencies told my agent that, if I could again swear I wasn't a Communist, I'd have my own TV program! Which meant one hundred fifty thousand dollars a year to me.

CM 2. Mr. Stander—

Mr. Stander. So I had a hundred-and-fifty-thousand-buck motive—

CM 2. Mr. Stander, will you subside?

Mr. Stander. —for coming before the Committee!

CM 2. If you will just subside and answer the questions—

Mr. Stander. Are you inferring—

CM 2. Now, just a minute, Mr. Stander—

Mr. Stander. —anything I said wasn't the truth?

CM 2. Unless you do that, your performance is not going to be regarded as funny.

Mr. Stander. I want to state right now I was not—

CM 2. Will you please subside?

Mr. Stander. —trying to be funny.

CM 2. If you continue, I am going to ask the Chairman to turn on the cameras so your performance may be recorded for posterity!

Investigator. Now, Mr. Stander, the investigation the Committee has made would indicate that you have special knowledge of things that the Committee is inquiring about. Harold J. Ashe was asked the names of professional units whose membership was kept secret. Here is his testimony: "Lucy Stander, the wife of J. Stander, also known as Lionel Stander—"

Mr. Stander. I'm not married.

Investigator. Or your former wife.

Mr. Stander. Which one?

Investigator. Well, the name mentioned here was Lucy.

CM 1. Do you remember that name?

Mr. Stander. Yeah, I remember her. Vaguely.

Investigator. Let me read that again: "Lucy Stander, at that time the wife of J. Stander, also known as Lionel Stander—"

Mr. Stander. What year was that?

Investigator. Along about '36.

Mr. Stander. I wasn't married to Lucy in '36.

CM 3. It was evidently the time you *were* married to Lucy. You would know when you were married to Lucy, wouldn't you?

Mr. Stander. Yes. We were separated in '35.

Investigator, *reading.* "Lionel Stander was definitely a member of this group." Then, the testimony of Mr. Martin Berkeley: "I met Lionel Stander who later became chairman of the actors' fraction." Were you a member of the Communist Party at any time between 1935 and 1948?

Mr. Stander. I swore in 1940 that I was not a member of the Communist party—

CM 3. Why don't you swear under oath now?

Mr. Stander. You want me to give you the reason?

CM 3. Yes.

Pause.

Mr. Stander. Because by using psychopaths—and I have the letter here giving the mental history of Marc Lawrence, who came from a mental sanitorium—he suffered a mental breakdown, and you used that psychopath and this man Leech, who the district attorney and the grand jury didn't believe, and they cleared me— so, I don't want to be responsible for a whole stable of informers, stool pigeons, psychopaths, and ex-political heretics, who come in here beating their breasts and saying, "I'm awfully sorry, I didn't know what I was doing, please, I want *absolution,* get me back into pictures!" They will do anything *to get back into pictures!* They will mention names! They will name *anybody!*

Investigator. Are you acquainted with Martin Berkeley?

Mr. Stander. Any question by stool pigeons, informers, psychopathic liars—for instance, Mr. Berkeley—First, he said he wasn't a member of the Communist Party, then, when he realized you had the goods on him, he came here and rattled off 150 names. This is an *incredible* witness!

The Chairman. Do you decline to answer the question?

Mr. Stander. I resent the inference that anyone who invokes the Fifth, which our forefathers fought for, is guilty of anything. My name is Stander. The name was adopted because in feudal Spain my ancestors didn't have the protection of the United States Constitution and were religious refugees. And you know that the Puritans, the people that established this country, used the right. I have done a little research since you called me. The first instance was—

Investigator. Will you answer the question I asked you?

Mr. Stander. —and I am not being sacrilegious—when Jesus Christ was asked by Pontius Pilate, "These judges have a lot of witnesses against you?" And he said nothing.

Pause.

The Chairman. Will you answer the question?

Pause.

Mr. Stander, *quietly.* I decline under the First Amendment, which entitles me to freedom of belief, under the Fifth Amendment—in which there is no inference of guilt—and under the Ninth Amendment, which gives me the right to get up in the union hall, which I did, and introduce a resolution condemning this Committee for its abuse of powers in attempting to impose censorship upon the American theatre.

Investigator. Now, Mr. Stander—

Mr. Stander, *still quiet.* And finally, I can't understand why a question dating back to 1935 concerning statements made by a bunch of stool pigeons and informers can aid this Committee in recommending legislation to Congress. The question is not relevant to the purposes of this Committee.

Lionel Stander remained on the blacklist.

Arthur Miller, May 21, 1956.

Investigator. In 1953 did you criticize Elia Kazan as a renegade intellectual?

Mr. Miller. No.

Investigator. As an informer?

Mr. Miller. No.

Investigator. After Kazan had been your producer, worked with you in your plays, and came down to Washington and testified before a

Committee, "Yes, I have been a Communist, yes, I identify so-and-so and so-and-so as people who were in the conspiracy with me," did you break with him?

Mr. Miller. I broke with him—though that word is not descriptive of my act. There are private reasons involved which I don't believe are of interest here.

Pause.

Investigator. Tell us about these meetings with Communist writers which you said you attended in New York City. Who invited you there?

Mr. Miller. I don't know.

Investigator. Who was there when you walked into the room?

Pause.

Mr. Miller. I understand the philosophy behind this question and I want you to understand mine. I am trying to—and I will—protect my sense of myself. I could not use the name of another person and bring trouble on him. I ask you not to ask me that question.

CM 1. We do not accept your reasons for refusing to answer. If you do not answer, you are placing yourself in contempt.

Investigator. Was Arnaud d'Usseau chairman at this meeting of Communist writers in 1947 at which you were in attendance?

Pause.

Mr. Miller. My conscience will not permit me to use the name of another person.

By 373 votes to 9 the House of Representatives found Arthur Miller in contempt of Congress.

Paul Robeson, 1956. In the late forties, the screenstar Adolphe Menjou advised the Committee that Communist tendencies in American citizens could be spotted in a certain type of behavior. Congressman Richard Milhous Nixon asked him what type. Menjou replied:

> Attending any meeting at which Mr. Paul Robeson appeared and applauding or listening to his Communist songs. I would be ashamed to be seen in an audience doing things of that kind.

During the early fifties, an attempt was made by the government and the press to wipe Paul Robeson off the record. Willingness to denounce Robeson was made the test of a star's patriotism. One star to denounce Robeson was the black actor Canada Lee. Another was

Robeson's old friend José Ferrer. Otherwise Ferrer's new movie, *Moulin Rouge,* would be picketed and shut down by friends of HUAC. Director Willand of the American Legion stated:

> The American Legion expresses disapproval of the distribution of *Moulin Rouge* until such time as the personnel connected with it evidence sincere cooperation with their government. The Legion disapproves of the distribution of the picture because of the various front records of José Ferrer and John Huston.

Whereupon, *The Hollywood Reporter* announced:

> José Ferrer blasts Soviet Peace Prize. "I condemn Paul Robeson's acceptance of Stalin's so-called Peace Prize," Ferrer said as he lambasted Robeson.

The columnist George Sokolsky summed up:

> No one has ever denounced Paul Robeson with such accurate pinpointing of his unforgivable sins against his native land as José Ferrer.

The Legion's opposition to *Moulin Rouge* was then withdrawn. What HUAC saw as its contribution to the war against Paul Robeson was to help the State Department keep the singer from traveling abroad. Robeson commented:

> I am not in any conspiracy. It should be plain to everybody and especially to Negroes that, if the Government had evidence to back up that charge, they would have tried to put me *under* their jail. They have no such evidence: In 1946 I testified under oath I was not a member of the Communist Party. Since then I have refused to give testimony to that fact. There is no mystery in this. I have made it a matter of principle to refuse to comply with any demand that infringes upon the constitutional rights of all Americans.

Investigator. Paul Robeson, will you please come forward?
Mr. Robeson. Do I have the privilege of asking who is addressing me?
Investigator. Richard Arens.
Mr. Robeson. What is your position?
Investigator. I am Director of Staff. Did you file a passport application on July 2, 1954?
Mr. Robeson. I have filed about twenty-five in the last few months.
Investigator. Are you now a member of the Communist Party?

Mr. Robeson. Oh please, please, please.

CM 1. Please answer, will you, Mr. Robeson?

Mr. Robeson. Would you like to come to the ballot box when I vote and take out the ballot and see?

Investigator. Mr. Chairman, I respectfully suggest that the witness be directed to answer the question.

The Chairman. You are directed to answer that question.

Mr. Robeson. I invoke the Fifth Amendment.

Investigator. Do you honestly apprehend that if you told this Committee truthfully—

Mr. Robeson. I invoke the Fifth Amendment. And forget it.

Investigator. I respectfully suggest the witness be ordered to answer the question whether, if he gave us a truthful answer, he would be supplying information which might be used against him in a criminal proceeding.

The Chairman. You are directed to answer, Mr. Robeson.

Mr. Robeson. Gentlemen, in the first place, wherever I have been in the world, the first to die in the struggle against Fascism were the Communists. I laid many wreaths upon the graves of Communists. *Pause.* The Fifth Amendment does not infer criminality. Chief Justice Warren has been very clear on that. I invoke the Fifth Amendment.

Investigator. Have you ever been known under the name of "John Thomas"?

Mr. Robeson. Oh, please, does somebody here want—are you suggesting—do you want me to put up for perjury some place? "John Thomas"! My name is Paul Robeson, and anything I have to say I have said in public all over the world. That is why I am here today.

CM 1, *to the Chairman.* I ask that you direct the witness to answer the question. He is making a speech.

Mr. Robeson's Attorney. Excuse me, Mr. Arens, may we have the photographers take their pictures and then desist? It is rather nervewracking for them to be there.

The Chairman. They will take the pictures.

Mr. Robeson. I am used to it. I have been in moving pictures. Do you want me to smile? *Indicating the Investigator.* I can't smile when I'm talking to *him.*

Investigator. I ask you to affirm or deny the fact that your Communist Party name was "John Thomas."

Mr. Robeson. I invoke the Fifth Amendment. This is really ridiculous.

Investigator. Now, tell this Committee whether or not you know Nathan Gregory Silvermaster.

Mr. Robeson laughs.

CM 1. Mr. Chairman, this is not a laughing matter.

Mr. Robeson. It *is* a laughing matter! This is complete nonsense! I invoke the Fifth Amendment.

Investigator. Do you honestly apprehend that if you told whether you know Nathan Gregory Silvermaster you would be supplying information that could be used against you in a criminal proceeding?

Mr. Robeson. I have not the slightest idea what you are talking about. I invoke the Fifth.

Investigator. I suggest, Mr. Chairman, that the witness be directed to answer that question.

The Chairman. You are directed to answer the question.

Mr. Robeson, *quietly.* I invoke the Fifth Amendment.

CM 1. The witness talks very loud when he makes a speech, but when he invokes the Fifth Amendment I can't hear him.

Mr. Robeson, *quietly.* I have medals for diction. I can talk plenty loud.

CM 1. Will you talk a little louder?

Mr. Robeson, *loudly.* I invoke the Fifth Amendment loudly!

Investigator. Do you know a woman by the name of Louise Bransten?

Mr. Robeson. I invoke the Fifth Amendment.

Investigator. Who are Mr. and Mrs. Vladimir P. Mikheev?

Mr. Robeson. I have not the slightest idea, but I invoke the Fifth.

Investigator. Mr. Chairman, the witness does not have the slightest idea who they are. I respectfully suggest he be directed to answer that question.

The Chairman. You are directed to answer the question.

Mr. Robeson. I answered the question by invoking the Fifth Amendment.

Investigator. Have you ever had contact with Gregory Kheifets?

Mr. Robeson. I invoke the Fifth Amendment.

Investigator. Gregory Kheifets is identified with the Soviet espionage operations, is he not? Tell us whether you have had contact *and operations* with Gregory Kheifets.

Mr. Robeson. I invoke the Fifth Amendment.

Investigator. Do you know a Manning Johnson?

Mr. Robeson. He was dismissed from the FBI. He must be a pretty low character when he could be dismissed from that.

Investigator. I would like to read you some testimony of Manning Johnson: "In the Negro Commission of the National Committee of the Communist Party, we were told, under threat of expulsion, never to reveal that Paul Robeson was a member of the Communist Party because his assignment was confidential and secret."

Mr. Robeson. Could I protest the reading of this? If you want Mr. Manning Johnson here for cross-examination, ok.

Investigator. Tell us whether Manning Johnson was lying.

Mr. Robeson. I invoke the Fifth Amendment.

Investigator. Do you know Max Yergan?

Mr. Robeson. I invoke the Fifth Amendment.

Investigator. Max Yergan took an oath—

Mr. Robeson. Why don't you have these people here to be cross-examined? Could I ask whether this is legal?

The Chairman. This is not only legal but usual. By a unanimous vote, this Committee has been instructed to perform this very distasteful task.

Mr. Robeson. To whom am I speaking?

The Chairman. You are speaking to the Chairman of this Committee.

Mr. Robeson. Mr. Walter?

The Chairman. Yes.

Mr. Robeson. The Pennsylvania Walter?

The Chairman. That is right.

Mr. Robeson. Representative of the steelworkers?

The Chairman. That is right.

Mr. Robeson. Of the coal-mining workers? Not United States Steel, by any chance? A great patriot!

The Chairman. That is right.

Mr. Robeson. You are the author of the bills that are going to keep all kinds of decent people out of the country.

The Chairman. No, only your kind.

Mr. Robeson. Colored people like myself. And just the Teutonic Anglo-Saxon stock you would let come in.

The Chairman. We are trying to make it easier to *get rid* of your kind, too!

Mr. Robeson. You don't want any colored people to come in?
Pause.

The Chairman. Proceed.

70

Investigator. Max Yergan testified: "There was a Communist core within the Council on African Affairs." Was there a Communist core?

Mr. Robeson. I will take the Fifth. Could I read from my statement here?

Investigator. Will you just tell this Committee, while under oath, Mr. Robeson, the Communists who participated in the preparation of that statement?

Mr. Robeson. Oh, please.

Investigator, *reading.* "The Chairman: Could you identify that core clearly? Of whom did it consist?"

Mr. Robeson. Could I read my statement?

Investigator. As soon as you tell the Committee the Communists who participated in the preparation. *Pause. Reading:* "Dr. Yergan: Paul Robeson was chairman of the council and a part of that Communist-led core." Now, tell this Committee, while you are under oath, was Dr. Yergan *lying?*

Mr. Robeson. The reason I am here today, from the mouth of the State Department itself, is: I should not be allowed to travel because I have struggled for the independence of the colonial peoples of Africa. For many years I have so labored, and I can say modestly that my name is very much honored all over Africa. The other reason I am here today, again from the State Department and from the record of the Court of Appeals, is that when I am abroad I speak out against injustices against the Negro people of this land. I am not being tried for whether I am a Communist. I am being tried for fighting for the rights of my people who are still second-class citizens in this United States of America. My mother was born in your state, Mr. Walter, and my mother was a Quaker, and my ancestors in the time of Washington baked bread for George Washington's troops when they crossed the Delaware. My own father was a slave. I stand here struggling for the rights of my people to be full citizens in this country. And they are not. They are not in Mississippi. And they are not in Montgomery, Alabama. And they are not in Washington. They are nowhere. You want to shut up every Negro who has the courage to fight for the rights of his people, for the rights of workers, and I have been on many a picket line for the steelworkers too. And *that* is why I am here today.

The Chairman. Now just a minute. You ought to read Jackie

Robinson's testimony.

Mr. Robeson. I know Jackie Robinson, and I am sure that in his heart he would take back a lot of what he said about me. I addressed the combined owners of the American and the National Leagues, pleading for Robinson to be able to play baseball, like I played professional football.

Investigator. Would you tell us whether you know Thomas W. Young?

Mr. Robeson. I invoke the Fifth.

Investigator. Thomas W. Young is Negro president of the Guide Publishing Company. I would like to read you his testimony: "Paul Robeson has no right to place in jeopardy the welfare of the American Negro to advance a foreign cause. In the eyes of the Negro people this false prophet is unfaithful to their country, and they repudiate him." Do you know the man who said that?

Mr. Robeson. May I read from other Negro periodicals? May I read from a statement by Marshall Field, when I received the Spingarn medal from the NAACP?

The Chairman. No.

Mr. Robeson. Why not? You allowed the other statements.

The Chairman. This was a question, Mr. Robeson.

Mr. Robeson. Would you give me a chance to read my statement?

CM 2. Would you read some of the citations you have received from Stalin?

Mr. Robeson. I have not received *any* citations from Stalin.

The Chairman. From the Russian government?

Mr. Robeson. No. I received citations and medals from the Abraham Lincoln High School, and medals from many parts of the world, for my efforts for peace. Are you for war, Mr. Walter? Would you be in the category of this former Representative who felt we should have fought on the side of Hitler?
Silence.

CM 2. Were you in the service?
Silence.

Mr. Robeson, *beginning to read the statement.* "It is a sad and bitter commentary—"

Investigator. Did you make a trip in 1949?

Mr. Robeson. Yes.

Investigator. And, while you were in Paris, did you tell an audience the American Negro would never go to war against the Soviet government?

Pause.

Mr. Robeson. Two thousand students who came from populations that would range to six or seven hundred million people asked me to say in their name that they did not want war. No part of my speech in Paris says fifteen million American Negroes would *do* anything. I said it was my feeling that the American people would struggle for peace. It was unthinkable to me that any people would take up arms, in the name of an Eastland, against *anybody.* This United States Government should go down to Mississippi and protect my people.

Investigator. I lay before you an article, "I am Looking for Full Freedom," by Paul Robeson, in *The Worker,* July 3, 1949: "I said it was unthinkable that the Negro people of America could be drawn into war with the Soviet Union. I repeat it with hundredfold emphasis: They will not."

Mr. Robeson. And, gentlemen, they have not! No Americans are going to war with the Soviet Union!

Investigator. On that trip to Europe, did you go to Stockholm?

Mr. Robeson. I did. Some people in the American Embassy tried to break up my concert. They were not successful.

Investigator. While you were in Stockholm, did you make a little speech?

Mr. Robeson. All kinds of speeches.

Investigator. Let me read you a quotation.

Mr. Robeson. Let me listen.

Investigator. Do so, please.

Mr. Robeson. I am a lawyer.

CM 2. It would be a revelation if you would listen to counsel.

Mr. Robeson. In *good* company, I usually listen. But you know, people wander around in such fancy places.

Investigator, *reading.* "I belong to the American resistance movement, which fights against American imperialism, just as the resistance movement fought against Hitler . . ."

Mr. Robeson. Just like Frederick Douglass and Harriet Tubman were underground railroaders, and fighting for our freedom, you bet your life.

Investigator, *reading.* "Why should the Negroes ever fight against the only nations of the world where racial discrimination is prohibited, and where the people can live freely? Never! They will never fight against either the Soviet Union or the Peoples' Democracies." Did you make that statement?

Mr. Robeson. I don't remember, but nine hundred million other colored people have told you *they* will not. Four hundred million in India, and millions everywhere, have told you that!

CM 2. The witness has answered the question. He doesn't have to make a speech.

Investigator. Did you go to Moscow?

Mr. Robeson. Oh, yes.

Investigator. And while you were there, did you make a speech?

Mr. Robeson. I spoke many times and sang.

Investigator. Did you write an article in the U.S.S.R. *Information Bulletin?*

Mr. Robeson. Yes.

Investigator, *reading.* "I want to emphasize that only here, in the Soviet Union, did I feel that I was a real Man with a capital M." Did you say that?

Mr. Robeson. I would say—what is your name?

Investigator. Arens.

Mr. Robeson. I am quite willing to answer the question. When I was a singer years ago—this you have to listen to—

Investigator. I am listening.

Mr. Robeson. I am a bass singer, and so for me it was Chaliapin, the great Russian bass, and not Caruso the tenor. I learned the Russian language to sing their songs—I wish you would listen now—

CM 1. I ask you to direct the witness to answer the question.

Mr. Robeson. Just be fair to me.

CM 1. I ask regular order.

Mr. Robeson. The great poet of Russia is of African blood—

The Chairman. Let us not go so far afield.

Mr. Robeson. It is important to explain this—

The Chairman. Did you make that statement?

Mr. Robeson. When I first went to Russia in 1934—

The Chairman. Did you make that statement?

Mr. Robeson. When I first went to Russia in 1934—

The Chairman. Did you make that statement?

Mr. Robeson. In Russia I felt for the first time like a full human being. No color prejudice like in Mississippi. No color prejudice like in

Washington. Where I did not feel the pressure of color as I feel it in this Committee today.

CM 1. Why do you not stay in Russia?

Mr. Robeson. Because my father was a slave, and my people died to build this country, and I am going to stay here, and have a part of it just like you.

CM 1. You are here because you are promoting the Communist cause!

Mr. Robeson. I am here because I am opposing the neo-Fascist cause. Jefferson could be sitting here, and Frederick Douglass could be sitting here, and Eugene Debs could be sitting here.

The Chairman. Now, what prejudice are you talking about? You were graduated from Rutgers and the University of Pennsylvania. I remember seeing you play football at Lehigh.

Mr. Robeson. We beat Lehigh.

The Chairman. And we had a lot of trouble with you.

Mr. Robeson. That is right. DeWysocki was playing in *my* team!

The Chairman. There was no prejudice against you.

Mr. Robeson. Just a moment. This is something I challenge very deeply: that the success of a few Negroes, including myself or Jackie Robinson can make up—and here is a study from Columbia University—for seven hundred dollars a year for thousands of Negro families in the South. My father was a slave, and I have cousins who are sharecroppers. I do not see success in terms of myself. I have sacrificed hundreds of thousands of dollars for what I believe in.

Investigator. While you were in Moscow, did you say Stalin was a great man?

Mr. Robeson. I wouldn't argue with a representative of the people who, in building America, wasted the lives of *my* people. You are responsible, you and your forebears, for sixty to one hundred million black people dying in the slave ships and on the plantations. Don't you ask me about *anybody*, please.

Investigator. I am glad you called our attention to that slave problem. While you were in Soviet Russia—

Mr. Robeson. Nothing could be built more on slavery than *this* society, I assure you. Can I read my speech?

The Chairman. You have *made* it without reading it. The hearing is adjourned.

Mr. Robeson. You should adjourn this forever.

After two more years of waiting and struggle, Paul Robeson got his passport. By that time—1958—a whole profession had been brought to heel. Some had died by their own hand, others of heart failure, many were blacklisted, many maintained their position—or improved it—by fake repentance. The investigation of show business was complete.

The Recantation
of Galileo Galilei

Respectfully dedicated to Friedrich Heer—like Galileo, a good
Catholic

Preface

Dean Inge has wittily said: "Events in the past may be roughly divided into those which probably never happened and those which do not matter." Galileo may not have risen from his knees whispering, *"Eppur si muove!"* ("it's still moving")—though nowadays the scholars are returning to the thought that he might have—but that whisper, whatever its source, is the only message the world ever received on the whole Galileo story. One tends not really to believe that William Tell shot an apple off his son's head, yet except for that story one would certainly never have heard of William Tell. That apple was the making of William just as surely as another was the unmaking of Adam.

Scholars and scientists are still debating many aspects of the Galileo case.* The most sophisticated argument is, as often, the most conservative one. In this instance, it is that there was much that was wrong about Galileo's theorizing, and the Church was right, even scientifically, in being slow to bow to his claims to higher authority.

If such arguments are meant to debunk Galileo completely, they are too sophisticated by half. The point was never that he was right about everything but that he was responsible for certain substantial advances and that the Church, not really on scientific grounds, refused to accept those advances, forcing him to seem to wish to cancel them. The Church itself certainly does not think Galileo has ceased to be anything but a source of embarrassment. Here is a report from the *New York Times* published 335 years after the trial:

---

*One scholar wrote me: "You cannot 'prove' astronomical theory; you can only show that one works better than the other . . . The Ptolemaic system still 'works' . . . but the Copernican is more 'economical' and therefore more acceptable. But neither one is 'true' in the true sense of the word." And again: "The interesting thing is that the Church's position at that time corresponds to the 'relativists' of our time (Einstein, etc.) And Galileo's [absolutist] stand is the one that modern physics and astronomy have discarded."

Vatican May Lift Censure of Galileo

Special to The New York Times

BONN, July 1—Franz Cardinal König, Archbishop of Vienna, announced today that the Roman Catholic Church might revise its censure of Galileo Galilei, the 17th-century Italian scientist who was declared a heretic for asserting that the earth moves around the sun.

Pope Paul VI authorized Cardinal König to make the announcement at a meeting of Nobel Prize winners in Landau, on Lake Constance, a spokesman for the church in Bonn said today.

More than 20 Nobel Prize winners were present when the Austrian Cardinal declared in his lecture in "Religion and Science" that the Vatican might institute a special commission to "retry" Galileo.

Galileo, who lived from 1564 until 1642, recanted his theory under threat of torture before the Inquisition in Rome in 1633. He had to spend the last years of his life in strict seclusion at a villa in Florence.

By 1616, consulting theologians of the Holy See had already condemned as heretical the theory first advanced by Copernicus in the 16th century that the sun is the center of the universe and that the earth performs a diurnal motion of rotation.

Cardinal König said that revision of the Galileo judgment "could heal one of the deepest wounds between religion and science." He did not say when the commission would start its work but he stressed that "steps to achieve a clear and open solution are already under way."

Cardinal König was the first churchman to address the traditional meeting of Nobel Prize winners.

The Cardinal said that the world was still being ruled by "bankers, generals and professional politicians" and that, now as before, "their practical intelligence" was in charge of "deadly arsenals." The scientists, as representatives of "modern intelligence," still did not have sufficient say in important matters, he added.

There was no reason, the Cardinal continued, why theologians who severed all links with political forces should not cooperate with "those scientists whose misgivings about political developments are generally known."

That was in 1968. In 1973 I received a letter that seems to show that the only reason the Church has not gone ahead with such a retrial is that the embarrassment would only thereby be renewed. The latter was from Father Ernan McMullin of the University of Notre Dame, who graciously permitted use of his words in the theatre program:

I notice in the printed version of your play that you reprint the news item about a possible "retrial" of Galileo. I am glad to say that I had a hand in persuading Cardinal König not to proceed with the idea. History has already vindicated Galileo. Besides, he *was* technically guilty (because of the mistaken Index Decree of 1616) so that a retrial—under the ecclesiastical law of that time at least—would not, I think, reverse the result.

An excellent paradox: a man vindicated by history who is not otherwise vindicated—not vindicated legally or, perhaps, theologically—even after 340 years.

Various dramas can be found in the situation that Father McMullin's words describe. There is the small drama of legalism versus history, a liberal melodrama in which legalism is wrong and history right. There is the large drama of history versus theology, fact versus truth, which could go to the making of an antiliberal melodrama exalting eternity over time, God over Clio, history's Muse.

The nineteenth century produced the phrase "martyr of science," and often saw Galileo as a sacrifice to the new religion or counterreligion. It was equally possible—the ambivalences being pervasive in the material—to be so devoted to Science or Scientism that one could only see Galileo's ambiguous action as a guilty fudging of matters, in short, a betrayal. Today's audience knows this view chiefly from Brecht's *Galileo* but, first, it is considerably older than Brecht and, second, it had been restated in a popular book about Galileo in those very 1930s when Brecht himself went to work. Brecht could very well have read it. The book I mean is *The Star Gazer*, a "fictional biography" of Galileo by Zsolt de Harsányi. Since it was a Book-of-the-Month Club selection, we can learn from the *Book-of-the-Month Club News* just what version of the Galileo story was at that time being fed to the millions:

> His theses proved, his fame spread through Europe, an oldish man, afraid of pain . . . he was broken by the Inquisition. He recanted shamelessly, dragging his belly on the ground before his potential torturers. He knew the earth moved, and that the skies were not immutable, but eagerly denied his knowledge to escape burning at the stake . . . And, at the end, it is the Inquisition itself that, by proclaiming his denials throughout the world, advertised their evident falsity.

One hears the not very still or small voice of liberal mythology. Your liberal smells the martyr's burning flesh considerably before even one faggot has caught fire. Galileo was no Joan of Arc. Was he even a Giordano Bruno? Rather, there would seem to be a polar contrast between these two great thinkers, Bruno being an archrebel, Galileo what we would call apolitical and friendly to the authorities. Is it not fair, then, to connect this friendliness to the authorities with shameless recantation and dragging of the belly on the ground? Here one would like to ask: Is recantation shameless by definition, or can it really be shown that Galileo recanted in some unusually outrageous manner? The same question must be asked about his alleged dragging of his belly on the ground, since he didn't do it literally.

The conventional wisdom of the Book-of-the-Month Club also entails a contradiction. By proclaiming Galileo's denials throughout the world, the Inquisition, we are told, advertised their evident falsity. Well, if this is so, Galileo, not being entirely stupid, would know that it was so. If he knows it is so, he has an excellent reason for recanting: to advertise the falsity of recantation throughout the world. And, this way, his belly can be well above ground and his sense of shame delicate and inviolate as ever.

Jerome Clegg has summed up my *Recantation of Galileo Galilei* thus:

> This Galileo is seen as the darling of an Establishment, his aim, until the crisis of 1633, nothing more nor less than to win that Establishment over to his view of the universe. Only when he definitively fails in this campaign does he rebel, and thus become a revolutionary in a social as well as a scientific sense: he will spend his last years in conscious conflict with the hierarchy, a smuggler of spiritual contraband. Even at this point, though, he is no nineteenth-century radical, denouncing Christianity and crying, "neither God nor master!" He is closer, rather, to some of the Catholic radicals of the twentieth century who, instead of challenging the church as such, challenge current office-holders and power-wielders. It was, however, much harder for this man to really recant his assumptions about the Establishment than to pretend to recant his assumptions about the universe.

The *Recantation* had its first full production in the Bonstelle Theatre, Detroit, Michigan, under the auspices of Wayne State University Theatre, October 19, 1973. In an earlier version entitled *The Good Catholic* there had been a staged reading at the HB Studio, New York City, directed by the author, with Herbert Berghof as Galileo.

Wayne State University
Bonstelle Theatre

1973-74 Season

The Recantation of Galileo Galilei
Scenes from History Perhaps

Directed by	Don Blakely
Scenic Design and Technical Direction by	Norman Hamlin
Costumes Designed and Executed by	Michael Pullin
Lighting by	William J. Rynders

CAST

Virginia Galilei	Zdzislawa Jablonski
Benedetto Castelli	Donald Dailey
Father Sarpi	David Calvin Berg
Signor Sagredo	Michel Cullen
Galileo Galilei	Martin Molson
Dean Bruciano	Tom Kjellberg
Professor Rizzi	Eric R. Dueweke
Professor Seggizzi	Dennis Pfister
Professor LoVecchio	Frederick E. Lehto
Professor Guarini	Ron Turek
Professor Lorini	Justin Rashid
Father Scheiner	Nick Calanni
Caccini, a Dominican Priest	Michel Cullen
The Inquisitor	Gregory Olszewski
Cosimo de' Medici	Justin Rashid
Medici Attendants	Steve Raptis, Paul Koponen
Niccolini, the Medici Chamberlain	Samuel Pollak
Cardinal Bellarmine	Mack Palmer
Secretary to Bellarmine	Stephen V. Isbell
Firenzuola	Philip Fox II
Secretary to Firenzuola	Blake Cumbers

Cardinal Silotti	Tom Kjellberg
Cardinal Girardi	Eric R. Dueweke
Cardinal Bandolfi	Dennis Pfister
Cardinal Gorazio	Ron Turek
Cardinal Sordi	Frederick E. Lehto
Cardinal Lucignano	Justin Rashid
Pope Urban VIII	Charles Geroux
Swiss Guards	Steve Raptis, Paul Koponen, Samuel Pollak, Stephen V. Isbell, Blake Cumbers

The play covers about 25 years, from 1608 to 1633.

It is easy to be a martyr. It is much more difficult to appear in a shady light for the sake of the idea.

—Rabbi Eybeschütz in Feuchtwanger's *Jud Süss*

Today the hero is ideally the man who resists without being killed. Cunning, as the mental faculty which is the equivalent of endurance, has become, not the better part of valor, but certainly an essential part.

—John Berger

The scenic pattern is as follows:

Prologue
1. On Revolutions
2. The Telescope
3 a. A Villa in Florence
   b. A Watchdog of the Lord
   c. The Investigation
   d. A Philanthropist
4. The Master of Controversial Questions
5. Two World Systems
6. The Inquisition
7. A Friendly Commissar
8. A Sincere Statesman
9. On Recantations
   Epilogue

Prologue

June 22, 1633. In the great hall of the Convent of Santa Maria Sopra Minerva in Rome, a man in a penitential shirt is on his knees before the Congregation of the Holy Office. A Bible on the stone floor beside him, he reads from a scroll as follows:

I, Galileo Galilei, do now, with a sincere heart and unfeigned faith, abjure, detest, and curse the heretical belief that the earth moves around the sun, and take my oath that never again will I speak, write, or otherwise assert anything that might lend plausibility to this belief. Should anyone suspected of subscribing to this heretical belief be known to me, I shall denounce him to this Holy Office in Rome or to the Inquisitor in whatsoever place I shall be, so help me God and this Holy Book.

ONE

On Revolutions

The city of Padua in the Republic of Venice. A room in the home of Galileo Galilei, professor of mathematics at the University of Padua. Books, scientific apparatus. A huge volume is on a special reading stand in the middle of the room. Sunday evening. Someone is playing a lute on the floor above. After a few moments there comes a quiet knocking at the door. A girl in her early teens crosses the room to answer it. She admits a young man, evidently a student, about eighteen years old.

Student. Is Professor Galilei at home?

Girl. He's not expecting you, is he?

Student. He said to come over any evening soon around nine.

Girl. This is Sunday. And he has people coming.

Student, *starting to leave.* I'll try again tomorrow then. You're not his daughter, are you?

Girl. Oh, yes.

Student. Your name's Virginia, isn't it?

Girl. Yes.

Student. Mine's Castelli. Benedetto Castelli.

Virginia. One of father's students?

Castelli. Yes. He told me he needed a student assistant. I'm applying for the job.

Virginia. Well, look, if you want to wait, I can put you over here. *She indicates another room.* He may find a minute for you later. Do you have something to read?

Castelli. Yes, yes. *The music has continued.* Is that *him* playing?

Virginia. Yes. He always plays on "exciting occasions."
But the music is serene.

Castelli. He doesn't sound excited.

Virginia. He is, though. He plays to calm himself down.

Castelli. What's he excited *about?*

Another knock at the door, a less timid one this time.

Virginia. Oh dear, they're here already!

Castelli. Is he having a party tonight?

Virginia. His weekly meeting with Signor Sagredo and Father Sarpi. Do you know them?

Castelli. Everyone knows Father Sarpi—by reputation.

Virginia. He's not at all the way people say—

Castelli. Dangerous? He teaches at the university and most of the faculty think he's a dangerous nut. Who's Sagredo?

Virginia. A fine gentleman. With a huge villa and four dozen servants. Knows all about science too—

A slightly insistent knock. Virginia by now has placed Castelli where he can stay and read—in the next room—and she is back at the outer door. A middle-aged priest enters, wiry, intense, virile, and with a twinkle in his eye. When he hugs Virginia, one senses that she is still an even smaller girl to him.

Sarpi. Virginia, my dear!

Virginia. Sorry to take so long! There's a student here waiting to see daddy.

Sarpi, *with the ease of a family friend.* How's the convent school?

Virginia. Oh, I love it, Father. I . . . think I may stay in the convent . . . *after* school.

Sarpi, *quite surprised.* You want to be a nun? Really?

Virginia. You're not shocked, are you, and you a priest?

Sarpi. The name Galilei would then signify the union of science and religion: a pretty thought. But you have to be sure our church and you can get along together.

Virginia. Oh, I hope the church can put up with me!

Sarpi. The question sometimes is if we can put up with it, my dear Virginia.

Another knock at the door.

Virginia. That'll be Signor Sagredo.

She hurries to the door. The man she admits is a thirty-year-old Venetian who combines the hauteur of an aristocracy with the sophistication of an intelligentsia. A little spoiled but intelligent enough to know it, Sagredo treats himself, as well as others, with a touch of irony.

Sagredo. Well, how's my god-daughter? *He picks her up and kisses her.* I saw your mother yesterday. With your step-father—

Virginia. Oh! How is she?

Sagredo. She likes being married for a change. She likes living with a non-genius, for a change, too, eh, Sarpi? *He shakes hands with Sarpi.*

Sarpi. Certainly the genius upstairs is glad he never got married at all . . .

Evidently Galileo was coming downstairs when this was said since his voice is heard answering it before he actually appears.

Voice of Galileo. Would *you* like to get married, Sarpi? I thought you priests favored celibacy.

Galileo enters now with a telescope in his hand. The man we thus encounter is at first indistinguishable from many another brilliant academician in early middle age. We become aware of the high voltage of his personality only as he talks or paces the room. Even then it may only be nervousness, not brilliance, that reveals itself. His manner soon informs us that he is one who tends to brush obstacles aside and get on with the job, a propensity which friendly observers see as singleness of purpose or even purity, yet which the less friendly can see, with equal reason, as impatience or ruthlessness. He recites playfully:

The world is full of woes, I've heard it said
But of all these, the worst is—to be wed.

Sagredo. Enter Galileo, quoting Ariosto.

Galileo. A yet profaner spirit, my dear Sagredo.

Sarpi. Francisco Berni, poet of the Roman taverns and whorehouses.

Galileo. The Vatican is right, Father Sarpi, the Jesuits are right: You are a dangerous fellow, you keep bad company. *He points at Sagredo and himself.* You even read the wrong poets. How are you both? *He shows them where to sit but they remain standing.*

Virginia. A student came, daddy. I put him in the study. Wants to be your assistant.

Galileo. He'll have to wait. For, gentlemen, I come before you tonight with a proposal of some weight. You can run along, little lady. *He gives his daughter a hug and packs her off.*

Sagredo. What's that you've got there? *He points at the telescope, which is a very primitive affair, little more than the simplest of tubes.*

Galileo. This? Oh, I use it as an effective prop. So one of my students will come up with a drawing: "Galileo at the blackboard, pointer in hand." *He holds the telescope like a pointer.*

Sarpi. But it's a tube.

Galileo. Yes. I'm at my old game of stealing other people's ideas.

Sagredo. Who invented the tube?

Galileo. I haven't the slightest idea. I bought it in a toy shop. The shopman said the kids love it. A new type of magnifying glass, using two lenses instead of one. The tube is just somewhere to put the lenses.

Sagredo. What use is it?

Sarpi. How much does it magnify?

Galileo. You two do know the right questions to ask, don't you? But can we shelve this?

Sarpi. Yes, yes. Let's hear your proposal.

Galileo. Sit down, gentlemen. *He takes the big book from the stand, and sits at the end of a table. They sit at his left and right hand.* To cut a long story short, we three have been reading this together now for—how many years, is it?

Sagredo. Five or six.

Sarpi. More.

Galileo, *reading the title off the cover. On Revolutions* by Niklaus Copernicus. And its main idea is the greatest revolution of them all.

Sagredo. Its main idea is worth all the books of the Bible put together.

Sarpi. Ts, ts, ts, Sagredo: the Holy Bible will continue to have its uses!

Sagredo. Yet your enthusiasm for Copernicus is as great as mine.

Sarpi. Greater.

Galileo. Now that we have absorbed this very great conception, now that we have agreed together that it is *true,* a gratifying and thrilling conclusion awaits us: We must give this gospel, these tidings of great joy, to the world.

Sagredo. Make a public announcement?

Sarpi. With our names on it?

Galileo. "The great vision of Copernicus is hereby endorsed by Galilei, Sarpi, and Sagredo." Yes.

Sarpi. You're convinced the time is ripe?

Galileo. Overripe. Copernicus wrote his book more than half a century ago. It has been read from one end of Christendom to the other. In Protestant Germany, our colleague Kepler has been able to come out for it; nothing has happened to him; and now he challenges me, in the name of science, to do the same in Catholic Italy. I'm not even the first: Giordano Bruno has already come out for it—

Sagredo. I'm surprised to hear you use *that* argument.

Galileo. Why?

Sarpi, *with a glance at Sagredo.* Well, you know where Bruno now is, don't you?

Galileo. No.

Sagredo. On trial before the Inquisition in Rome.

Galileo. But he was here just the other day!

Sarpi. The Inquisition had him kidnapped.

Galileo. Sarpi, your idea of the Inquisition comes straight from Protestant London.

Sagredo. But Sarpi's right.

Galileo. I don't believe it. But where was I? Yes, I was saying the Italian people are now ready for our new view of things.

Sagredo. I see no grounds for believing that.

Sarpi. Our own students, even the most brilliant, are not yet ready.

Galileo. I beg leave to test that remark.

Sagredo. What?

Sarpi. Here and now? How is that possible?

Galileo. One moment. *He strides to the doorway of the room where Castelli is reading. To Castelli.* Hello. What's your name, by the way?

Castelli. Castelli.

Galileo. Gentlemen, this is Castelli, a student of mine. *They murmur a greeting.* May we use you as a guinea pig?

Castelli. I don't quite understand.

Galileo. Well, we want to get a student reaction to . . . something.

Castelli. Oh. Go right ahead.

Galileo. Have you attended my lectures on the structure of the universe?

Castelli. Oh yes, sir.

Galileo. What view did I set forth?

Castelli. That of Ptolemy: cycles and epicycles, the earth in the center, the sun revolving around it, the spheres. . . .

Galileo. What other view is there?

Castelli. Oh, Giordano Bruno has all *sorts* of notions. . . .

Galileo. Bruno. Who else?

Castelli. I don't know.

Galileo. Copernicus. My question to you is: Should I endorse him?

Castelli. Would that mean you don't believe what you teach in your lectures?

Galileo. That might follow, mightn't it?

Castelli. What *is* the new view?

Galileo. Hear that, Sagredo? Sarpi? Well, young man, the earth is *not* in the center and is *not* stationary. It moves. Will your mind receive that notion? If not, you're out of luck, because the earth moves twice over: once by rotation about its own axis and again by revolution about the sun.

Castelli. That's . . . incredible.

Sagredo, *an "I told you so."* Aha!

Castelli. It's contrary to fact!

Sarpi turns with a smile to Galileo. Galileo raises his hand.

Galileo. Wait a minute, Sarpi. *To Castelli.* Is it contrary to fact?

Castelli. You ask me seriously? After your own lectures. . . . Oh, but then you don't believe your own lectures, do you? I'm confused.

Galileo. You have the right to be. We three oldsters are only just emerging from that confusion. Let me ease the strain with an *if*. If this view were true, what difference would it make?

Castelli. We would have to . . . see *everything* differently, wouldn't we?

Galileo. Go on.

Castelli. We'd have to see the earth as . . . a sort of *flying machine,* such as Leonardo da Vinci imagined. We'd have to see ourselves as *voyagers* on a flying machine, voyagers through space!

Galileo. That's very good, I wish I'd said that. May I remove the *if?*

Castelli. The *if?*

Galileo. I said *if* the Copernican view were true. It *is* true, so help me God! As for my lectures, Castelli, well, I lead a double life. On weekdays, I'm a disciple of Ptolemy. On Sunday evenings, when I meet with Sarpi and Sagredo, I say a black mass, cook a spiritual minestrone in a witches' cauldron, and whisper a magic incantation that makes my faculty colleagues toss uneasily in their beds: *The earth revolves; the sun stands still.*

Castelli. Can I study the new view, sir?

Galileo. Now, Signor Castelli, would you do something for me? Go out and get the latest news sheets on the Square. Ask especially for news of Giordano Bruno. *Castelli leaves the house.* He wants to study the new view.

Sarpi, *laughing.* This is one student.

Sagredo. And one that likes you.

Galileo. All right. Was this one student, drawn from the large class of young people that likes me, ready for the news?

Sarpi. He certainly was.

Sagredo. I enjoyed every moment of it: I'd like to have him as a student.

Galileo. Well then?

Sarpi. Well, Sagredo, we are not conceding there are no risks. But shall we take a chance?

Sagredo. I have misgivings.

Noise of opening door. Castelli rushes in.

Castelli. The news is terrible, sir!

Galileo. Yes? What then?

Castelli. Giordano Bruno is *dead.*

Sarpi, *jumping up.* He was—

Sagredo, *ditto.* Executed?

Sarpi, *seizing the news sheet, and reading from it.* ". . . taken from his prison in the Tower of Nona to the Campo dei Fiori, he was there stripped naked, bound to a stake, and burned alive."

Sagredo, *grabbing the sheet from Sarpi.* "Two Dominicans and two Jesuits showed him his errors yet he stubbornly held onto his vain-glorious fantasies. One of the Jesuits, thinking he might repent, held up the image of Jesus before him on a pole, but Bruno turned his face away, weeping wildly. The sentence was then read by the Lord Cardinal Bellarmine."

Sarpi. The most important Jesuit of them all. Did Bruno say anything?

Sagredo, *scanning the sheet.* Yes. "He said, 'Better a spirited death than a craven life.' At this, Bellarmine called on him in a loud voice to repent, but Bruno answered, 'Clearly you fear me more than I you.' "

Pause.

Galileo. Couldn't there be some mistake? These news sheet editors—

Sarpi. To print this—if it was a lie—would be more than any editor's life was worth.

Galileo. It's just too awful. I don't understand.

Sarpi. No one understands.

Sagredo. Yet this is how things are.

Sarpi. And it's good we've been reminded—in time.

Sagredo. That's true. We were on the brink of a colossal blunder.

Galileo. Huh?

Sagredo. To make your announcement now is to ask for what Bruno got.

Sarpi. We were crazy to even consider it. I've been asking myself for years if I shouldn't drop these scientific studies altogether and concentrate on the prior necessity.

Galileo. Which is?

Sarpi. To restore this church of ours to health. Well, now I know. From now on, just that must be my mission.

Galileo. You are unfair. If Bellarmine agreed to . . . this, he had his reasons. . . . I *hate* to hear you talk against our church!

Sarpi. The hierarchy is not the church.

Galileo, *petulantly.* And what is? You?

Sarpi, *calmly.* Yes. And you. Wherever two or three are gathered. All.

Galileo, *sarcastically.* Even Protestants, I suppose?

Sarpi. Even Jews. Moslems. . . . All. That is my vision. Our vision. The vision of a church that is *really* catholic.

Sagredo. It is staggering.

Pause.

Galileo. No more Sunday evenings anyway. From now on you will be a professional agitator, huh? What about you, Sagredo?

Sagredo. Oh, I'll live on my estates. And never venture outside this Republic of Venice. Don't worry about me. What will *you* do?

Sarpi. You will *not* make that announcement.

Galileo. No. I'll be silent, don't worry. For a while.

Sagredo. Forever, if you ask my advice.

Galileo. No. One day I will have physical evidence. The Copernican theory mustn't be something that needs endorsement, even mine. It must be independent of all authority, even mine.

Sagredo. Is that going to be possible?

Galileo. A true proposition, in physical science, is one for which there is physical evidence.

Sagredo. In principle, yes, but can you find any? Copernicus didn't manage it. Bruno didn't manage it.

Sarpi. The trouble being that the heavens—the infinite spaces about us—are inaccessible.

Sagredo. We cannot sail to the moon!

Galileo, *slowly.* If we cannot—as yet—sail to the moon, can we make the moon sail to us?

Sagredo. Magic, eh?

Galileo. Well then, *seem* to sail to us. Can we strengthen our eyesight until it penetrates space. Better spectacles, better magnifying glasses. . . .

He picks up the telescope again.

Sagredo. All right: go ahead and perfect that tube till you can see the secrets of the skies through it!

Galileo. Hm? Is that an idea of yours I'm allowed to steal?

Sagredo. For what little it's worth.

Sarpi. Galileo's ideas were seldom worth much to those he stole them from.

Sagredo. Will you work on it then?

Galileo. I shall work on this idea and a hundred others. The evidence is there: I have only to find it.

Sagredo. Well, let me know if you ever do find this evidence. I can always be dragged off my vineyards.

Sarpi. Let *me* know too, Galileo. I can always be dragged off my soapbox.

Galileo. I am going to find this evidence and hale you over here if I have to come for you into the very dungeons of the Inquisition.

Sagredo. Venice for the Venetians! You can postpone all thoughts of the Inquisition till you leave these parts, which I trust will be never. Goodbye.

Sarpi. Goodbye, dear friend. *They embrace.* I fear for you: but you must do what you must do. I wish you the pagans' luck and our own God's care. You will need both.

Sarpi and Sagredo leave.

Galileo. Well, young man, it was you who brought the fateful news of Bruno's death. Are you also the last to leave me?

Castelli. I don't want to leave you, Professor.

Galileo. It's a mouthful, though, isn't it? A new universe? And a burning at the stake in prospect? *Pause.* Do you know what you want, Castelli?

Castelli. I want to be your assistant, Professor.

Galileo. Hm. Know anything about optics?

Castelli. No.

Galileo. Nor do I. Maybe we can learn it together?

Castelli. Am I hired, then?

Galileo, *nodding.* Bring me everything the library has on optics.

TWO

The Telescope

The same room, but time has passed. Evening. The telescope, set up on a stand, now dominates one side of the room. Galileo is peering through it; Castelli sits ready to take notes. No dialogue for a while. Only the grunts of Galileo as he moves the instrument and changes the field of vision. A relaxed atmosphere: Both men are happy. Then a knock at the door.

Galileo. Not to be disturbed till ten o'clock! Go away!

Virginia's voice. It's me, daddy. There's mail for you.

Galileo. Not interested! The committee's coming!

Virginia. But this is special. From foreign parts. One letter has "Grand Duke of Tuscany" on the envelope!

Galileo. Oh, it does? Excuse me a minute, Castelli. *He opens the door to Virginia.* So you call Florence foreign parts, eh? *He has opened one letter. He lets out a yell of triumph.* Hey! Castelli! He says he will!

Castelli. Who will what, maestro?

Galileo. The grand duke has been deluging me with offers for several years. Double my Padua salary. Half the teaching load. So I kept leading him on. Asked him in my last if he would come out for the new view of the universe, should I take the job. He now says he would!

Castelli. Does he know what's involved?

Galileo. I'm not going to Florence anyway. After the meeting this evening, we shall have the endorsement of the University of Padua. That will suffice.

Knock at the door.

Virginia. They're early.

Galileo. No, no, that will be Sarpi and Sagredo. I asked them to come first. Let them in, Virginia. *She does.* Sarpi! Sagredo! *They embrace.*

Sarpi. Galileo!

Sagredo. You haven't changed a bit.

Galileo. Well, old friends, you asked to be brought back on The Day: this is The Day. And that's the offending party. *He points to the telescope.* No words. Point that thing at the sky and tell me what you see. Or rather, tell yourselves what you see, since I know. *He leaves Sarpi and Sagredo to experiment with the telescope, while he moves over to the other side of the room.* What was the other letter, Virginia?

Virginia. Here.

Galileo. Ah! This one really is from foreign parts, Austria anyway, and I recognize the handwriting. It's Herr Kepler's. I sent him one of my telescopes. Would you like to read it to me?

Virginia, *taking it back.* "O spy glass, instrument of much knowledge, more precious than any scepter, is not he who holds thee in his hand made king and overlord of the works of God?" I don't quite get it.

Galileo. *pacing to and fro in what we shall come to regard as a characteristic manner, nervous yet purposeful.* Nature is the work of God, and Nature isn't just the garden and the vineyard opposite and the cypresses on the ridge beyond, it's the whole green earth with the blue air around it and the white clouds overhead, and it's more again than these: It is the sun and moon and stars and the infinite silent spaces.

Virginia. The same as the Bible: "The heavens declare the glory of God."

Galileo. The same as the Bible.

From the other side of the room.

Sagredo. That's Jupiter all right, but what's going on all around?

Sarpi. I thought there were specks on the lens but now I've cleaned it.

Sagredo. They are objects. In the sky. Near Jupiter.

Sarpi. Let me look again.

Back to Galileo and Virginia.

Virginia, *still reading.*

"All that is overhead, the mighty orbs
With all their motions Thou dost subjugate
To man's intelligence."

Galileo. The Bible says that too, remember?

Virginia. The eighth Psalm. "When I consider Thy heavens, the work of Thy fingers, the moon and the stars, which has ordained. . . ."

Galileo. "Thou madest him to have dominion over the works of Thy hands."

Virginia. So Herr Kepler thinks you're a god.

Galileo. No, not at all—

Virginia. I used to think you were a god myself. The kind that comes down from Olympus to make a conquest of the ladies.

Galileo. And you want to be a nun? Why, I'll report you to the Jesuits, and they'll burn you as a heretic.

Virginia. The Jesuits have been expelled from Venice.

Galileo. You know everything, don't you? Except the interpretation of the Bible. In "Thou madest him to have dominion," "Thou" is God, "him" is man. . . .

Back to Sagredo and Sarpi.

Sarpi. *Four* objects. Jupiter is surrounded by four. . . .

Sagredo. Just a minute. Let me take another look. *He puts his eye to the telescope.* How do you know which is Jupiter?

Sarpi. It's bigger.

Sagredo. Right. It's bigger. But, Sarpi, that is the *only* difference.

Sarpi. How *can* it be the only difference? That would be to say that . . . let me look again.

Galileo begins to listen to his friends' conversation.

Virginia. But the man that "has dominion" is you—

Sarpi, *very slowly and distinctly, with amazement.* The four specks are also planets.

Sagredo. Let me look.

Galileo. Listen to this, Virginia.

Sagredo. There are four planets around Jupiter.

Sarpi. Four planets never before beheld by the eye of man!

Gelileo. Well, how is that, gentlemen, for a beginning? The universe has other secrets up its sleeve, several of which I am about to divulge to the Faculty Committee on the Sciences.

Sarpi. You have physical evidence for the whole Copernican theory?

Galileo. Enough.

Sarpi. I can't wait to hear it.

Sagredo. The faculty committee is on its way here? What do you hope to get out of *them?*

Galileo. See for yourselves. Dean Bruciano was here already, looked through the telescope at the surrounding landscape, and became an ally. He is bringing the group in his coach tonight.

Knocking at the door.

My God, here they are. Virginia!

She goes to the door and lets in seven men. Not seven clowns. Rather, citizens of some distinction, from the viewpoint of most of whom Galileo is the clown. Men of the world, they would not wish the world to be mocked.

Dean Bruciano, I'd like you to meet my old friends Father Sarpi and Signor Sagredo. My daughter Virginia and my assistant Castelli you already know. *Bowing on all sides.*

Scholar 1, *evidently Dean Bruciano.* Rizzi, Seggizi, LoVecchio, Guarini, Lorini, Scheiner. *Each of these bows as his name is spoken.*

Galileo. You are seven. Isn't it a committee of nine?

Scholar 1. Oh, um, yes, Sforza and Magrini were, um, indisposed.

Galileo. That's too bad, they're in my field. Anyway, gentlemen, I see where your eyes are tending, that contraption is indeed the telescope. I have several others you can take away with you when you leave. Dean Bruciano has already witnessed some of the telescope's powers. As have Sarpi and Sagredo. Nevertheless, the pith and point of these proceedings have been saved for the present moment. Gentlemen, I did not invent the telescope. What I did was realize what to point it at.

Scholar 2. How's that?

Galileo. The children had been using it this way. *He places it horizontally.* They could see down the street, across country, over the sea, even through lightly curtained windows. But one evening, by a stroke of genius, I fell over it, knocked it into this position, *he places it vertically,* lay on my back to use it, and saw—

Scholar 3, *a wag.* God Almighty?

Galileo. Well, to be frank, absolutely nothing. But it gave me an idea. "I will lift up mine eyes unto the hills: from thence cometh my help." Or rather, just above the hills, thus. *He has been playing with the telescope. It now points upward but aslant.* And saw the next best thing to God, Professor Seggizi: the sun and the moon. Castelli, are both of them perfect, unblemished, crystal spheres?

Castelli. That's what you said in your lectures.

Galileo. When observed through the telescope, the sun is seen to have spots on it. Not spots on the lens, Father Sarpi, spots on the sun. As for the moon, does it have a smooth, even surface?

Castelli. That has been the assumption.

Galileo. Whereas actually the moon has a rugged surface, being mountainous.

Scholar 3. Does the man in the moon live in a valley or on a mountain top?

Galileo. The topic has changed now: We shall begin to think, instead, of a man *on* the moon. Lacking, of course, is the right kind of ship to sail there on. . . . Which of you is familiar with the planet Venus? Oh come, the shape of Venus has been of perennial interest to the male sex, but the shape of her namesake in the sky will astonish the human race, male and female, for, gentlemen, it keeps changing. Can the changes be accounted for?

Castelli. Not on the supposition that Venus revolves around the earth.

Galileo. But on the supposition that she revolves around the sun? What did you learn in my class about Jupiter?

Castelli. That he shines in lone splendor.

Galileo. Sarpi and Sagredo, when you arrived this evening the telescope was trained on Jupiter. What did you see through it?

Scholar 3. Jupiter! A miracle!

Galileo. Jupiter. And what else?

Sarpi. Four other planets.

Galileo. I call them the satellites of Jupiter. Physical evidence that Ptolemy's view of the universe was wrong. Physical evidence that Copernicus was right.

Scholar 1. Now, let me get this straight, Galilei. Have you brought us here to—

Galileo. You represent the University of Padua. This University now has the opportunity to announce to the entire civilized world a truth of majestic proportions and unbounded possibility.

Scholar 1. You told me nothing of this! All I saw through that tube was landscape—

Scholar 2. Galilei, like yourself I have been teaching the Ptolemaic universe for decades. D'you want me to throw away my lecture notes and go to school to you?

Galileo. Don't you think it might do you a great deal of good? *Scholar 2 turns on his heel and leaves.* Oh dear, I've said the wrong thing. Wouldn't some of you like to look through the telescope? *Scholar 6 goes and does so.*

Scholar 3, *shifting from a playful to an insolent tone.* Galilei, if I don't look through your spy-glass, it is not because I don't believe you see what you say you see. That, however, is no proof that it is there. The overthirsty man sees extra oases in the desert; the overcurious man sees extra stars in the sky.

Galileo. Can a scientist be *over*curious?

Scholar 4. He can be overambitious. What is not discovered can be invented.

Galileo. You are imputing fraud.

Scholar 5. Not necessarily, my dear Galilei. Human beings avoid deliberately deceiving others by involuntarily deceiving themselves.

Galileo. Would you care to look through the telescope and report whether or not I have deceived myself?

Scholar 5. Lorini's been looking through it for several minutes. I'm willing to take his word on what is presently visible through it.

Scholar 6. I wish I knew. I was all set to see Jupiter and four little Jupiters, as Galilei suggested. There are a few things bobbing about there that *could* be planets but. . . .

Galileo. Like other machines, the telescope may take a little getting used to. Visibility varies, the moon changes, there are differences from night to night. . . . I did not mean to imply, gentlemen, that you owed me an answer. Take a telescope home with you. Or return and use mine some other night. I would only request that you keep an open mind.

Scholar 1. Oh, but, Galilei, this is not at all what any of us bargained for. . . . You never even hinted that astrology—excuse me, astronomy—was involved. . . . Please realize that none of us here is more than a dean. The rector would have to be consulted. And the regents. And I doubt that they would take kindly to switching unverses on us.

Galileo. Not even if they got all the credit? "Universes switched by order of rector and regents"?

Scholar 1. So, finally, you mock me too, Galilei? I was shielding you from the real reason why Sforza and Magrini didn't come. Neither one of them can stand you. Sforza says you stole his ideas. Magrini feels he failed to get a promotion because you elbowed him out. Even tonight, when more might have been expected of you, you have caused Rizzi to walk out. I shall now follow him.

Galileo. I imagine he's waiting for you in your coach. Good night!

They all leave. A long pause.

Sagredo. Well, Galileo my friend, as I've told you before, you are incorrigible.

Sarpi. You never did do anything by halves, did you?

Sagredo. Your method, however, has the merit of leaving nothing in doubt. At least we don't have to discuss how you will mend your bridges and win the faculty over on a future occasion.

A knock at the door.

Galileo, *going to the door himself.* Who can this be?

Reenter Scholar 7, a younger man than the others, and much less the academician. His eyes are earnest and fiery. He is gaunt.

Scholar 7. I came back for one of your telescopes.

Galileo. The coach drove off.

Scholar 7. Yes, there was a slight altercation.

Galileo. You will walk home for the sake of a telescope? A man after my own heart! And I don't even know your name.

Scholar 7. Scheiner. Christopher Scheiner. Astronomy is my passion.

Galileo. Then there is hope in Padua.

Scheiner. I am leaving for Rome.

Galileo. But there the Jesuits have a monopoly on science.

Scheiner. I am joining the Jesuit order.

Galileo. Well, young man, you don't do things by halves either, do you? *Gives him a telescope.* I shall follow your career carefully.

Scheiner. And I yours, Professor Galilei.

Galileo lets him out.

Galileo. Signor Scheiner is right. Padua is a provincial dump.

Sagredo. The grass is greener on the other side of the street?

Galileo. Where's that letter, Castelli? *Castelli supplies the letter from the grand duke.* "Finally, we shall hope on your behalf to make that announcement to the world by which the world shall learn its true relation to the universe. Signed: Cosimo de' Medici."

Sagredo. "We shall hope." Florence hopes a lot of things. That the Vatican and the Jesuits won't be so strong. That its own Dominican preachers will be less influential. Don't you realize that the provincialism of Padua is your shield? No Jesuits. No Inquisition. No Vatican. No extradition. Leave this Republic of Venice, and you are naked among the wolves.

Galileo. Don't you think I can take care of myself?

Sagredo. You're too *naive,* Galileo. Supersubtle in science, in politics you are a babe in arms. Take tonight's exhibition! Good God, man, if you can't bend the Padua faculty to your will, how do you hope to fare with the Medici, the Dominicans, the Jesuits, the Holy Office, the Inquisition, and the Pope? Help me, Sarpi. Help me save a great man for his own greatness. This may be our last chance.

Pause.

Galileo. Sarpi isn't helping.

Sarpi. Sarpi is thinking. What Sagredo says is true, Galileo, but it influences you in the opposite direction. And while he was talking you made your decision. *You are going to Florence.*

Galileo. Quite right. Is that perverse of me?

Sarpi. Sagredo said it was *dangerous.* Your friends want you alive and free.

Sagredo. I also said it was *futile.*

Sarpi. I *cannot* help you, Sagredo. As you say, this is probably our farewell to our friend, and in this solemn hour, all I want is to feel I understood him. What do you live for, Galileo?

Galileo. Hm? I want to get certain truths accepted.

Scarpi. Why?

Galileo. Isn't it normal?

Sarpi. Why?

Galileo. Oh, you mean I'm vain? I'm proud?

Sarpi. I want to understand you.

Galileo. Well, certainly, there must be a big selfish element in it. Not just my desire for prestige and honors. My yearning to be released from this awful silence.

Sarpi. You said years ago you lived for the day when the silence would cease. Can a man demand that?

Galileo. The world owes him that.

Sarpi. The world owes you something?

Galileo. I'm even persuaded it's not such a bad world as you and Sagredo suppose. It not only owes, it will pay.

Sarpi. *This* world? *This* church? *This* Italy?

Galileo. *This* world, *this* church, *this* Italy.

Sarpi. Suppose you prove wrong, and the world refuses to pay?

Galileo. I hate supposing!

Sarpi. On the contrary, you are a master of hypothesis.

Galileo. Should the world refuse to pay, a man can do what Bruno did.

Sagredo. Good God!

Galileo. "Better a spirited death than a craven life."

Sarpi. It's a beautiful answer, Sagredo. May an old priest be permitted a piece of advice on parting?

Galileo. To this old priest everything is permitted.

Sarpi. Should you ever, which God forbid, find yourself in Bruno's position, ask yourself if Bruno's response is, for you, the bravest and the . . . most appropriate. That's all. And goodbye.
He embraces Galileo.

Sagredo. Goodbye, my friend. As a counsellor I'm no match for Father Sarpi, but let me say this: you have most value—you will always have most value—alive and kicking. *He embraces Galileo. Sarpi and Sagredo leave.*

Galileo. Virginia! *Virginia comes in.* Virginia, Castelli, this is a family council. I am going to Florence. To Rome, first, on a visit; then to Florence, to live. As mathematician to the grand duke. Things can work out well there. I believe they will. But they may not. Some of my friends think they will not. So, Virginia, it would be better if you took the veil here and stayed here. Castelli, you are almost ready to enter upon a career as a scholar-priest, a priestly scientist. You too must stay here in the free Republic of Venice.

Castelli. So I'm fired?

Galileo. I didn't say *that.*

Castelli. You said it was a family council. That makes me a son—who might prefer to cling to house and home.

Galileo, *smiling.* Could you get a release from your priestly obligations and work with me in Florence?

Castelli. I must.

Virginia. And I could enter a *Florentine* convent, and keep an eye on you!

Galileo. What? But I don't know any Florentine convents!

Virginia. I do. I know *about* them. No problem!

Galileo, *looking at her.* You're serious. You're both serious. Very well, I reverse myself. Come to Florence, both of you. Keep an eye on me, Virginia. But, Castelli, do either of you have any idea what you're taking on?

Castelli. Do you?

Galileo. No. *He laughs.* No! *All three laugh.* What was it Sarpi said once? Yes: "No one goes so far as the man who doesn't know where he's going."

THREE

a.

A Villa in Florence

Galileo's villa in Florence. More lavish than the Padua house but not extravagant.
Enter Galileo with Virginia. He is just finishing showing her the premises.

Galileo. So how d'you feel to be back?

Virginia. Back? We never lived in Florence.

Galileo. Our ancestors did, we're authentic Florentines, I myself was born just a stone's throw from here . . .

Virginia. Fancy being able to see the Arno and the Ponte Vecchio from the master bedroom!

Galileo. From all four bedrooms. That was the real estate man's big selling point. And this is my workroom, Virginia. Let's sit down and relax.

They sit.

Virginia. It's charming. Inspiring, I should say: It's got to inspire you to write masterpieces. But I'm not Virginia any more. I'm Sister Maria.

Galileo. My God, I was forgetting I have a nun for a daughter.

Virginia. I'm not a nun yet, but my name—

Galileo. How can a father remember to call his daughter his sister? Let me look at you. *He takes her face in his hands.* It seems like centuries since I saw you.

Virginia. You were in Rome, or I'd have come long since.

Galileo. Are you happy? Will you be happy as a nun?

Virginia. With you just an hour away I'll be very happy. How about you?

Galileo. The pope granted me six audiences, Virginia—

Virginia. Sister—

Galileo. Maria! Now what happens if I call you Virginia?

Virginia. God will forgive you.

Galileo. It's his job, huh?

Virginia. You're incorr—What's Sagredo's word?

Galileo. Incorrigible. *Picking up the thread.* Bishops came and looked through my telescope in the Pincio Gardens. Old Cardinal Bellarmine himself expressed interest, and a young cardinal called Barberini wrote a poem in honor of Galileo and the new astronomy.

Virginia. Wonderful! What about the Grand Duke, here in Florence?

Galileo. He's been vacillating as grand dukes do. When I've inquired, he's always been in Leghorn inspecting his fleet. But even in Leghorn they can't ignore the writing on the walls of Rome. Cosimo de' Medici will return to Florence and make that long-awaited announcement.

Noise of outer door. Castelli rushes in.

Galileo. I have a visitor for you.

Castelli. Virginia!

Galileo. Sister Maria!

Castelli and Virginia embrace.

Castelli. Sister Maria now? God bless you, sister.

Virginia. What is it you've got on your mind?

Castelli. I must talk to you alone, maestro.

Galileo. As bad as that? Well, Virginia's staying to make the supper this evening. She's brought something very special from the convent.

Virginia. Tagliatello. I'll go get on with it.

She heads for the kitchen.

Galileo. Well?

Castelli. A preaching campaign has started. Last Sunday ten different Dominicans preached the same sermon. A diatribe against you.

Galileo. And?

Castelli. This morning, after mass, a man came up to me and said, "Are you Father Castelli?" When I said I was, he just hurried off.

Galileo. Police spies were never very long on subtlety.

Castelli. They're long on hostility. Their masters are long on power . . . *Exasperated at having no effect.* Does none of this faze you one bit, Galileo?

Galileo. Should it?

Castelli. Suppose Caccini preached against you.

Galileo. He hasn't, has he?

Castelli. He was not one of the ten—

Galileo. Good. Caccini is a formidable demagogue but not entirely devoid of common sense. He knows which side his bread is buttered. The pope—

Castelli. Granted you six audiences. Caccini couldn't care less.

Galileo. He will not come out against *me*.

Castelli. My information is he will do just that. Next Sunday. From the pulpit of Santa Maria Novella. Preaching on a text from the Acts of the Apostles—get this—"Why stand ye gazing into Heaven, O Galileans?"

Galileo. I don't believe it.

b.

A Watchdog of the Lord

A Dominican preacher in his pulpit. His eyes are earnest but slightly watery and shifty. His speech is loud but tends toward incantation; he listens to himself, and what he hears makes him sad.

Dominican. "Why stand ye gazing into Heaven, O Galileans?" *He drinks water.* Dearly Beloved, we look up toward heaven to see there the works of God as in fact they are and always have been and as our church has found them to be. But I need not tell you, in this Florence of ours, that there are those among us—a small minority but a minority organized, ruthless, and backed by foreigners—who are encouraging another attitude. Let us call it the mathematical attitude. For what is this so-called science of mathematics? What else but the Devil's sign language? Does it not go hand in hand with astronomy, astrology, horoscopes, sorcery, and black magic? What else is a mathematician but a male witch? Even the Protestants—even the Protestants—have admitted that their great mathematician, *looking for the name in his notes*, Giovanni Keplero—alias Johann Kepler, a German, hiding out in Austria—is the son of a convicted witch. And here in this Florence of ours— well, what have they ever done in Florence, these scientists, I'd like to know, with their long hair and their noses in books and their fingers in experiments and other hocus-pocus? Take their latest attack on our beliefs and institutions. Look up with me into the heavens, look through the windows of this lovely Church of Santa Maria Novella, and what do you see? The sun. Where? There. *He points to the sun.* And where was it when you entered this church an hour ago? Was it not there? *He points to the east of the sun.* It has moved, has it not? And you know it. You know it. You are not rabble, and filth, and ignoramuses, as these so-called scientists say. You were in Florence before they crept out of their German holes, and you'll be here when they've been sent back where they came from, and you have eyes and can see. *Very quiet again.* But there is an element in our midst, underground, like reptiles, like vermin, without the courage to show its face in the Christian city, in league with the Devil, and believing, not in religion, but in magic, that says we must not believe our own eyes or Aristotle or Ptolemy or Mother Church, we must believe *them!* There is a word, my children, that I do not like to use from this sacred pulpit. That word is heresy, but I use it now because I am going to end this sermon with an announcement. Each of us does what he can, is that not so? and what I have done this week is report some of these . . . heretical activities where each and everyone of us must report them as he sees them: at the headquarters of the Holy Inquisition. Then we shall see changes in Florence! Yes, for though the prime mover himself may for the present be able to hide behind, shall we say, ducal robes, behind Medicean ermine, the watchdogs of the Lord will sniff him out in the end! Glory be to the Father, and to the Son, and to the Holy Ghost, Amen. *He crosses himself.*

c.

The Investigation

An office. Quite bare. Castelli and an Inquisitor at either end of a long table. The Inquisitor is equipped with documents and a writing pad. Nothing grand about this Inquisitor: he is just a plump, cantankerous, small-time investigator, "most ignorant of what he's most assured."

Inquisitor. We are collecting information on Galileo Galilei. You work for him?
Castelli. Yes.

Inquisitor. Why?

Castelli. I am interested in science.

Inquisitor, *consulting papers.* The science taught by Galilei is based on the work of one Hibernicus, correct?

Castelli. Copernicus.

Inquisitor. A Russian?

Castelli. A Pole.

Inquisitor. Are you quibbling with me?

Castelli. It isn't a quibble. The Poles are Catholic, the Russians aren't.

Inquisitor. Hibernicus's book is called *On Revolution.* Is that a Catholic title?

Castelli. It's called *On Revolutions.* Plural. Of the globe, that is.

Inquisitor. What globe?

Castelli. This one.

Inquisitor. Are you telling the Holy Roman Inquisition that we are sitting on a globe, and that it revolves?

Castelli. I am reporting that Copernicus believed this; and that he was a Pole and a Catholic.

Inquisitor. A bad Catholic!

Castelli. A canon of the church. A friend of His Holiness Pope Paul III.

Inquisitor. You were not asked for a lecture on church history. Does Professor Galilei also believe that the earth revolves around the sun?

Pause.

Castelli. I am not entitled to speak for Professor Galilei.

Inquisitor. Has he not taught the opposite theory for years?

Castelli. I think he has.

Inquisitor. When did he stop doing so?

Castelli. I couldn't say.

Inquisitor, *writing in his book.* He has stopped doing so, but you couldn't say exactly when.

Castelli. I am confused now.

Inquisitor. Is Galilei currently teaching that the earth is stationary?

Castelli. I couldn't say.

Inquisitor. You said his view was based on Hibernicus. You said Hibernicus believed the earth goes round the sun. You have therefore affirmed that Galilei believes the earth goes round the sun. I'm asking you if he is currently teaching what he believes?

Castelli. I'm not sure.

Inquisitor. So that Galilei is a teacher whose own pupils don't know what he is currently teaching. Or whether he is sincere and teaches what he believes. What does he mean by saying, "God is an accident"?

Castelli. I don't know.

Inquisitor. Then he did say it. You just didn't understand. How about when he pictured Our Lord as laughing?

Castelli. I don't recall . . .

Inquisitor, *making a note.* It was said but it has been forgotten. Do you recall if you tried to correct him? You are in holy orders. It would be your task to correct such a statement.

Castelli. No, but then—

Inquisitor, *another note.* No attempt to correct. Does he believe in miracles?

Castelli, *more and more distressed.* How can I answer that question for another man?

Inquisitor. Claiming to be a Christian, Galilei leaves it doubtful, even to his intimates, whether he accepts the miracles of Christ. Is he a bachelor?

Castelli. Yes.

Inquisitor. And yet he has a daughter?

Castelli. Yes.

Inquisitor. Where is the mother?

Castelli. In Venice, I believe.

Inquisitor. The mother in Venice. Galilei in Florence. What are his sex habits in Florence?

Castelli. I have no idea. I—

Inquisitor. Is there a woman on the premises?

Castelli. No, there is no one—

Inquisitor. Except you, eh? Does Galilei become too intimate with male companions? You are blushing. Who is Monteverdi? Another Hibernican? He is often mentioned in Galilei's conversation.

Castelli. A musician. Chorus master at St. Mark's.

Inquisitor. St. Mark's, *Venice?* Once again, Venice?

Castelli. St. Mark's *is* in Venice.

Inquisitor. Don't pretend you don't know what the word *Venice* means. When did Galilei launch his attack upon Holy Scripture?!

Castelli. What attack upon Holy Scripture?

Inquisitor. So there were several?

Castelli. But he would *never* attack the Bible—

Inquisitor. You say he "wouldn't." You are asked when *did* he. You are not very cooperative, Father Castelli. This is serious: a priest who is not willing to fight heresy. But it is also *not* serious: This investigation will continue.

d.

A Philanthropist

Galileo's villa. Galileo in earnest talk with Castelli, Galileo pacing the room in agitation.

Galileo. Will continue how? Will continue through whom? Hibernicus! Picturing Our Lord as laughing? Monteverdi a dangerous heretic? Galilei too intimate with male companions?

Castelli. You yourself said Caccini is formidable.

Galileo. I was wrong. If all he could do was report his gripes to a little twirp like this Inquisitor—

Castelli. Who will take them further. Who will stop at nothing, at nobody—

Galileo. What can he do? Who would pay any attention to him?

A knock. Castelli goes to the door. A courtier enters.

Galileo. *very surprised.* Niccolini! Castelli, this is Niccolini, the grand duke's chamberlain. *To Niccolini.* This is Father Castelli.

Chamberlain, *with quiet urgency.* I have the honor to announce the grand duke.

Castelli. What?

Galileo. How do you mean that? He isn't *here*, is he?

Castelli. That would be impossible, he never—

Chamberlain. Exactly. The grand duke never pays calls on commoners. Officially. If, however, he chooses to do so incognito, he does so without appointment—from one moment to the next. Ready?

Flunkeys enter and take up their stand on either side of the door. Grand Duke Cosimo enters with his chamberlain. The grand duke is a neat, "dynamic," self-assured young man, effusive without being warm, and bright without being intelligent, who today might be chosen to hand out funds for a philanthropic foundation. Like the Rockefellers, the Medici distributed largesse for cultural purposes. How the wealth had been acquired in the first place was and is a question not to be asked.

Cosimo. No, no! No formalities! This is a strictly informal visit. Incognito, one might say, except that everyone in Florence knows me. Well, so this is our celebrated mathematician! How do you like Florence? *One soon realizes that he never expects answers or comments.* It's a good city, isn't it, a handsome city! I want to thank you for your contribution to our culture. The city of Michelangelo—I say nothing of the Medici—appreciates culture. And since we've covered art and architecture, I think we should give science a whirl, don't you? Well, you're a biased witness on that one. I just wanted you to know our motives for bringing you here. You've got to cause future historians to write, "What Michelangelo was to painting and sculpture, Galileo was to science and philosophy." Let Bologna compete with that! And Venice too! Even Rome may get worried! You know how you got the job, I suppose? You don't? Well, that's important. There's a moral in it that I don't want you to miss. The man first in line for the job was a friend of yours— Father Sarpi? The combination of priest and scientist seemed pretty unbeatable. But it turns out he's a malcontent. Hostile to the Vatican, the Jesuits, all established authority. Regards the whole country as decadent, and so forth. Now there was criticism of you too, of course. You're a genius, after all. Temperamental. Make enemies wherever you go. But you don't hate established authority, do you? "Erratic, yes, but a law abiding citizen and a good Catholic," said one your testimonials. I said, "I'll buy that," and here you are. Now, Galilei, if you remember all this, everything is going to be all right. If you forget it, however, I won't be able to help you. Think it over and goodbye. My men will leave you some goodies to nibble on.

As they withdraw, Galileo plucks the chamberlain by the sleeve.

Galileo. What happened, Niccolini?

Chamberlain. That agent of the Inquisition had an audience with Cosimo this morning.

He follows the others. When all have left, we realize they have left a pile of expensive food behind.

Galileo. So?

Castelli. Galileo, I came to Florence in good faith, and ever since I've tried to make your wishes come true. But Sarpi and Sagredo were right.

Galileo. We're in for a battle royal with the Dominicans and the Inquisition.

Castelli. The grand duke has proved a broken reed! We'll have to go back to Venice!

Galileo. Venice?!

Castelli. What other escape route is there?

Galileo. So Galileo's assistant talks the language of Sarpi. Escape route! I am not against the Inquisition. If it is against me, I must face up to it. At worst, appeal from its bureaucrats to its leaders. Not back to Venice and the past: forward to Rome!

Castelli. Rome! "Rome is a hoax. Rome is a whore."—Galileo Galilei.

Galileo. All right, but Rome, for Catholics, is past, present, and future; and I *need* Rome.

Castelli. What can you do there, maestro?

Galileo. What did I do when my Paduan colleagues refused to look through the telescope?

Castelli. You went over their heads to the grand duke, and where has that got you?

Galileo. Into hot water with the Dominicans and Inquisitors, so I'll go over *their* heads.

Castelli. Over the head of the Inquisition?

Galileo. Over the head of its hirelings. For, if the hierarchy is not the church, your little preachers and investigators are not the hierarchy.

Castelli. Who *is* the hierarchy?

Galileo. The man who condemned Bruno has "expressed a friendly interest" in the person and views of Galileo.

Castelli. Cardinal Bellarmine?

Galileo. I shall go to Rome and appeal to Bellarmine in person. Are you coming with me?

Pause.

Castelli. Oh, I'll come with you.

Galileo. We leave at dawn.

FOUR

The Master of Controversial Questions

Rome. Cardinal Bellarmine's audience chamber, which is empty save for Galileo and Castelli who sit waiting.

Galileo. How many days has he kept us waiting?

Castelli. Fifty-five.

Galileo. I made a mistake presenting my case in writing. I should have got an appointment two months ago and refused to leave till every point was driven home.

Castelli. Your project is hardly one that a cardinal could take in stride.

Galileo. My project?

Castelli. Asking the Catholic Church to change its mind.

A secretary enters.

Secretary. The Lord Cardinal Bellarmine.

The man who now enters in the red robes of his office is a wizened little creature with keen, mischievous eyes. He has the poise of one who both enjoys the exercise of power and is accustomed to it. He is so far from feeling the need for an aggressive style that he invites characterization as a frail old man and cups an ear in his hand from time to time to suggest deafness. Certainly one feels that he does not hear certain things; whether he is deaf or not is another question. He is not senile.

Bellarmine. Professor Galilei?

Galileo, *kissing his ring.* And this is Father Castelli, my assistant.

Castelli kisses the cardinal's ring too.

Bellarmine, *placing himself presidentially behind a table, smiling.* Well! A historic occasion. The meeting of Bellarmine and Galileo could hardly fail to be a historic occasion. Forgive me if I do not

115

underestimate my own importance. Do you know what the king of England calls me? The Red Menace! Also the Devil's best friend. So I *am* important. Ironically speaking. You are important *un*ironically speaking. . . . The best friend of the Devil is meeting the best friend of Science!

Galileo. I'm flattered that you've interested yourself in my little exploits, Your Eminence.

Bellarmine. My God, you have all the mock humility of a bishop! Little exploits! Young Barberini knows all about science and can't stop talking about you. Quotes you by the yard—delights to go "wandering and discoursing with you among truths"!

Galileo. You have been reading *me*, Your Eminence!

Bellarmine. Did I quote you correctly?

Galileo. "How great a sweetness to go wandering and discoursing together among truths!"

Bellarmine. "How great a joy to proceed from true principles to true conclusions!" Correct?

Galileo. Correct.

They chuckle.

Bellarmine. But of course you're anxious to get down to business?

Galileo. I won't say no to that, Your Eminence.

Bellarmine, *to the secretary.* Ask Father Scheiner to come in. *To Galileo.* You know Scheiner, of course.

Galileo. We met in Padua. Since which time he has become the leading Jesuit scientist.

Bellarmine. Quarreled with you lately, didn't he?

Galileo. He claimed to have discovered the sun spots before I did. That was . . . inexact.

Castelli. That was false.

Galileo. Oh, come, Castelli, Scheiner is an ally. Through him, Jesuit science has committed itself to Copernicus. And what the Jesuits say today, the church will say tomorrow, eh, Your Eminence?

Bellarmine, *who has been consulting documents.* Eh, what? Oh, yes, we Jesuits have a certain standing these days. The church cannot easily ignore us. No, indeed.

While he is saying this, Father Scheiner is shown in. The two scientists eye each other. Bellarmine talks right on. He consults documents from time to time throughout his presentation.

Another historic encounter! Our greatest scientific priest meets our greatest scientific layman! Well, be seated, gentlemen, and let's proceed at once. I must first enjoin secrecy upon you pending our public announcement. Father Scheiner, you will keep the minutes for the Inquisition records. That way we will be sure they are scientifically correct.

Castelli. May I keep notes for Professor Galilei?

Bellarmine. Good idea, good idea. Now, let me begin by putting you out of your agony, Galilei. The goings-on have been scandalous. They will stop. Forthwhile and forever. All harassment will cease. No sermon will be preached against you ever again. No gossip will be spread against you by monks and priests. As for the blunders of the Inquisition itself, or rather of some of its officious menials, they will not recur. Father Castelli, our apologies if some of the Lord's watchdogs have proved to be donkeys.

Galileo. You see, Castelli, what did I tell you?

Bellarmine. Not only, Professor, does your church apologize for the clumsiness of its servants, and free you from all suspicions spread by them, we come to you in gratitude for the service you now render us. While our people squander their energies in slander and intrigue against you, you recall us to our proper duties. For seventy-three years this book of Copernicus has lain around. A few of us read it. None of us came to grips with it. You have forced us to study it, reflect upon it, and commit the church to a definite view of it. *He pauses grandly.*

Galileo, *on tenterhooks.* Yes? Yes, Your Eminence?

Bellarmine. *searching among his papers.* I was looking for our official formulation. Of the main point, you know: The universe? Earth-round-sun or sun-round-earth? Ah yes. *He coughs, then reads.* "The following opinions, having been submitted to the experts of the Inquisition, namely, that the sun does not move round the earth and that the earth does move round the sun, both opinions have been declared false, absurd, and contrary to the Bible."

Galileo. What?

Scheiner. But our observations confirm Professor Galilei's, Your Eminence! We now know that the sun does *not* move round the earth and that the earth *does* move round the sun!

Bellarmine, *still immersed in his document.* Father Scheiner, we shall get to you in a minute. *Coughs again and reads.* "The Lord Cardinal Bellarmine is therefore instructed to summon Galilei before him and advise him not in future to defend these opinions."

Galileo. They have turned me down flat? I can't believe it.

Bellarmine, *continuing.* "As for researches of a Copernican nature within the confines of the church herself, they will cease. Laboratories and observatories will close down. Our physicists all being Jesuits, they will scarcely need reminding of their vows. The Vicar-General is hereby instructed to enforce that absolute obedience for which the Society is so justly renowned."

Scheiner. But this is impossible, Your Eminence! The earth does move round the sun! Who has advised you to the contrary? On what grounds? Why didn't you respect our own Jesuit observatories?

Bellarmine. It's a shock, yes. You'll need time to adjust, I realize that. All this work for nothing! Very galling for you both, I realize that too. But we shall make it up to you. You're ambitious men. We shall not frustrate your ambitions. For luckily, you are versatile. Your ambitions will take a different direction when they must. *Turning to Galileo.* The man who could invent the pendulum, the thermometer, and the telescope can invent something else. Why don't you invent me a gun, Galilei? Some firearm that the Protestants don't have. Then the right side will always win, hm? Invent me a gun. As for you, Father Scheiner, the Inquisition needs a man who knows more of heresy than the heretics themselves. You are that man. You shall be our Special Adviser on Scientific Affairs and as such have far more power than you ever had as a mere researcher.

Scheiner, *his eyes starting out of his head.* This is a nightmare! How can I sit in judgment on people I agree with? And "agreement" isn't the word. These are not opinions, they are objective facts. How can I renounce facts for fantasies? Perhaps I *am* a man who enjoys power. But as a priest I seek purity. As a scientist I revere truth. How then shall I—

Bellarmine. Father Scheiner, you are overexcited, which is excusable in the circumstances. Leave us. You need time, solitude. You also have a job to do: enter this day's business in the minutes. Here's the original I was reading from. *Gives him a couple of sheets of paper, but Scheiner seems rooted to the spot.* Leave us.

Scheiner, *in a low voice.* Has it not occurred to you what this experience will do *to me?*

Bellarmine. What? What are you talking about?

Scheiner. An ambitious Jesuit. No saint. An intellectual. And now a frustrated intellectual. An intellectual whose arm has been twisted. Whose soul will have been twisted. Don't make a dangerous man of me, Your Eminence!

Bellarmine. By no means. Of every Jesuit we make an obedient man. Obedient men are the reverse of dangerous. Obey me now by leaving—without another word. *Scheiner is starting to speak.* Without another word. *Scheiner leaves.*

Bellarmine. I trust you understand, Professor, why this must be?

Galileo. What is that?

Bellarmine. You know how things are, in the Christendom of today?

Galileo. How are they?

Bellarmine. You are unworldly in a new sense, Galilei. Your thoughts are in those other worlds of yours and not in this one!

Galileo. Does this one insist on being stationary?

Bellarmine. Ask rather if it insists on becoming Protestant. When one country falls to this new enemy, must they all go—like dominoes?* At least we can say this much, not one more will go. Further encroachment will be stopped on all fronts! *Smiling at his own fervor.* Well, Professor, I am Master of Controversial Questions. Commander in Chief on the intellectual front, so to speak.

Galileo, *unsmiling.* Copernicus was no Protestant. His teaching was dismissed as folly by both Luther and Calvin.

Bellarmine. And they were *really* the Devil's best friends! For a hundred years now, Protestantism has drawn to itself all elements of doubt and dissent. In combating this evil thing, we combat the incarnate spirit of innovation.

Galileo. But I can't see you rejecting a doctrine, not because it's false, but because it's new!

Bellarmine, *mildly.* My dear Professor, the new is bound to be false. We Catholics say to the Protestants, "Since you are changeable, you

---

*Dominoes do not seem to have been traced back earlier in Europe than the eighteenth century. But this is hardly the first time that a history play contained anachronisms. In any case, what characters say should seem to be what such persons (give or take elements of style imposed by the context) would indeed say. Seem—to whom? To the audience. And our audiences have no clue to the answer except their own experience of such people. It was the opinion of the present author that his audience had often heard their Bellarmines talk about dominoes. (Actually, dominoes here are not "out of time" but "out of place," since they did exist in China.)

cannot be the truth."

Galileo. We Copernicans say to scientists who will not learn, "Since you are unchangeable, you must be dead."

Bellarmine, *cupping his ear in his hand.* What? What was that?

Galileo. I was taught: "We limit not the truth of God."

Bellarmine, *still seeming not to hear.* What? What's this?

Galileo. "The Lord hath yet more light and truth to break forth from his Word."

Bellarmine. Oh. By whom? By whom were you taught that?

Galileo. By my dear departed mother.

Bellarmine. Hm. Were she alive, we should have to have that looked into. The truth has been revealed once and for all. It has also been brought down to us by a mother who has not departed. Mother Church. *Again relaxing, with a smile.* What would you think, after all, of a God who withheld the truth from countless generations and then popped it exclusively into the brains of Canon Copernicus and Professor Galilei?

Galileo, *again not returning the smile.* What do *you* think of the curiosity which God implanted in Copernicus and Galilei—through which they must inevitably discover things and formulate new truths?

Bellarmine. Hm. Curiosity is as curiosity does. Today, "daring" thoughts are the Devil's favorite bait. What is your field? Yes, mathematics—a subject that has its fascination, that's the trouble! We know, from the Bible, that, at Doomsday, the stars will fall from the sky. All right, find me one modern mathematician who doesn't want to contest this! Some of them have even proved that stars cannot fall! *The smile vanishes.* Men, my dear Galilei, are like frogs: open-mouthed to the lure of things that don't concern them. The Devil, being a good fisherman, catches them in shoals. *Sadly.* So when I hear the word curiosity, I summon my Inquisitors, and we prepare the faggots for the stake.
Pause.

Galileo. Suppose I say, "the earth does move round the sun." What do you reply?

Bellarmine. That it does not. What could be simpler?

Galileo. I provided physical evidence. Did you understand it?

Bellarmine. No.

Galileo. Well then.

Bellarmine. Well then what? Evidence must be understandable, or it is not evidence.

Galileo. I will not ask, understandable by whom? But if I were to come back to you at some future date with outright proof would you then be willing to say that the earth moves round the sun?

Bellarmine. Of course!

Galileo. Of course?

Bellarmine. I am a logician, and you have asked me a question to which the logical answer is, Yes. But you placed an *if* before the question. I do not regard the condition it implies as fulfillable—except insofar as all things are possible to Him above. *He crosses himself.*

Galileo. But since all things are possible to Him above, this too is possible to Him above.

Bellarmine. Persuasion would be needed as well as proof. And up to now you have shown little interest in persuading us. Mother Church, my dear Professor, cannot be raped!

Galileo. Can she be seduced?

Bellarmine. By proof and persuasion.

Galileo. But I'm not allowed to offer proof and persuasion.

Bellarmine. How's that?

Galileo. To quote your decree, now being entered in the Inquisition minutes by Father Scheiner.

Bellarmine. To misquote it. Read him the text, Castelli.

Castelli, *consulting his notes.* ". . . Summon . . . Galileo . . . and advise him not in future to defend these opinions."

Galileo. Exactly.

Bellarmine. They wouldn't be *opinions* if you proved them to be facts. Nor do facts need a defense. Merely a persuasive presentation.

Galileo. You are suggesting, then—

Bellarmine. Mother Church is never indifferent to truth or deaf to persuasion. Remember that.

Galileo. I shall.

Ballarmine. You will be with me in my prayers tonight, Galileo. May I be in yours?

And Bellarmine leaves, followed by the secretary. Galileo and Castelli do not move.

Galileo. "Not an opinion but a fact"—Scheiner's words. He will have to eat them. But I am not a Jesuit. I don't have to eat them. *Pause.* What *do* I have to do?

Castelli. Can you face exile?

Galileo. I am not interested in exile. Am I a Protestant?

Castelli. Of course not.

Galileo. If I left Catholic soil, I *would* be giving the Protestants aid and comfort.

Castelli. Then there's nothing for it but knuckling under. *Trying to smile.* Your next book wasn't to be about the universe anyway, was it?

Galileo. It's to be about motion. Mechanics.

Castelli. What are you thinking, maestro?

Galileo. The book on motion will have to wait.

Castelli. How's that?

Galileo. Do I really have to choose between exile and silence? Between outright mutiny and utter servility?

Castelli. Yes. Yes!

Galileo. You are forgetting Bellarmine's lesson in logic. *If* I can be persuasive, *if* I can present what are conceded to be proofs, I can still "defend Copernicus," can still study cosmology.

Castelli. "Persuasiveness" is not a scientific category. Bellarmine can find you unpersuasive to all eternity.

Galileo. Bellarmine won't live to all eternity. I will write a new book— on this subject, not some other. Bellarmine won't be around by the time it's finished. Think of the new generation. They say Barberini will be the next pope. He'll free us from this bondage.

Castelli. I fear Scheiner.

Galileo. What can he do?

Castelli. Well, suppose what he writes into the minutes is inaccurate?

Galileo. He would hardly falsify Inquisition records.

Castelli. He lied about the sunspots.

Galileo. Under pressure of acute professional rivalry.

Castelli. Exactly.

Pause.

Galileo. Did you get down what Bellarmine said?

Castelli. Yes.

Galileo. Go back to him. Ask him to certify that your transcript is correct.

Castelli. I'll catch him before he leaves the building.

Starts to leave.

Galileo. Oh, and Castelli, when you have his signature, just casually throw out that I'm on the track of a new explosive. Far more damaging than anything on the market so far.

Castelli. But is that true?

Galileo. No. Yes. Only don't tell him this part: It is for use "on the intellectual front." For blowing up the world—all the worlds—in which Bellarmine believes.

Castelli. You mean the book.

Galileo. Yes. Are you going to stay with me to work on it?

Castelli. How long will it take?

Galileo, *after a moment's thought.* Oh, give me fifteen years.

    Castelli leaves.

FIVE

Two World Systems

The same Florentine villa as in Scene Three. But many years have passed since the previous scenes.* It is almost sunset on a bright March afternoon. The table is already laid for supper. Sound of a coach halting outside. A knock on the house door. Castelli emerges from an unseen room and crosses to the door. He is now in his thirties. He opens the door. Virginia—Sister Maria—enters. She is no longer a girl.

Castelli. Sister Maria! At last! Why, it's so good to see you!

He embraces her.

Virginia. Your message was so mysterious. "Come at once. Explanations on arrival." The mother superior almost didn't let me come.

---

*Why not say *how* many? History has not concealed the answer. It is seventeen. But to the extent that our scenes are viewed as drama, rather than pure chronicle, they are also viewed as performance and in the theatre the passage of time can easily become obtrusive. Seeing Helen Hayes present Queen Victoria, her audiences used to ask, how old will she be in the next scene? and often asked nothing else. In the present script, the number of years is left unstated so that the actors need not focus their attention, and the public's, on time and its effects upon the human body, the greying hair, the stooping shoulders, the quavering voice. This was the more important because the time span from the death of Giordano Bruno to the trial of Galileo was all of thrty-three years. The literal-minded stage director would face many problems. Not only would his Galileo have to age inordinately, two actresses would be needed for the one role of his daughter (little girl and woman). Yet these are problems which not only can but should be avoided. Though passage of time is important in this action as a painful process of waiting and also as developing conflict, the biological aging process has no part in it whatever. This Galileo is not shown in the blindness of his later years. He is never even shown as an old man. The thirty-three years of history may properly seem about twenty. If an audience never even asks itself how many years have passed, that is perhaps the most desirable result of all.

Castelli. She never lets you come these days. How many months since the last time?

Virginia. Six. It was before the death of the holy father. We went into strict seclusion after that.

Castelli has taken her cloak and shawl and brought her into the living room.

Castelli. I'm afraid the holy father's death didn't sadden *your* father. *She winces.* I shouldn't have put it that way.

Virginia. *I* shouldn't be so touchy. You see, at the convent, I'm the one whose father quarreled with the pope.

She knows her father's home and finds her own way to a seat. In his personal life, Galileo belongs to these two, Virginia and Castelli, and they especially feel their common proprietorship when they meet after long absence and when they are alone together. Both conditions are met now.

Castelli. Well, he won't now. When Barberini was elected pope your father staged a celebration. All Florence was here. The archbishop of Florence read a message from Barberini to the assembled company. From Pope Urban, I should say.

Virginia. Where *is* my father?

Castelli. Out gardening. He got tired of sitting here waiting for the mailcoach.

Virginia. Mailcoach?

Castelli. That belongs to the "explanations on arrival."

Virginia. Oh? I thought they'd have something to do with The Book.

Castelli. They do.

Virginia. Don't say it's finished? After how many years is it?

Castelli. It was as if he couldn't bear to finish it while the old pope was still around. Less than three weeks after Barberini's accession, he marched in here one morning, and plonked the completed manuscript down on that table.

A small, high table occupies pretty much the same proud place in this room as the reading stand had in the Padua house in Scene One.

Virginia. You don't mean *that's* it? *She jumps up to touch some pages of the manuscript.* Hm. Is this the only copy?

During this speech, her father has entered by a door that leads directly to the garden. He is dressed in old gardening clothes, has a couple of gardening tools dangling from his waist and some foliage in one hand. Since we last saw him he has passed from early to late middle age. He is a little frailer in body but, if anything, even more purposeful and vigorous in mind.

Galileo. "Explanations on arrival"!

Virginia, *turning round.* Father! *And she runs to embrace him.*

Galileo. Well, my dear, you're so pretty these days, a father could have unmonastic thoughts.

Virginia. And you're still the Greek god: ageless. Your eyes are about nineteen.

Castelli realizes that father and daughter would like to be alone for a while.

Castelli. I'll go see if the mailcoach has come. *He leaves by the house door.*

Galileo. Will you drink a little wine with me before supper? I sent to the ends of the earth for it.

Virginia. Sicily, you mean. I'd love some. But why don't you put those leaves down first?

Galileo. They're for the wine. Watch. I take this leaf, fold it like this, make little holes in it with a pin like this, dip the stalk in the wine like this, take the leaf in my mouth like this, and suck up the wine through the little holes like this.

Virginia. What for?

Galileo. To get more pleasure from the wine. Watch again!

He continues with his experiment.

Virginia. "The body, like the mind, should imbibe delicately."

Galileo, *between imbibings.* What?

Virginia. You made me write that out three times—when I was ten.

Galileo. Heavens, was I that stuffy? Well, today I thought of a definition of wine.

Virginia. Oh?

Galileo. "Wine . . . is light held together by moisture."

Virginia. That's beautiful!

Galileo. It would even be clear—but for one thing.

Virginia. What's that?

Galileo. I don't know what light is. Want to try this? *He offers her a leaf.*

Virginia, *who has already been drinking from a glass.* I'm very content with this. *Silence. They sit drinking, each in his own way.* Castelli told me about the book. It must give you a deep feeling of satisfaction to have finished it at last.

Galileo. I'm on top of the world. Never been so happy before. *Another sip.* People sneer at success. I wonder if they should: It seems to do one good. I'm savoring it—as I do this wine—and finding a lot more nourishment in it.

Virginia. And now what?

Galileo. Castelli hadn't finished his story? Where'd he leave off?

Virginia. I was asking if that, *pointing to the manuscript,* was the only copy.

Galileo, *jumping straight in.* It's one of two copies.

Virginia. Where's the other?

Galileo, *with relish.* The other? On Pope Urban's desk in the Vatican.

Virginia. Good heavens, is it that kind of book?

Galileo. How d'you mean?

Virginia. Well, d'you need the Holy Father's special . . . patronage?

Galileo. You don't know what it's about, do you?

Virginia. You have never breathed a word in all the years.

Galileo. Because I'm going to present you with a *fait accompli:* a book on a "highly controversial subject" licensed by the Holy Father.

Virginia. So *that's* why you're on top of the world. When did the news come?

Galileo. It should have come several hours ago. We tried to time your arrival for right afterwards. But the mailcoach is late.

Virginia. So that's what Castelli's doing out there—

Galileo. Getting the pope's letter from the mailman—

Virginia. The letter authorizing publication of your book!

Galileo. Such was the "explanation on arrival."

Virginia. So it's quite certain? Pope Urban has let you know he *will* approve?

Galileo. Oh, he committed himself to our views years ago.

Virginia. But now he's pope.

Galileo. Pah! Barberini is a man of character.

Virginia. And couldn't have reasons for changing?

Galileo. You can't withdraw support from a case that has been proved.

Castelli comes hurrying in, holding up an envelope.

Castelli. The papal coat of arms on the envelope!

Galileo snatches the letter, opens it with trembling fingers, quickly skims the contents in silence, then grunts noncommittally.

Virginia, *also on her feet by now.* Has he *not* approved the book?

Galileo. Sit down, both of you. Now, Castelli, read this letter for the three of us.

Castelli, having taken the letter back, reads, sitting.

Castelli. "Dear Professor Galilei, the Holy Father has received your request for a license to publish your manuscript *The Two World Systems. . . .*"

Virginia. *Two World Systems!* So that's what the book is!

Castelli. " . . . Kindly present yourself without delay at the address below. Signed, Firenzuola, Commissar General." The address below is the Palace of the Inquisition in Rome.

Virginia. The Inquisition!

Galileo. So how do my two henchmen take this new turn in the story?

Virginia. That subject has always made trouble between you and the church.

Galileo. "The hierarchy is not the church."

Castelli. You're prepared to take on the hierarchy now?

Galileo. What should I do? Present myself without delay at the address below?

Virginia. You have to. When the Inquisition sends for you.

Castelli. This is a very great setback.

Galileo. And?

Castelli. In going to Rome you are putting your head in the she-wolf's mouth.

Galileo. But as Virginia says, I have no alternative. Save flight, save exile. And I would rather all my books were burned, I would rather tear our my right eye, then lend comfort to the enemies of our church.

Castelli. In Rome you confront the top men of the hierarchy.

Galileo. They have my confidence!

Castelli. But this letter!

Galileo. The pope is busy. He had the right to hand the book on to—

Castelli. He can understand the book. The commissar of the Inquisition can *not*.

Galileo. The commissar has the cardinals of the Holy Office to advise him—

Castelli. The cardinals! But the cardinals are—

Virginia. You're wasting your breath, Castelli. Look at his face. He is going to Rome.

Galileo, *to Castelli.* And once again you are coming with me.

Castelli, *sighing.* I suppose I am.

Galileo. Enough gravity then. *To Virginia.* You are our guest at supper tonight. Drink a toast with me. *He has poured the wine. They take their glasses.* I give you the friendship of both your fathers, Virginia, the holy one in Rome and the somewhat less holy one here in Florence! *They touch glasses.*

SIX

The Inquisition

Rome. In the Palace of the Inquisition. Again, as before Bellarmine years earlier, Galileo sits with the faithful Castelli awaiting word from above.

Galileo. So here we are: in the Palace of the Inquisition. Is it so terrifying?

If he means the surroundings, they are indeed unterrifying: They are elegant.

Castelli. The room is set up for a formal proceeding.

Tables and chairs are arranged for a council or other such proceeding.

Galileo. But when the secretary said the Commissar General will be here in a moment, I got the impression he'd come alone. What do you know about him?

Castelli. He's one of the new men. Name of Firenzuola. Very close to the Vatican. Not so close to the Jesuits.

Galileo. In other words, it's *preferable* to deal with him alone.

Castelli. Definitely.

A secretary enters.

Secretary. Father Commissar Firenzuola.

The Commissar General of the Inquisition enters. Father Firenzuola is a pleasant-looking young official, and in his handling of the business in hand will prove brisk, efficient, and correct. All associations with the word "Inquisition" would only mislead us as to his character, since he is not a scoundrel either of the blustering or the smooth variety. He sees himself—and after all is not alone in this—simply as a man with a job to do for an organization that has made certain commitments. He is not an ideologue and feels no animus against Galileo.

Firenzuola. Would you sit here, Professor?

They have never met, but Firenzuola takes in Galileo at a glance, Castelli at a second glance. The secretary has already left.

And perhaps we should be alone for a few minutes.

Galileo. I would prefer it if Castelli could remain.

Castelli. The professor isn't as young as he once was, Father Commissar.

Galileo. I'm not as bright as I once was. I need Castelli to prompt me, these days.

Firenzuola. As a priest Father Castelli knows the meaning of secrecy. He shall stay if you say so.

Galileo. Thank you.

Firenzuola. Galilei, you have submitted a manuscript for a publication license. I have to report that your petition has been denied.

Galileo, *turning to Castelli, unable to believe his ears.* What? The request . . . denied?

Firenzuola, *who does not leave such questions for others to handle.* The book cannot possibly be approved. We are amazed that you should ever have supposed it could be. But since you did, we recognize that this news must come to you as a shock. And we know a good deal about shocks. One needs time to get over them. Would you care to return to this room in exactly forty-eight hours?

Galileo, *and it is not clear now if he is speaking to Castelli, to Firenzuola, or himself.* The book "cannot possibly be approved"?

Firenzuola. That is correct.

Galileo. Not even in amended form?

Firenzuola. Not even in amended form.

Galileo. Selections from it could appear perhaps?

Firenzuola. No, no, Professor. There are no if's or but's. The answer is an all-inclusive no.

Galileo. I can't take this in.

Firenzuola. That is why we suggest a two-day recess.

Galileo, *suddenly much clearer in his mind.* Oh, no, no, no. Time won't help. I'll stay.

Firenzuola. Are you sure?

Galileo. I'll stay.

Firenzuola. You are a strong man, and we admire strength. To proceed. As you must know better than anyone, Professor, in this book you have championed a view of the universe which the church condemned years ago. We will not discuss that view, or the church's condemnation of it, nor yet your . . . defiance of the condemnation. We will content ourselves with a repetition of our first statement. *Your book is banned.* It has been condemned by the congregation of the Holy Office, and this condemnation will be enforced by the Inquisition. Need I say more? You know why the Inquisition exists. You know how it operates. You know you mustn't oppose its wishes. You know you would get nowhere if you did. . . . You follow me?

Galileo. Hm? Oh. Oh, yes, I am following you very intently, Father Commissar.

Firenzuola. Good. Because I am going to propose something. Doing it will hurt, but believe me when I say that not doing it would hurt far, far more. And we know a good deal about hurts, too. *He stops as if for a reaction.*

Galileo. Yes, yes?

Firenzuola. Allow us to destroy your manuscript. Destroy any other copies you may have made. Drop the whole matter. And the world will never know you have been condemned by us, nor even that we ever received a manuscript. No punishment, no disgrace, no censure, no slur on your good name. You will walk out of here a free man.

Galileo. I see. *Slowly.* Free to do what?

Firenzuola. *You* tell *us.* To pursue your researches in mathematics and physics . . . in any direction whatever, any *other* direction whatever . . . perhaps something more practical . . .?

Galileo. Ah yes, I should invent a gun.

Firenzuola. What was that?

Galileo. Oh, just something Bellarmine told me.

Firenzuola, *not to be sidetracked.* So you do accept our proposal?

Galileo. Of burning my book?

Firenzuola. Of . . . wiping the slate clean?

Galileo. No, no, I can't.

Firenzuola. Galilei, we are *prepared* for a negative answer, and our preparations are cruel. Humiliating. Are you determined to make us use them?

Galileo. I cannot burn my book.

Firenzuola. If you and I fail to reach agreement, the entire matter will be placed in the hands of six cardinals of the Holy Office. At once. They are waiting in the next room now. None of them has read your book. They will be dependent on a single reader: your old rival Father Scheiner, the Special Adviser on Scientific Affairs.

Galileo. I am sure Father Scheiner can do a good job.

Firenzuola, *hesitating.* He is a Jesuit. *Pause.* So are three of the cardinals.

Galileo, *smoothly.* I am not prejudiced against the Society of Jesus, Father Commissar.

Firenzuola. You know best. *He rings a bell. A secretary enters.* Ask the cardinals to come in now, would you? *The secretary at once admits six cardinals who take seats obviously prepared for them and soon look like a bench of judges. What manner of men are they? Are they religious? Are they recognizably ecclesiastical, even? It is debatable. What is certain is that these are men in important positions in an organization that dominates the life of the time. They resemble other such men.*

Firenzuola. Would you now care to reconsider my proposal, Professor? *Galileo shakes his head.*

Firenzuola, *to the secretary.* Ask Father Scheiner to come in. *To Galileo.* You may find him somewhat changed. *Father Scheiner comes in. He is recognizable but terribly changed. He was gaunt before but is now gaunter. His eyes were fiery before but are now deep-set, haunted. His face is unnaturally pale. He too takes a place obviously prepared for him. When all are in position, Firenzuola continues.* My lords, the question before you this morning is whether to license the book *The Two World Systems* by Galileo Galilei, who has generously consented to be present with us. You will be assisted in making this decision by the Special Adviser on Scientific Affairs and myself. Your decision will be reached unanimously, as per the regulations. Yes, Cardinal Silotti? *Cardinal 1 has held up his hand.*

Cardinal 1. May not a decision also be reached by five votes to one?

Firenzuola. That is correct. *Reading from a small book on his desk.* "Provided an honest and exhaustive attempt at unanimity has been made and on no account on the first day of such proceeding."

Cardinal 1. Thank you.

Firenzuola. The Special Adviser has studied the book and researched the entire career of its author. Father Scheiner?

Scheiner. Yes, Father Commissar?

Firenzuola. Question Galilei on his meeting with Cardinal Bellarmine.

Scheiner, *stepping forward.* Galilei, it is my understanding that you met with Cardinal Bellarmine, on a single occasion, more than ten years ago, is that so?

Galileo. That is so.

Scheiner. Could you tell the tribunal what the upshot of the meeting was?

Galileo. I was advised not to defend the forbidden doctrine of Copernicus.

Scheiner. Not to . . . What was the verb?

Galileo. Defend.

Scheiner. Galilei, I have here in my hand the words of Bellarmine as set down in the Inquisition records at the time. Would you be exact in your account?

Galileo. I have been exactly exact, that is my profession.

Scheiner. Then, Father Commissar, may I read the actual words of Bellarmine?

Firenzuola. Please do.

Scheiner. "Galilei was enjoined to relinquish the opinion that the sun is the center of the world and stationary and that the earth is not the center of the world and is not stationary and forbidden to discuss *or even mention it in any way,* orally or in writing, which injunction the said Galilei agreed to and promised to obey."

Galileo. *Discuss or even mention in any way?!* But Bellarmine even went on to say that I could offer proofs and persuasions—which is exactly what my new manuscript does!

Firenzuola. Is there anything to that effect in the minutes?

Scheiner. No, Father Commissar.

Firenzuola. Are the Inquisition minutes generally accurate and complete in such matters?

Scheiner. They are the most accurate and complete records in the world.

Firenzuola, *to Galileo.* Now you know what I mean by cruel and humiliating. You have forced us to convict you of breach of faith with your church.

Galileo. But I deny it! A man couldn't forget being ordered not to mention his favorite subject, the theme of his whole life's work!

Firenzuola. Precisely.

Galileo. I know I never agreed to that.

Castelli. May we see those minutes, Father Commissar?

Scheiner. That would be extremely irregular, Father Commissar.

Firenzuola. Let him see them.

They are handed to Castelli.

Castelli. It is as I feared. The handwriting is different. The minute was not written by the same hand as everything else in this section of the book.

133

Scheiner. May I speak to that?

Firenzuola. You may.

Scheiner. The minute in question was written by me. Castelli already knew that. He heard Bellarmine order that.

Firenzuola. Father Castelli, scientific notes written up by Father Scheiner could only be considered more than usually dependable.

Castelli. He had always been jealous of Galileo. And it was a moment of very great stress for him.

Pause.

Firenzuola. You couldn't be suggesting that Father Scheiner falsified our records?

Galileo. It *is* a falsification, so, if Scheiner wrote it. . . .

Firenzuola. In any event, wild accusations made on the spur of the moment by way of effective speechmaking cannot weigh in the balance against official records.

Galileo. What would you accept as legitimate evidence on our side?

Firenzuola. We would need Bellarmine's signature on a written document.

Galileo. We have that.

Castelli, *rooting among his papers.* Indeed, yes. I noticed at the time the state Father Scheiner was in. Here. *He hands it to Firenzuola.*

Firenzuola. "The following opinions . . . that the sun does not move round the earth and that the earth does move around the sun . . . have been declared false. . . . Cardinal Bellarmine is therefore instructed to summon Galilei before him and advise him not in future to defend these opinions. Signed, Robert Cardinal Bellarmine."

Silence.

Scheiner. May I see that document, Father Commissar? It will be a forgery.

The Commissar General hands it to him.

Firenzuola. Is the Bellarmine signature genuine?

Scheiner, *examining it.* It does seem to be his handwriting. I don't understand.

Galileo. But I do. The official minutes are inaccurate and defamatory!

Scheiner, *quietly.* I formally request that Galilei be asked to withdraw.

Firenzuola. Would you step outside for a moment, Professor?

He does so, with Castelli.

Scheiner. The whole thing is now quite clear. Bellarmine was in his dotage, and Galileo got him to sign a document he didn't even read.

Cardinal 1. Thus compounding his own crime. . . .

Cardinal 2. By adding forgery to disobedience!

Cardinal 3. Yes, that's *obviously* what happened.

Cardinal 4. But then we don't know, do we, actually?

Cardinal 5. No, suppose this document really was approved by Bellarmine?

Cardinal 1. How can we suppose a thing like that?!

Cardinal 6. Well, if this document was really approved by Bellarmine, then not only was Galileo not guilty of forgery; he would not be guilty of disobedience either.

Cardinal 2. Which side are you on?

Cardinal 1. We're here to find this man guilty, not hold student debates on the English model!

Cardinal 2. The Protestant model!

Pause.

Cardinal 6. I wonder if our true objective should not be stated thus: *At all costs avoid a public crisis. One Giordano Bruno was enough.* More than enough. For an *auto da fé* which was supposed to deter heretics and help us only aroused indignation among heretics and made us repellent. Today, certainly, such an execution would serve only the Lutherans. If I am right, what follows? That, instead of making the name of Galilei a rallying point for our enemies, we should come only to conclusions which he himself will voluntarily accept.

Cardinal 1. In which statement do we not read the fine Roman hand of Urban VIII?

Cardinal 6. Can I not agree with my pope? No vows of absolute obedience limit *my* choice!

Cardinal 2. That is an insult to the Society of Jesus!

Cardinal 3. It certainly is!

Firenzuola. Order, my lords! Cardinal Lucignano's point is well taken. Just as we should not be fighting each other, so also we should not be fighting Galilei.

Cardinal 6. What we are apparently engaged in is a prize fight of which Galilei has won the first round.

Cardinal 5. It was a mistake to urge an offence he couldn't possibly plead guilty to: writing a book on a topic he's been forbidden to mention!

Cardinal 4. Besides, his version of what happened had Bellarmine's signature on it. Father Scheiner's had not.

Scheiner. Are you insinuating that—

Firenzuola. Cardinal Gorazio, you are out of order. My lords, you are here to judge Galilei, not each other.

Cardinal 4, *pouting*. Well, well, ancient Rome had emperors: modern Rome has commissars. Tell us what to think, Firenzuola, tell us what to think!

Firenzuola. Well, my dear Cardinal, would you have Galilei give the signal for protest and revolt to his admirers throughout Christendom?

Cardinal 4. Of course not.

Firenzuola. What is the injunction Galileo admits receiving, Father Scheiner?

Scheiner. An order stating that he must not *defend* the forbidden views.

Firenzuola. We have to concede, my lords, that he is licensed to *mention* the forbidden views. We do not have to concede that he may *defend* them. Very well, Father Scheiner will present the evidence that he has indeed defended them; and Galilei will be forced to agree. We can then ban the book *with his blessing*.

Cardinal 1. Well, let's see if this works.

Cardinal 3. Scheiner will find a way if anyone can.

Cardinal 2. He certainly will.

Firenzuola, *to secretary*. Ask Galilei to return.

Secretary, *in doorway*. Professor Galilei.

The professor returns with Castelli.

Firenzuola. Father Scheiner, have you read Galilei's manuscript?

Scheiner. Yes, Father Commissar.

Firenzuola. Tell the tribunal whether Galilei has not only mentioned but also defended the forbidden view of the universe.

Scheiner. I have made notes on that.

Firenzuola. Read them.

Cardinal 4. How long is this going to take? Some of us have appointments.

Scheiner. Oh, about two hours.

Cardinal 5. Two hours? What do you take us for?

Cardinal 3. Sh, sh, sh. Sordi, let's show that English virtue shall we? What's it called—tolerance?

Cardinal 1. Go on, Scheiner.

Scheiner, *looks to Firenzuola. Firenzuola nods*. Very well. *He reads*. "Does

Galilei teach the forbidden view? What is teaching? asks Saint Augustine, and answers, it is to communicate knowledge. Does Galilei communicate the knowledge of the forbidden view? He does. See pages 4 through 53, 72 through 96, 113 through 147, 196 through. . . ."

He continues in this vein for more than an hour.

". . . To summarize, the knowledge of the forbidden view is therefore communicated on a sum total of 364 pages. Nor is that all. Saint Thomas Aquinas states that a teacher indicates both his own approval of the doctrine taught and his desire that others should accept it. Such approval and such desire are clearly indicated on pages 33, 47, 68, 89, 113. . . .

He continues in this vein for more than another hour.

". . . To summarize, approval of the forbidden view and a desire for others to accept it is clearly indicated on a sum total of 166 pages. The fact that the book is written in Italian, not the customary Latin, must also be urged as evidence that Professor Galilei wished to ingratiate himself with the public."

Firenzuola. Any comments, Professor Galilei?

Galileo. Am I supposed to remember all those page numbers? Father Scheiner has been talking for two and a half hours.

Cardinal 3. Father Commissar, if the Holy Office is to be insulted, I move that the session be adjourned.

Firenzuola. Galilei, tell the tribunal if Father Scheiner's report is just or unjust.

Galileo. I can make an uninterrupted rejoinder?

Firenzuola. Of course.

Galileo, *after a pause.* As Father Scheiner spoke I was reminded of Roman Law—in which the omission of relevant truths coupled with the cunning suggestion of untruths constitutes lying. At no point did Father Scheiner weigh the pro and con; at no point did he let the relevant fact and falsehood confront each other; at no point did he attempt to measure differing degrees of relevance. But let us forget Father Scheiner, even if that will be difficult, and let us remember Cardinal Bellarmine, whose advice I have either flouted or not flouted. He "advised" me not to "defend" the "erroneous" view of Copernicus. But I don't believe that view to *be* erroneous. The church, in its infallible wisdom, has never proclaimed it so, has never made this a matter of dogma. Even in the opinion of the church, therefore, such a view can only be erroneous till it is proved correct. I did not "defend" this view. I spent long years proving it correct, so that it would no longer be held "erroneous," after which no one could disapprove if I taught it.

Father Scheiner jumps up.

Firenzuola. One moment, Scheiner. Cardinal Silotti has the floor.

Cardinal 1. Has your secretary taken all this down, Firenzuola?

Firenzuola, *giving the secretary a glance.* Oh yes, of course.

Cardinal 1. That is all I care to say at this time.

Firenzuola. Cardinal Girardi?

Cardinal 2. Galilei, if you publish these . . . so-called proofs, then you *are* teaching them.

Galileo. But first, before they are published, you yourselves have the chance to judge if the proofs are better than "so-called" or not. If you should judge that they are, then I would be authorized to teach them.

Cardinal 3. But then you are teaching *us* in advance of such judgment.

Galileo. How am I to present a subject without teaching it? Would you have me present truths as untruths?

Firenzuola. I must disallow these questions, Galilei. The prisoner does not cross-examine his judges.

Galileo, *shrugging.* What does he do?

Firenzuola. He gives his version of the truth.

Scheiner. If he has what it takes.

Galileo. Hm?

Scheiner. He has what it takes to denounce others as liars. Dare he reveal what he himself holds to be true?

Galileo. This is a charade we have been playing. I will end it. *Short pause.* What Bellarmine told me was: the truth is old and the truth is known. In my field, that of physical science, we call truth "new" because it is not known but is in the process of being discovered. What passes for the known is progressively revealed to be error. You see what Bellarmine proposed to me? The Copernican view was new and therefore, as far as he was concerned, wrong; but if I wanted to spend my life trying to prove it right, that was my affair. I risked failure. A double failure. Should the doctrine prove false, I would have willfully spent my life defending what I was advised not to defend because it was known to be false all along. But what else could I do? To me, Catholicism is true. I believe that,

being dedicated to truth, the church must and will accept *anything* that can be proved true. Some truths are more important, no doubt, than the truths of physics, but, for a Catholic physicist, this can hardly mean that, in physics, the church prefers falsehood to truth. *Pause.* Bellarmine, God rest his soul, is dead. The church lives. It is the church in which I place my hopes. My church *cannot* be hostile to "new" truth in physical science, for truth in physical science is "new". My church will be hospitable to scientific discovery. I appeal from Bellarmine—to you, my lords.
Silence.

Cardinal 5. I'm flabbergasted.

Cardinal 4. Did I hear you right, Galilei? You are asking not only to be let off but celebrated as the hero of the occasion?

Galileo. I am asking that we drop all pretense, admit that what is at stake is our view of the universe, and accept the view which has been proved true.

Cardinal 5. You would turn the tables on us!

Galileo. Cardinal Lucignano, I appeal to you.

Cardinal 6. I'm afraid, Galilei, you have now passed the bounds. I too would have to concede that your book must be banned.

Cardinal 1, *to Firenzuola.* I request that the prisoner be asked to withdraw.

Firenzuola. The guards will escort you to your quarters, Galilei.
Galileo and Castelli leave.

Cardinal 1. The book, says Cardinal Lucignano, must be banned. What triviality is this? Galilei has come right out with it at long last! Father Scheiner is to be congratulated on prying this statement loose. Do you realize, my lords, what it amounts to?

Cardinal 2. An admission.

Cardinal 3. An outright admission of guilt.

Cardinal 1. Yes. And what guilt?

Cardinal 3. Disobeying Bellarmine.

Cardinal 2. Disobedience—the sin of Adam.

Cardinal 1. Adam and Eve were guilty of a single act of disobedience, over in a moment, but this man persisted in his sin for many years—only to end, here, today, with the Holy Office itself as witnesses, condoning his disobedience, nay, even asking holy church to sanction it!

Firenzuola. Are you asking the tribunal to take a new position, Your

Eminence?

Cardinal 1. Most definitely. We came here to judge a book. We are now compelled to judge a man.

Cardinal 3. Galilei used the phrase, *he consults his notes,* "even in the opinion of the church." As if church doctrine were no more than personal preference!

Cardinal 2. To be pitted against the preferences of Professor Galilei!

Cardinal 1, *definitively.* Compounding disobedience with defiance, this man has proved himself an out-and-out heretic.

Cardinal 3. That is exactly it.

Cardinal 2. And must be punished as such.

Firenzuola. To be specific, my lords. . . .

Cardinal 1. "Specific!" Since when do commissars talk like schoolteachers? The Holy Inquisition has made its presence felt throughout Europe by one thing and one thing only!

Cardinal 2. The stake!

Cardinal 6. I object. The stake is for heretics. The Copernican view of the universe—though an error—has never yet been pronounced a heresy.

Cardinal 1. Is this the Holy Office or a theology seminar? How many of the Inquisition's victims have been openly committed to a declared heresy?

Cardinal 3. They're far too smart.

Cardinal 2. Like this man before us now.

Cardinal 1. Need I remind you, Lucignano, heresy today is not a matter of doctrine only: it is a *spirit* that bloweth where the Devil listeth by the agency of unquiet souls spreading disaffection as dungflies spread disease.

Cardinal 6. Even so, it has to be proved, by overt acts, that they have done this. Galilei has written an unpublished book that has been submitted to us alone—

Cardinal 1. Giving us the chance to *prevent* catastrophe.

Cardinal 6. Is that a Christian approach?

Cardinal 1. Who was it that said to think adultery was to commit it? Our Lord Himself. It behoves us, therefore, to see into men's thoughts in advance of "overt acts." See into them, and punish them. *Sharply.* The three Jesuit members of this tribunal demand the death of Galilei.

Firenzuola. Cardinal Gorazio ?

Cardinal 4. I agree to that.

Cardinal 5. And I.

> *Silence.*

Unanimity being lacking, may I make a suggestion?

Cardinal 1. What is it?

Firenzuola. When there is no clear mandate from the tribunal, the Inquisition has a way of securing one from the accused.

Cardinal 3. Extracting a confession?

Cardinal 1. Galilei's present stance does not suggest that he would give you one.

Cardinal 2. Though we have seen these "stances" crumble often enough.

Cardinal 3. Under torture.

Cardinal 6. I will not agree to the use of torture in this case.

Firenzuola. Nor would I propose it. I would propose only to talk to Galilei—alone.

Cardinal 6. What will you have him confess? This is not a man who will put himself in the wrong to save his skin.

Firenzuola. That is why it will be advisable only to ask him to admit that he did disobey Bellarmine. And, at that, unintentionally—not by malice but through vanity.

Scheiner. A venial sin! A nothing! Why, he has already confessed more than that before this tribunal!

Cardinal 1, *softly.* Gently, Scheiner. *Scheiner recognizes that this is an order.* Lucignano, do you agree to Firenzuola's plan?

Cardinal 6. Very well.

Firenzuola. Then I have your authorization, my lords? *Silence.* Good. We reconvene tomorrow morning. I shall visit Galilei this afternoon.

SEVEN

A Friendly Commissar

Palace of the Inquisition. Galileo's quarters. Guards in the entrance hall. Castelli is eating lunch from a tray.

Guard. The Commissar General.

Firenzuola enters.

Firenzuola, *to Castelli.* I wish to see the professor alone.

Castelli goes out to a back room where, we can assume, Galileo has been resting. Enter Galileo. The two men stand facing each other.

Firenzuola. Please be seated, Professor. *Galileo sits.* A private conference between the two of us has been deemed desirable before the tribunal reconvenes. Is that agreeable to you?

Galileo. Has nothing been decided yet?

Firenzuola. I represent the Inquisition. May I use *our* method of procedure?

Galileo. By all means.

Firenzuola. I shall begin by sounding you out a little. What is your own sense of the situation?

Galileo. Do I know what the situation now is?

Firenzuola. Of the situation . . . as it has developed during the hearing. How would you say you were doing?

Galileo. Not too badly. I nailed down the main weaknesses in Scheiner's position.

Firenzuola. You maintained—correct me if I'm wrong—that he is a liar. Even a forger.

Galileo. I *proved* those things.

Firenzuola. And proof lies very near to your heart, isn't that true?

Galileo. That is very true.

Firenzuola. Would you expect Scheiner to enjoy being exposed?

Galileo. No.

Firenzuola. Yet you needed him. No one but he had read your book.

Galileo. The others *could* read my book.

Firenzuola. And understand it?

Galileo. I could help them understand it.

Firenzuola. Between now and tomorrow's session?

Galileo. The world has waited for centuries for these truths. The tribunal could wait another week or two.

Firenzuola. And in that spirit you have appealed from Scheiner to the six cardinals?

Galileo. Yes.

Firenzuola. Three of whom, like Scheiner himself, are members of the Society of Jesus. *Silence.* Any comment?

Galileo. Your own irony is a comment. But not mine.

Firenzuola. You wouldn't, of course, have made this appeal if you didn't think it could succeed?

Galileo. I wouldn't. No.

Firenzuola. What are—or were—its chances of success?

Galileo. Oh, about fifty-fifty.

Firenzuola. Yes?

Galileo. Lucignano's friendly, isn't he? Gorazio and Sordi will jog along behind him, I should think. That's half the tribunal.

Firenzuola. You need five votes.

Galileo. Are you assuming that the individual Jesuits don't think for themselves?

Firenzuola. What would *you* assume?

Galileo. That they have to. Because they respect themselves. And their Order knows about science. . . . They are not inquisitors, they are Catholics, Father Commissar!

Firenzuola. Ah, then you have a *better* than fifty-fifty chance?

Galileo. Maybe. If this must be regarded as a gamble. I'd have said *faith* had something to do with it. You know, the faith which can move mountains.

Firenzuola. Very good, very good. I am not employing our inquisitorial method to torment you. Merely to bring the truth home to you. You have certainly brought home to me your illusion. *Quietly.* Galilei, after you left this morning, the tribunal dismissed your appeal. Unanimously.

Galileo. What? My book is to be banned?

143

Firenzuola. Which was inevitable, as I told you in advance.

Galileo. The tribunal will not even entertain the *possibility* that the earth moves round the sun?

Firenzuola. Will not even entertain the possibility.

Pause.

Galileo. It's unbelievable.

Firenzuola. Tell me *why* it is unbelievable.

Galileo. Because what my book provides is not opinion but proof.

Firenzuola. Proof of what?

Galileo. Of the truth. Obviously.

Firenzuola. The truth. Obviously. Is what is "obvious" to Galilei "obvious" to a tribunal of the Holy Office? Could it be?

Galileo. Be plain with me, Father Commissar. Proving things true has been my life's business, my personal vocation. Proving certain things true to the Holy Office has occupied me continuously for over fifteen years. The results are in that manuscript. Now if truth did not interest the Holy Office, what would that show?

Firenzuola. What *would* that show?

Galileo. A career, a whole life based on a total misunderstanding. A life thrown away. Wasted.

Firenzuola. I should not have enjoyed formulating those phrases.

Galileo. Then it is so ? There is no interest in truth here in Rome *at all?*

Firenzuola. I am not trying to instruct you but to help you to . . . certain conclusions.

Galileo, *suddenly.* Do you think you're God? But God could never be indifferent to truth. *You* can? Firenzuola, you're a human being, aren't you, let me address you as such. Are you totally unconcerned with truth? *Silence.* Then what *are* you concerned with?

Firenzuola, *unruffled.* What *is* a Commissar concerned with?

Galileo, *bitterly.* Power. Just naked power. I suppose that's what you are trying to tell me.

Firenzuola. Let's say administration. A Commissar has very little power. He does what he's told.

Galileo. By the cardinals. Are you saying they're a lot of power-hungry politicians?

Firenzuola. Heaven forbid! I've got you too excited, Galilei. Let me ask you an academic question. What is a church?

Galileo. What?

Firenzuola. Not what does it stand for. What is it?

Galileo. An institution, of course—

Firenzuola. An institution. Among other institutions of this world. Matching itself against other institutions of this world. Matching itself as to what? As to power. Its power against theirs. Or it will no longer exist in this world. What way out is there, except to exist only in other worlds? But the Catholic Church was placed *here* by Christ Himself. Upon this rock. Upon this earth.

Galileo. I'm naive in politics, the point is not new. But how, in God's holy name, is the church threatened by wholly unpolitical activities such as mine? How is it threatened by the motion of the earth around the sun?

Firenzuola. I think Bellarmine must have explained that years ago.

Galileo. He said all new views were wrong.

Firenzuola. Would that we still had his simplicity! *Pause.* The church is a fabric of traditions, nothing else. None of these traditions must be broken or the fabric as whole would fray, wear through, disintegrate. Now, if Bellarmine could feel that a generation ago, how much more strongly must any good Catholic feel it today! Protestant power was *not* stopped, as Bellarmine hoped. Throughout Central and Northern Europe, a so-called war of religion has been raging fifteen years, and no end in sight. Not just that, but—

Galileo, *stopping him rudely.* Yes, yes! *Silence.* But this preoccupation of yours with power and the struggle for power, this disregard of truth and the struggle for truth, this is just your viewpoint, Firenzuola, an inquisitor's viewpoint. The cardinals of the Catholic Church could not, dare not, permit themselves—

Firenzuola, *cutting in just as abruptly.* You appealed to them from Scheiner. Would you now appeal to them from me?

Galileo. Yes. I reject this "private conference." *Much louder.* Let me go back before the cardinals. Let me set my proofs before the tribunal.

Firenzuola, *gently.* Very good. I can now complete my report. This morning, Galilei, five of the six cardinals voted for your execution. *Pause.* By burning. *Pause.* At the stake. If, like Scheiner, I am suspected of lying, you may send Castelli to check.

Galileo. Burning at the stake!

Firenzuola. The verdict was halted by a single opposing vote, but till tomorrow morning only. Hence the decisive importance of this meeting this afternoon.

Galileo. Not burning at the stake!

Firenzuola. I see you have believed me.

Silence.

Galileo, *suddenly.* I have been living in a fool's paradise.

Firenzuola. Had I said so myself, at the outset, you wouldn't have believed me.

Galileo. My whole life *has* been based on a misunderstanding. All these efforts, these years, *have* been wasted.

Firenzuola. And there is very little time left.

Galileo. For what?

Firenzuola. As things stand you will be condemned to death tomorrow. You do not have to be.

Galileo. What are you talking about?

Firenzuola. Even as the captive Arab king can escape the stake by a last-minute genuflection before the cross, so you can escape it by one small token gesture of submission.

Galileo. What?

Firenzuola. Read this. *Hands him a scroll.*

Galileo, *reading tonelessly.* "I, Galileo Galilei, do hereby confess to the sin of disobedience, which sin, however, was committed unintentionally, in zeal prompted by idle vanity, and not in malice as an enemy of Holy Church."

Silence.

And in this way my lifelong attempt to change the church's mind is abandoned forever.

Firenzuola. As you have just demonstrated, your attempt to change the church's mind has definitively *failed.*

Galileo. Definitively? Are *you* the church?

Firenzuola. The Holy Office speaks for the church; the Holy Inquisition acts for it.

Galileo. No, no, no! I had heard the Jesuits were slippery; I had heard the Inquisition was arbitrary and had not dared to believe it. It's true. But they are not the church. And a final appeal still remains open, the appeal that all Catholics may make when others have failed.

Firenzuola. The appeal to the pope? You have already appealed to him.

Galileo. The book was snatched from his grasp by the Inquisition. As a good Catholic, I demand the right to present my case to him in person.

Firenzuola. Today? At a couple of hours' notice?

Galileo. That is for you to say. I don't mind if the tribunal does not meet tomorrow!

Firenzuola. The pope cannot commute a sentence passed by the Holy Office.

Galileo. Will the Holy Office pass sentence if the pope agrees to state in public what he has already conceded in private?

Firenzuola. Namely?

Galileo. That the earth moves round the sun.

Firenzuola. That, my dear Galilei, would be more than his triple crown is worth.

Galileo, *loudly.* I believe in my Barberini! I have the right to see him!
Silence.

Firenzuola. I shall try to get you an audience for this evening.

EIGHT

A Sincere Statesman

The Vatican. A modest audience chamber. Pope Urban VIII is seated, not on a throne, but on a straightbacked chair. If Firenzuola is an administrator, Urban is every inch the statesman, the kind that lies awake nights. Reality gnaws him, and he owes his success in life not least to his conspicuous and authentic sincerity. Sincerity such as his has a function that does not go unappreciated. It gives the impression that something is to be hoped from the established order; and through such men this order seeks, if not the realization of the hopes concerned, at least a modus vivendi. *Firenzuola and Castelli are also present, as Galileo winds up his presentation.*

Galileo. . . . Put it then, that, in my human weakness, I have been unable to persuade the tribunal of the truth of these views. In the light of this unhappy fact, your own prior knowledge of the truth gains a unique importance. For you are in a position to see for yourself that a condemnation of it at this time would set back science 200 years throughout Catholic Europe, thus giving the lead to Protestant Germany and England, not to belabor the point that for You, Your Holiness, truth needs no testimonial but is itself of God.
Pause.

Pope, *nervously.* That's the plea, then, is it? You've finished?

Galileo. Yes, Your Holiness.

Pope. Never become pope, Firenzuola, or these things will happen to *you.* An hour ago We were asked to stop the war in Germany. Now We are asked to open up a few new worlds. Can't you take a hint, Galileo? Can't you see the writing on the wall? No one kneels in the snow before the pope these days. They file their petitions with the cardinals and the commissars.

Galileo. I have been learning that. But I have come to you just because you are not one of these . . . men of power.

Pope. My dear Galileo, how should We have more power than the men of power?

Galileo. Because there is more than "power" in this world, in our church. Because people respect you and your office. Because even cardinals and commissars would think twice before flouting you.

Pope. There is nothing We can do.

Galileo. I could write on a piece of paper, "The earth revolves about the sun, as was discovered by Copernicus, and proved by Galileo." And you could sign it.

Pope. Are you out of your mind?

Galileo. Have *you* read my proofs?

Pope. No.

Galileo. Then you must, Your Holiness. At once. Everything hinges on that.

Pope. My dear fellow, nothing hinges on that. We were "persuaded," as far as that goes, years ago. It does not follow that We are in a position to favor such views now.

Galileo. I am not asking for favor. Only for you to state in public what in private you know to be true.

Pope. Galileo, enough is enough. We agreed to this audience at two hours' notice and in the evening of all times, not to help the universe but to help you: The universe must wait till We have halfway settled the German problem. The father commissar has shown us the confession he wrote for you. We shall simply add our prayers to his. Show him the document again, Firenzuola, would you? Read it again, Galileo, and this time—sign it.

Galileo. Adding your prayers to his? You want me to . . .? You too?

Pope. Sign it. Sign it. We might add that Cardinal Lucignano is also backing this little plot: it is the only way to save your life.
Pause.

Galileo. I am going to have to see Your Holiness alone.

Firenzuola. That is against protocol, Galilei, His Holiness *never*—

Galileo, *loudly.* I will not sign any confession! I refuse!

Pope. Leave us, Firenzuola, Castelli. We shall grant his request.
They leave.
So His Holiness is alone. Does it help?
Pause.

Galileo. I think I understand. This is the only way you can save a life. But I am old. More important to me than continued life is the knowledge that the life I have already had has not been lived in vain.

Pope. But of course it hasn't! The list of your achievements—

Galileo. I have lived for one truth. To put it through. To convince the church of it.

Pope. It has been explained to you—

Galileo. *When* will the church be convinced? Just answer me that. *If not now, when?*

Pope. Galileo—

Galileo. *You* are convinced already. Were convinced long ago. Today, as far as public announcements go, your hands are tied. I understand that too. I resent it, but I understand. You cannot speak in front of the others. So I asked them to leave. Speak to *me*. No one is listening, and I swear before your God and mine that I will never repeat what you now say. *How long do you expect to keep up this pretence?*

Pope. Pretence? But, my dear Galileo—

Galileo. Yes, pretence. That the sun goes round the earth. For you it is a pretence. You're forgetting I know that! How long can you keep it up? *When, when* will you come out for the truth?

Pope, *trembling.* Galileo, I cannot allow this interview to continue! You are insulting me! No good can come of that!

Galileo. Insulting you? Just the contrary! I grant that you have no choice, no power, that you must do what you are pushed into doing, that it's the cardinals that rule, the Jesuits, the inquisitors—

Pope. Am I some petty politician that I must do what I think is wrong for the good of my career?

Galileo. For your decision you gave political reasons, and political reasons only.

Pope. My conscience is clear, let me tell you, my conscience is clear.

Galileo. Huh? Then you *will* come out for the truth? Yes! You *have* to!

Pope. Good God, man, can't you conceive of any other reason for keeping quiet? Other than politics, other than sheer opportunism?

Galileo. You didn't give me any. Nobody has given me any!

Pause.

Pope. True. We cannot give you the real reason.

Galileo. You *can* let me die.

Pause.

Pope, *almost in a whisper.* Then let me avail myself, after all, of the secrecy—the secrecy before our God—which you offered, and utter behind these closed doors that which till now we have not told a living soul. . . . What is it, this older view of the universe that the church accepts? A fiction that "saves the appearances." If the universe was created for the single purpose of being inhabited by men, science must content itself with showing how this purpose has been carried out. It could hardly be carried out by stars outside the range of man's natural eyesight. Therefore, there *are* no such stars. The earth *is* in the center. Believing these things, the intellect is quieted, and men may turn to the more important matter of their souls and the salvation thereof.

Galileo. But you know the answer to all this.

Pope. At one time, yes, I was willing to begin at the other end, not asking how things can be fitted into the Christian story, but asking how they are *in mere fact,* as seen through telescopes and measured with no further end in view. But don't you see where that leads, Galileo? To a question not to be asked: the question whether the Christian story can be fitted into the facts.

Galileo. The facts are not all known but—

Pope. Since the facts are as yet unknown, it follows that anything, *anything,* can turn out to be true. Giordano Bruno suggested that this universe is not the only one there is! Suggested that there are an infinite number of others! Suppose *that* should turn out to be true! What happens to the Christian doctrine of God and His only beloved Son? Did he send out an infinite number of only beloved sons—or the same son an infinite number of times—a celestial traveling salesman, selling an infinite number of parables and ending on an infinite number of crosses?
    Silence.

Galileo. Still, *if* it were true, you would have to *acknowledge* that it was true.

Pope. What? No, no, no! Haven't you followed me, even now? I would have to *refuse* to acknowledge that it was true!

Galileo. Don't you care? Don't you give a God damn *what* the truth is?

Pope. Not a God damn! Not a God damn! Let me employ your blasphemous phrase. For what I care about—what is entrusted to my care, by Him who damns and saves—is of greater import: The welfare of my Catholic people—in this world and the next. To Hell—yes, to *Hell*—with truth! For who knows if our poor notions of it, changing as they do like the colors of the chameleon, are not *from* Hell? One thing I do know: The people—the community of

151

believers—are my sheep. I am their shepherd. *Silence.* Let me, in the secrecy of this encounter, admit the irrelevance of all the arguments publicly used against you. In consideration of the supreme relevance of our secret, you as a good Catholic will sign this confession.

Silence. Then Galileo lets out a great cry of pain. The pope turns pale.

Galileo. Don't blanch, Barberini, I wasn't even listening to you. Oh yes, I heard you, but as your voice droned on, do you know what happened? My whole life passed in review before me. All the years I have willed one thing, and everyone urged me on. I would discover certain things, and everyone would be grateful. My mother, my schoolteachers, my professors, my students, even, it seemed at times, princes, churchmen, the whole established order, the whole world would be grateful. The church—and the church was and is my world—would be grateful. There were setbacks, yes. I was warned. But I refused to accept setbacks. I refused to take no for an answer, true to type in this also: always the go-getter, the top boy of the class, the gilded youth, the acknowledged genius. Well, here the road ends. Here the success story stops. For here I sit with the top man of all—Christ's deputy on earth—a pope, at that, by no means to be despised, one of the best, and my friend, the only pope in history, perhaps, who would ever have understood what a scientist was talking about—and he is sending me a message I can only translate into these words: *You talk of truth but you have spent your whole life on an illusion. You who live your life in the conscious possession of genius are, in the actual living of that life, a dunce! An idiot!!*
Silence.

Pope. You leave me with no alternative but to turn you back to the tender mercies of my cardinals. Firenzuola!

Firenzuola, *reentering.* Yes, Your Holiness?

Pope. He will not sign.

Galileo. Huh? You want me to sign that thing? Give it here. What difference does it make? What difference does anything make now?
Sobbing, he signs the confession.

NINE

On Recantations

Palace of the Inquisition, as in Scene Six. All are in their places as before. Firenzuola is just finishing the reading of Galileo's confession.

Firenzuola. ". . . Hereby confess to the sin of disobedience, which sin, however, was committed unintentionally, in zeal prompted by idle vanity, and not in malice as an enemy of Holy Church. Signed by me, this eighteenth day of June, 1633, Galileo Galilei."
Pause.

Cardinal 4. Well, what do we do now? Pass a vote of thanks to Firenzuola?

Cardinal 5. To line up an evening audience with the pope on two hours' notice is probably the most remarkable feat of practical acumen in the history of the church.

Cardinal 6. May I remind you, my lords, that a man's fate is in your hands? The death sentence having been canceled we are faced, I take it, with the sacred obligation of meeting penitence with forgiveness.

Cardinal 1. I beg to differ. We are faced with the sacred obligation of defining the offense and imposing appropriate penalties.

Cardinal 6. May I suggest that the offense is defined in the confession we have just heard—written as it was, by the commissar general and signed in the presence of the Holy Father?

Cardinal 3. The pope has no jurisdiction here.

Cardinal 4. It is still the case that penalties have to be decided on—and approved by at least five of us.

Cardinal 3. Well, it's clear that the book cannot be published in any shape or form.

Cardinal 2. Well, even you agree to that, don't you, Lucignano?

Cardinal 6. Alas, I see no way out.

Cardinal 4. So that's about it, hm?

Cardinal 3. I suppose so.

Cardinal 1. One moment. Are you proposing, my lords, to let Galilei go scot free?

Cardinal 6. That *would* be forgiveness.

Cardinal 1. I was addressing myself to Sordi and Gorazio.

Cardinal 4. Well, as I said yesterday, we have appointments.

Cardinal 3. We just wanted to get the whole thing over with.

Cardinal 1. I see. But first I want you to hear a statement I asked Father Scheiner to prepare.

Here Galileo begins to show signs of life, but only, so far, in exchanging a look with Castelli. Cardinal 1 looks to Firenzuola to give the signal.

Firenzuola. Father Scheiner.

Scheiner. During the early stages of the hearing, Galilei pleaded total innocence. If there was any guilt at all, he was at pains to attach it to my humble self. Which would have little importance, except that I was the main source of evidence against him. The thesis of the *poisoned source* being not only useful but *necessary* to him, I was guilty of mendacity, even of forgery. If he was innocent, his accuser had to be guilty. If he spoke truth, his accuser had to be a liar. But now Galilei, has pleaded guilty and the positions are reversed. He is guilty, his accuser is innocent. He lies and it is not the accuser who is lying. I therefore come before you in a new role, my lords: the accuser whose credentials are not in question. In this role, I would call the tribunal's attention to the *character* of Galilei's confession. Let us dismiss at once the qualification—that he didn't intend to be guilty, etcetera. Who does? What sin does he confess to? Disobedience. Now those of you who wish to favor the sinner may urge forgiveness. Those of you who have pressing appointments elsewhere may favor getting rid of the case as quickly as possible on any terms. But to the others of you—and indeed to *all* of you really, since no appointments are all *that* pressing, and "forgiveness" is not what the Inquisition is really all about—I say: If the prisoner is guilty of disobedience, as he attests, what follows? If he did disobey Bellarmine after all, we are back, are we not, with the account of things which I gave yesterday morning when the professor tried to discredit me as a liar and cheat. If the original offense was disobedience, then what ensued was consistent defiance of the church over a period of many years culminating in a brazen attempt to have you, my lords, set your seal of approval upon the whole iniquitous adventure. Five of you judged that the man was a heretic. This judgment has now been confirmed by the prisoner himself.

Silence.

Cardinal 6. Are you suggesting that he be punished . . . as my five colleagues yesterday decided?

Cardinal 1. No, no. In any case, Father Scheiner is here in an advisory capacity. We, we—

Cardinal 6. We?

Cardinal 1. The three Jesuits on the tribunal naturally meet in caucus between sessions.

Cardinal 6. Naturally. And with Scheiner present?

Cardinal 1. Of course. And therefore Scheiner will not—any more than the rest of us—ask for a death sentence. But as for setting the prisoner scot free, that is out of the question.

Cardinal 5. Then you have a counterproposal?

Cardinal 1. A very precise one.

Cardinal 4. Let's hear it then.

Cardinal 1. That the book is to be suppressed is already agr   Next: The heretic Galileo Galilei must be isolated from the co   ity. A condition of *quarantine* is indicated. Such an infection m   not be allowed to spread. If not in jail, this man must be under life-long house arrest.

Again, communication between Galileo and Castelli, though only to the extent that Galileo seems to be awaking more and more from his previous torpor. Castelli is excited.

Cardinal 5. You're right, of course, my lord.

Cardinal 4. I agree—without hesitation.

Cardinal 1. Third and last, the confession just made being inadequate and misleading, for the reasons Father Scheiner has given, there must be another confession—and no little private affair either but before the whole world—that closes up all loopholes.

Firenzuola. Loopholes? I wrote the confession, my lord, and left no holes—unless it was one through which, with God's help, the soul of Galilei might still creep to salvation.

Cardinal 3. Even though the same loophole might serve the Devil's purposes?

Cardinal 2. Might serve to spread this man's heresy throughout

Christendom?

Firenzuola. I do not follow you now.

Cardinal 3. Then it devolves upon the Holy Office to recall the Inquisition itself to duty.

Cardinal 2. Exactly. Galilei confessed a venial sin, vanity, instead of a deadly one, pride. Excessive zeal is all it amounted to, the sin of enthusiastic adolescents. But enthusiasm for what? For an error. Of that there is no hint in your confession, commissar general.

Cardinal 1. We therefore demand that, in the revised and public confession, the error be specified and denounced.

Cardinal 6. I object. This is to ask Galilei to spit upon his own ideas, his whole life's work.

Cardinal 2, *venomously.* The time has come to ignore you, Cardinal Lucignano. You are in a minority of one.

Cardinal 6. Do the other five agree to that sentiment? *Looks are exchanged. No one says no.* Then there is nothing more I can do, Galilei. God have mercy on us all.

He leaves the room.

Cardinal 1. Father Commissar, will you ask Father Scheiner to read the ▮▮▮▮ation.*

Firenzuola. The revised confession?

Cardinal 1. The recantation. With preamble and appendix.

Firenzuola. Father Scheiner.

Scheiner. "Galileo Galilei, wearing the white shirt of penitence, shall so proceed through the public streets of Rome to the Convent of Santa Maria Sopra Minerva, and there, upon his knees before the Congregation of the Faithful, shall speak aloud the following words:

I, Galileo Galilei, do now with a sincere heart and unfeigned faith, abjure, detest, and curse the heretical belief that the earth moves round the sun, and do take my oath that never again will I speak, write or otherwise assert anything which might lend plausibility to this belief. Should anyone suspected of subscribing to this heretical belief be known to me I shall denounce him to this Holy Office in

---

*Actually, the church called it an abjuration. It is only popular tradition that Galileo "recanted." In matters like this, however, a playwright must follow popular tradition.

156

Rome or to the Inquisitor in whatsoever place I shall be. Appendix: This recantation, translated into foreign tongues, shall thereafter be read in every church in Christendom."

Firenzuola. But, Father Scheiner—my lords—if this document is accepted, then mine was a decoy, a trap—

Cardinal 2. Oh, come, Firenzuola, don't pretend you are above such things.
Pause.

Firenzuola. The power is yours, my lords. But I cannot, any more than Cardinal Lucignano, share the responsibility. I hereby withdraw from this proceeding.
Exit Firenzuola.

Cardinal 1, *without hesitation.* In the absence of the commissar general, Father Scheiner will preside.

Scheiner, *taking Firenzuola's seat.* Is there now unanimity in the tribunal? Cardinal Gorazio?

Cardinal 4. As far as I'm concerned.

Cardinal 5. Yes, yes.

Scheiner. Then our deliberations would seem to be at an end.

Galileo. One moment. *Almost as if he were a forgotten figure in the proceeding, he arrests the attention of the tribunal with something of a start.* Weren't you expecting to hear from me?

Cardinal 1. For what purpose?

Scheiner, *gently.* The position you are in is well understood, Galilei.

Galileo. The position I am in?

Cardinal 4. In chess it is known as checkmate.

Cardinal 5. That is true, Galilei. The game has been a long one. But it ended last night when His Holiness Pope Urban VIII refused you his support.

Scheiner, *always quieter than the others.* For always you had gone over the head of your opponents. From the dean of your University—you recall *our* first meeting?—to the grand duke. From the grand duke to Bellarmine. From the Inquisition to the pope. Over the pope's head there is no one.

Cardinal 5. Cardinal Gorazio and myself are even very sorry about it.

Cardinal 4. We had no desire to make any trouble for you.

Scheiner. Here is your signed confession. Here is the recantation. You will tear up the former and sign the latter.

Pause. Then Galileo walks over to Scheiner's table, takes the confession and tears it up. Pause.

Scheiner. Which disposes of the confession. Now sign the recantation.

Galileo, *picking up the recantation and looking at him.* Your account was very correct, Father Scheiner. I've been on your mind a lot during the past twenty years, haven't I? The dean, the grand duke, the Master of Controversial Questions, the pope, and "over the pope's head there is no one." After which you can ask me to do anything, and I'll do it. "Sign this confession." And I signed it.

Scheiner. Indeed. And now the formality of replacing it with this one.

Galileo. A formality, and all is over. *He looks at the cardinals.* Let me drink in the . . . peculiar feeling of . . . the moment before the moment. *Pointing to the recantation.* Why am I signing this, Scheiner?

Scheiner. Because, at this point, no other course is open to you.

Galileo. Except, of course, death—at the stake.

Scheiner. You signed the confession to exclude *that* possibility.

Galileo. I signed it because nothing mattered any more.

Scheiner. Such are the rationalizations of cowardice.

The dialogue has been getting quieter and quieter as the two antagonists have talked less and less for the tribunal and more and more for each other. And now Galileo, who had walked away from Scheiner with the scroll bearing the recantation in his hand, returns and slaps him with it. Two sharp blows, one on each cheek. Scheiner jumps to his feet. The cardinals start to rise but sit again as Galileo takes over.

Galileo, *continuing where he left off.* What I was doing—what I had been doing all my life—had failed. I was nothing. I wanted to . . . do nothing. There was nothing I *could* do. *He looks again at the cardinals.* Nothing *of that sort:* fishing for compliments, staking claims for honors and rewards, seeking fame and fortune, petitioning for favors, soliciting approvals, requesting confirmations, endorsements, permissions, licenses . . . All on the assumption that you were my admiring schoolteachers, my smiling uncles and aunts, my adoring parents. Benign authority sits on the throne, and all I have to do is submit my proofs and practice my persuasions and there will follow that most indispensable boon: *recognition.* Only not any more. You have relieved me of that illusion along with others, and helped me to see you, not as my friends and allies and patrons, which you aren't, but as my enemies and nothing but my enemies, which you are. Enemies! Not just Scheiner. All of you master politicians! Including the nice ones who just walked out. And the sad one who sits in the Vatican, weeping for mankind, because he thinks our discoveries are too much for the people, such terrible things are going to be discovered. But, my lords, since God made the universe, nothing can be discovered that He didn't put there. And since God is wise, He can't put there anything we ought not to discover. I find in our Holy Father a deep mistrust of our Heavenly Father. As if the Lord God needed the hierarchy of the Catholic Church to make up for His own insufficiency. You would go God one better, my lords. And so when I come along with the faculties He gave me and read some heretofore undeciphered words in the open book of His heaven, what do you have to say to me? *"Stop* reading." When you thus set bounds to the mind of man, do you not sense in your actions an affront to man's Maker?

Castelli. Galileo, take care!

Galileo. Why? Why should I take care? For the first time in my life, I *want nothing* from the hierarchy of the Catholic Church. I am their enemy. And for an enemy there is only one question, that of strategy: how best to attack, when, where? Father Scheiner thinks I'm afraid to die. Wrong! Yesterday I *wanted* to be dead. Today I don't want to die, but if it is the best way to fight you, my lords, I will do it. And it *is* the best way because, as Scheiner explained, it is the only way. So I accept it. Gladly. And I can't tell you what a relief, what a joy, it is to shed at long last the servility and complaisance of life in this our Italy! Burn me! Yes! Burn me! The flames will be seen all the way to London!

Silence. But Scheiner is coming out of the state of shock the slap had put him into.

Scheiner, *very quietly indeed.* The prisoner will return to his seat.

Castelli gets Galileo back to his seat and the two of them whisper excitedly while Scheiner addresses the tribunal as follows.

Scheiner. My lords, we are confronted with a totally new situation.

Cardinal 4. Yes, indeed. I move that we adjourn till tomorrow.

Cardinal 5. First, he strikes Scheiner in the face! Next, he threatens to make a Protestant martyr of himself! I agree with Gorazio, let's adjourn!

Scheiner. You take the change to be one for the worse, Cardinal Sordi.

Cardinal 4. Certainly. How could it be for the better?

Scheiner. A dead heretic is less dangerous than a live one.

Cardinal 5, *amazed.* You mean we should take him up on it?

Scheiner. You are the tribunal, my lords.

He is passing the ball to the Jesuit cardinals. They handle it in gingerly fashion at first.

Cardinal 3. The prisoner is no longer young, of course. It is better if our enemies die of natural causes . . .

Scheiner. My information is that he has another book in his head. One that will be as subversive in mechanics as this other in astronomy.

Cardinal 2. We shall have him under guard, of course. The Inquisition can take care of that . . .

Scheiner. Alas, this is not the Spanish Inquisition. It is Italian, and therefore inefficient.

Cardinal 1. Scheiner has a point there. A very big point. We all know what the experience has been, here in Italy, with writers under house arrest.

Galileo gestures to Castelli to stop talking and listen.

Cardinal 4. What?

Cardinal 1. They have been a thorn in the flesh.

Cardinal 3. They have hangers-on, you see. Visitors. Admirers. Hardly surprising that their writings circulate in manuscript.

Cardinal 2. The notoriety of such manuscripts sometimes gives them a wider circulation than books.

Cardinal 1. In short, such imprisonment could be regarded as *desirable.* From the standpoint of a malcontent, I mean. As a spot to shoot from. A sniper's dream.

Galileo looks at Castelli. "Do you hear what I hear?" his eyes say.

Scheiner. And may I point out the special appeal the situation would have for Galileo Gailei? He gives us his authority to say the sun moves round the earth. But he has already taught his admirers not to believe anything on authority, including his. "The earth goes its way," he will be saying, *"and I go mine."*

Cardinal 2. One might almost ask what good is such a recantation anyway? Our countrymen are apt to see *everything* as pretence.

Cardinal 3. They'll certainly see through this.

Cardinal 1. Then are we agreed that the death sentence must be reintroduced?

Cardinal 4. I am still worried about another "martyrdom."

Scheiner. It is a worry, if I may so, my lord, that can be dispelled.

Cardinal 4. How?

Scheiner. A burning need not be public. An execution need not be a burning.

Cardinal 3. A *secret* execution could be arranged.

Cardinal 2. Or simply a . . . disappearance.

Cardinal 4. That would *certainly* head him off, wouldn't it?

Cardinal 5. How exactly, um . . . . *He looks nervously across at Galileo and Castelli. Scheiner gets the point.*

Scheiner. I might suggest, my lords . . . *He leans forward to whisper to the five cardinals, who are now all in a huddle together around a table. Galileo and Castelli are watching them. All of a sudden, without warning, Galileo walks to the center of the floor and sinks to his knees.*

Galileo, *intoning in Latin.* Mea culpa, mea culpa, mea maxima culpa! Quia peccavi nimis cogitatione, verbo et opere! Mea culpa, mea culpa, mea maxima culpa . . . !

The cardinals rise to their feet in consternation. Has the accused taken leave of his senses?

Scheiner, *firmly, as to a hysterical child.* What's the matter, Galilei?

Galileo, *stops intoning.* My guilt, my guilt, my guilt . . . .

Scheiner, *as before.* What about your guilt?

Galileo. I feel it now. Disobedience. Defiance. Encouragement of heresy . . . .

Cardinal 5. He has turned around?

Cardinal 4. Seen the light at last?

Galileo, *intoning again.* Confiteor! Deo omnipotenti, beatae Mariae semper Virgini, beato Michaeli Archangelo . . . .

Cardinal 1. Let's be clear about this. Are you agreeing to recant—in the words prescribed?

Galileo. I am! I am!

Cardinal 1. You know that you will be placed under house arrest for life?

Galileo. I do! I do!

Cardinal 1. And that your book is wiped from the record?

Galileo. Oh yes! Yes!

Pause.

Scheiner. He is putting on an act. The device is transparent.

Cardinal 2. That's true. We can't let him get away with this.,

Cardinal 5. You are questioning the sincerity of a confession?

Cardinal 4. The Inquisition's punishments are revocable upon confession of guilt. If we start questioning the sincerity of confessions, where will it end?

Cardinal 3. If *wants* to recant, we can't very well stop him. After all, it was our idea.

Scheiner. But, my lord . . . .

Cardinal 1. No, Scheiner. Bandolfi is right. Let things take their course.

Scheiner. But the advantages of his position—

Cardinal 1. The real advantages are always with those in power. Think back. This is a greater victory than we had any right to expect. The man will virtually be in prison for the rest of his days. What does it matter if we leave him free to wriggle and squirm a little? The sun will keep moving, and the earth will keep still, that's the thing. *Suddenly, as if he had been in charge all along.* The session is adjourned. *All begin to leave.* Give the prisoner his instructions, Scheiner.

Scheiner, *coming out of a daze.* Huh? Oh yes, yes. *And he is soon alone with Galileo and Castelli.* Your escort will be here in a moment. The ceremony is set for next Tuesday in the Convent of Santa Maria Sopra Minerva. At twelve noon.
Scheiner leaves. A long silence.

Castelli. When you began to recite the *mea culpa* I thought for a second you'd gone stark staring mad.

Galileo, *very slowly; he is drained of energy.* Scheiner knew better, didn't he?

Castelli. I'm just plain relieved. That you'll live, I mean. That you'll *not* be a martyr.

Galileo. I wouldn't have been a *martyr* anyway.

Castelli. In God's eyes you might have been. Even killed in a dark alley. Murder is not hidden from Him.

Galileo. I don't have a martyr's calling. Just lost control for a moment there. Their talk about the advantages of recantation and the possibilities of life under house arrest brought me to my senses.

Castelli. But, as Silotti explained, they exaggerated.

Galileo. They offered something. Something far more real, far more *me,* than martyrdom. And maybe just as useful. What was Silotti's phrase?

Castelli. He feared you'd be "a thorn in the flesh."

Galileo. Just what a good Catholic should be.

Castelli. You have always craved recognition—

Galileo. I hereby abandon that morbid—no, that *naive*—craving. Let this be the real recantation. The world owes me nothing. *With a* *change of tone, almost to a "lighter vein."* But there's something I owe the world, Castelli. Can you be in Florence by tomorrow?

Castelli. You want me to go on ahead?

Galileo. Get that second copy of my book. Take it to Van Gelder's.

Castelli. The Dutch merchant?

Galileo. Have one of his people take it to the Elzevirs in Leyden.

Castelli. That's the publishers?

Galileo. Then ride over to Virginia's convent. Break the news to her gently, and when she asks how I'm bearing up, say, quite well, considering, and that I've made a good resolution.

Castelli. Already? What is it?

Galileo. My next book will be on a quite different subject.

Castelli. The book on motion? But *that's* going to be even more revolutionary.

Galileo. Sh!

The clank of armor has been heard. It is the guard coming to take Galileo back to his quarters.

Guard. Professor Galilei!

Galileo, *preparing to leave. To Castelli.* Think of me next Tuesday at twelve noon.

Castelli. Will you be all right?

Galileo, *with the ghost of a smile.* The earth won't have stopped moving.

Epilogue

June 22, 1633. In the great hall of the Convent of Santa Maria Sopra Minerva in Rome, a man in a penitential shirt is on his knees before the Congregation of the Holy Office. A Bible on the stone floor beside him, he reads from a scroll as follows:

I, Galileo Galilei, do now, with a sincere heart and unfeigned faith, abjure, detest, and curse the heretical belief that the earth moves around the sun, and take my oath that never again will I speak, write, or otherwise assert anything that might lend plausibility to this belief. Should anyone suspected of subscribing to this heretical belief

be known to me, I shall denounce him to this Holy Office in Rome or to the Inquisitor in whatsoever place I shall be, so help me God and this Holy Book.

From the Memoirs of Pontius Pilate

These "imaginary conversations" about a brotherhood are dedicated to those brothers, sisters, and sons of mine who prompted me to write them and/or helped me improve them after listening to an early draft:

LK
RB
AB
AD
JB
EB
PB
IS (ZS)
PP
LO'N

Preface

Everything I want to say in the three plays of this book is implicit in the title of the first one—*Are You Now Or Have You Ever Been*—especially if a question mark be added thereto. I wanted to make each spectator ask himself if he existed, and, if he didn't, had he ever existed.

If, as Wilde said, most people are other people, have no selves, do not exist in their own right, then that is the big problem of "most people." What, on the other hand, is a *great* man? Greatness expresses itself in many ways, in many fields of action, but surely what it is—its foundation as against any superstructures resting upon it—is an identity operating unhindered, undisputed, undivided, an identity that has come out into the open and which, being accepted by its owner, has to be accepted, with whatever acts of rapture or rage, by the world.

Rage is commoner than rapture. The world crucifies the great man more readily than it celebrates him, or crucifies after celebrating, for one may confidently assume that those who cry "Crucify" on Friday are the same folk who cried "Hosannah" the Sunday before.

The mistake of Christianity was making its great man a god, and at that a god in the then most modern vein: a god unmarked by any human imperfections. That Matthew, Mark, Luke, and John believed Jesus to be a god frustrates all their efforts to dramatize (*i.e.*, create) what they would have us believe was his humanity. They would have us sympathize with him when Satan tempts him; we cannot do so because there is, *ex hypothesi*, no chance—not a slight chance, but none at all—that he will fall for it. They make him fake a little weakness in the Garden of Gethsemane but of course there is no chance—again, not a slight chance even—that he will not come through as Superman. Even the cross was quite tolerable, or at least a lot better than it was for the countless thousands who were accorded the same punishment without being promised that all would come out fine two days later, let alone that after a more prolonged delay they would return on horseback and give their oppressors . . . hell.

The Jesus of the New Testament succeeds so well in being a god that he has no humanity. For a human being has his contradictions, while here is someone uncontradictory by definition. A human being has to cope with his own weakness, but here is someone who has no weakness to cope with—only a seeming weakness that, hey presto! was the mask of not just strength but All Strength. Here is a "man" who wants you to feel bad when you threaten him with a table knife, while at the same time he has his finger on the button that will blow up not just you and the table but the whole globe.

Here is someone those dreadful Freudians can never get at because he *had no childhood.* Also no boyhood and no youth. Except for the Cecil B. DeMille prologue in Bethlehem, and the Charles Dickens vignette of an eleven-year-old lecturing the greybeards, there is nothing but a fast flash forward to Jesus at about thirty. His body has no innards. It makes no sense to ask whether his penis had other functions than just to urinate, because those are questions one simply does not ask of a god. Of a Roman god, perhaps—but not of this Semitic Supergod. No doubt the authors of the New Testament would like us to ponder the possibility that the penis of Jesus now and then began to swell a little and that he told it to go down again, showing what can be done if you really try, especially if you're the only Son of the One Who in any case can't miss.

Great men, as against great gods, are at the same time singularly nongreat. Powerful as they may be in the special line of their power— Beethoven so powerful in sound, Van Gogh on canvas, Baudelaire as a writer—they are in other respects as *powerless* as the rest of us, and more dramatically so since, while our weakness is all of a piece, theirs contrasts starkly, appallingly, with their extraordinary strength. The contrast is the source of their endless fascination. *We* are fascinated, because we can shuttle between the joys of simply admiring what is admirable (an elemental pleasure of this our life) and the more dubious joys involved in saying: "Think you're so great? and yet you die just like me," or: "Think you're so great? and yet you're as lousy a husband as me," or—illustrations can continue *ad infinitum,* and have indeed continued almost that far in the many debunking, or at least chatty and familiar, works of history and fiction concerning the foibles of the great—their nongreatness. What else should bring us consolation in our mediocrity?

Returning, as the preacher would say, to Our Lord and Savior Jesus

168

Christ, one story is that he was jeered at on the Cross with the reflection: "The man who talked so much about saving others cannot save himself." There is plenty of drama in that—if only it were true. But, alas, on the New Testament interpretation of things—the only *licensed* interpretation of these things in our culture—he was rather more "saved" than anyone else and had known it all along. At the moment he is waiting a mere forty-eight hours before vaulting up to the Right Hand of Power.

It has been said that Jesus saves. Not just said. Shrieked. And not just shrieked. It has been *smiled* at us by those who "know" that he has already saved them, from the guileless Salvation Army miss on the corner to the guileful Reverend Sun Myung Moon and his many colleagues and analogues.

What is clear is that Jesus has not helped. Just because he does not share our weakness. One with the All Wise and All Powerful, he is above the battle. His "sufferings" cannot change that, as, even in his sufferings, he was given special treatment throughout. Being One with the Father, he is not—and it is a fatal lack—our brother.

All of which, with the appropriate change of names, could have been said a hundred years ago. What has emerged since 1850 is that the "freethinkers"—those who deny that Jesus was an almighty god's only son—hoping to justify their audacity in gracious terms have hit on the notion that, if not the one son of the one god, Jesus must have been one of the most original spirits that ever existed. It has been said that all philosophy is but footnotes to Plato, and some wish us to believe that all religion is but footnotes to Jesus. Historically, however, he was himself a footnote to Judaism.

This can be denied, but what cannot? Many good Christian folk have suspected at one time or another that it *should* not be denied, and that it has been denied at a terrible price, a price still being paid in the 1940s in the ovens of Auschwitz. It is understandable that Christians have wished the Jews out of the way. They are *in* the way! They are the aboriginal *skandalon* and stumbling block! Hitler was right, and was, besides, far from original.

One should not appease Official Christianity by seeming to say: "That I cannot recognize your Jesus as a god may be my limitation: I wish to display modesty. I will make it up to you, as far as my modest mentality permits, by naming him, instead, Greatest of Great Men." It was probably Ernest Renan, more than any other single individual, who put this over on our semisecular, semi-Christian, wholly highminded culture. I grew up in that culture and was never told, but had to learn for myself, that the price Ernest Renan paid for this conclusion was the traditionally Christian one: slander against Judaism. The greatness of Renan's Great Man Jesus is that he was anti-Judaist. I avoid the word anti-Semitic, but is a question whether I ought to.

In his preface to *Androcles and the Lion,* Bernard Shaw wrote a trenchant analysis of the four Gospels, but, when he put together his own fifth Gospel, it retained as unquestioned assumption the Renanian idea that, if this fellow was to lose his throne in heaven, on earth he must be sent straight to the head of the class in philosophy, sociology, psychology, and any other subjects that strike G.B.S.'s fancy. All this amounts to is to make Jesus a brilliant, prophetic precursor of a Renan or a Shaw. Nor does the New Testament forestall such a development. It leaves itself open to such "misinterpretation" by being vague on many matters and contradictory on many others.

Another modern "approach" (I put the word in quotes because it is not clear that anything is really being approached) is that of Tolstoy. He set to work with a will to make the New Testament both less vague and less contradictory. He succeeded. But the resultant "religion" could have been arrived at without recourse to the New Testament at all.

There is one group of scholars in this field who have received little but scorn for their labors yet who should really be thanked for proposing a most suggestive hypothesis. I refer to the hypothesis that there never was any such person as Jesus, and that "he" is therefore a figure of legend, myth, or fairy tale. Although I am not myself of that school of thought, I acknowledge that this really radical hypothesis does stimulate thought—and, in the comments it elicits from the orthodox, reveals how unfriendly to all thought are so many of the friends of Jesus. It was shrewd of men like Albert Schweitzer, who were not going to give up Christianity whatever might be "dis-covered," to notice that, if you surrendered the divinity of Jesus, you might be surrendering everything. You might well be left, not with the great man of Renan and Shaw, but with zero.

Curiously enough, the theory that Jesus never lived at all must be seen, finally, as another evasion of the issue. To lose the god Jesus has been a shattering experience for our culture. No wonder those who brought about the loss for us also sought to soften the blow with their rationalizations: You have lost a god but found a great man. Et cetera. So those who think that "a historical Jesus" never existed *redeify* him: They think he is an analogue of gods like Orpheus and Osiris. But supposing he was neither a god nor a superman? Is this too great a disenchantment? Too steep an anticlimax? And what was he then? Just an ordinary guy? What interest would there be in that? If he is just a Jew, how is he more interesting than 6 million others who, not so long ago, perished in the gas chambers? I think the possibility must be faced that *he was not more interesting.* It is possible that, among six million, there were others who would have made a better subject for hero worship, hagiography, even ordinary biography.

What is known about Jesus, if anything? Just, really, that he was a Jew, who was given the standard, banal Roman punishment for political offenders. Let us assume he took it "like a man." Not like a god, but like those other men who were known to have taken it bravely, unbribed by promises of instant bliss in heaven. Let us make a second assumption: namely, that he was brought up to believe he might well be the Messiah and liberate Palestine. In this case his failure must then have taught him how mistaken he had been.

Can there also be something great about such a one? Well, why not? *Actual great men do not resemble the demigods of Renan and Shaw.* For, alongside their greatness, they bear witness to the same lack of self-knowledge as you or I—though, for whatever it's worth, they have larger selves to fail to know. In his fragment *The Triumph of Life,* the poet Shelley puts it thus:

> The wise
> The great, the unforgotten—they who wore
> Mitres and helms and crowns or wreaths of light,
> Signs of thought's empire over thought—their lore
> Taught them not this: to know themselves. Their might
> Could not repress the mystery within
> And for the morn of truth they feigned, deep night
> Caught them ere evening.

Which would be a real—that is, a human—Gethsemane. I have tried to create the sense of such a phenomenon in my play before trying, even more rashly, to answer the question: What would a real resurrection be like?

171

Pilate has this prehistory, too, which may hold a little interest for the student of Christianity. A couple of years ago the New York State Council on the Arts announced that it would like to commission some plays for younger audiences. They commissioned mine—and prepared the ground for a production by the Theatre of Riverside Church. That theatre, however, is or was advised by a Board, that, I was told, unanimously opposed production of my play on the grounds that it was "heretical." All of which would seem perfectly appropriate, except that Riverside Church—"the church of Harry Emerson Fosdick"—was originally, and that is not long ago—a pretty "heretical" sort of church. I should not complain, of course, if the play is controversial, since it was meant to be. Is it foolish to ask a hearing in a Christian church for an obviously Jewish view of Jesus? If so, I am happy to be a "fool for Christ's sake." Nor have I forgotten those "younger audiences" for whom I was commissioned to write. I think it would do young Christians a great deal of good to see how the other half lives—how the non-Christian world (or a part of it) thinks of the Christian Lord and Savior. The playwright George Tabori says my dialogue "sounds young, the way Ernst Busch at seventy sounds young, singing." Although at this writing I am a mere sixty, I shall take Tabori's remark as (a) a compliment and (b) a description of the play that follows, in which I am mediating between a youth movement—all revolutionary movements are that—and a youth audience.

From the Memoirs of Pontius Pilate had its first full production in the Pfeifer Theatre, Buffalo, New York, under the auspices of The Buffalo Project, the resident theatre company of the State University of New York, October 21, 1976. In an earlier version there had been a staged reading at the Yale Repertory Theatre, directed by Baker Salsbury, with Tom Hill as Pilate and Barry Primus as Yeshu.

The Buffalo Project

From the Memoirs of Pontius Pilate

Directed by   Donald Sanders
Space by   Vanessa James
Clothes by   Anna Marie Brooks
Lights by   Ken Tabachnik

CAST

Pilate, Roman Governor of   Jim McGuire
      Judea, later in retirement
      near Rome
Yeshu (Yeshua, Joshua, Jesus),   Evan Parry
      a Galilean prophet
Barabbas, Zealot leader   Mark Donahue
Stephen, a follower of Yeshu   Barry Cohen
Judas, another follower   Jerry Finnegan
      of Yeshu, and a Zealot
Caiaphas, high priest of Israel   Larry Turner
Herod Antipas, tetrarch of   Charles Wisnet
      Galilee, son of Herod
      the King of the Jews
Annas, former high priest   Jack Hunter
      father-in-law of Caiaphas
Soldiers (and Understudy)   Bill Maynes
                        Keith Watts

Assistant Director   Ray Munro
Stage Manager   Gary Musante
Asst. Stage Manager   Agim Huerisowic
Assistant Stage Designer   James J. Keller
Technical Director   Peter R. Kalven
Assistant Technical Director   Mitchell Bogard
Master Carpenter   Matt Russo
Master Electrician   Gary Gertz
Draftsman   Sandy DeCarolis, Matt Russo

These men who have been subverting the whole world have come here also . . . They all flout Caesar's decrees and proclaim a rival emperor, Jesus.

—Acts of the Apostles

On October 23, 1975, the New York Times *published a report of a "security index" kept by the FBI under J. Edgar Hoover—"a list of individuals targeted for detention in a national emergency." Clarence M. Kelley, the present director of the FBI, states that persons were placed on the list who had "exhibited a willingness or capability of engaging in treason, rebellion, sedition, sabotage, espionage, assassination of Government officials, terrorism, guerrilla warfare, or other acts which threatened to disrupt the operation of Government." The New* York Times *reported that the list "contained about 15,000 names at its peak, and at one point had included virtually all known members of the American Communist Party.*

The figures of poetry and history can only survive in the thoughts of men by endlessly transforming themselves. The people could take no interest in a person of ancient times if they did not invest him with their own interests and passions.

—Anatole France

The time is the First Century, A.D.

The scenic pattern is as follows:

A monologue is read by Pontius Pilate: these are his memoirs. Flashbacks show eight encounters in the form of these dialogues.

1. Conspiracy: Yeshu, Judas, Barabbas
2. Insurrection: Yeshu, Stephen, Judas
3. The Voice of an Informer: Yeshu, Stephen, Judas
4. Collaboration: Yeshu, Caiaphas, Herod
5. The Face of an Angel: Yeshu, Stephen
6. Capitulation: Yeshu, Annas
7. Crucifixion: Yeshu, Pilate
8. Resurrection: Yeshu, Pilate

Pontius Pilate, in retirement in a Roman suburb, is at work on his memoirs. Has just come to the end of a scroll and a chapter.

Pilate, *going back to the beginning of the scroll, to read this chapter over.* Chapter Five: "The Death of Yeshu, being the true story of a Jewish prophet now believed by some never to have died at all but to have really been a god, even the One Real God, or son of the same." I should know if he died or not since I killed him. But if I now tell his story, it is not to refute a crackbrained superstition, it is to help Rome know its enemy. For I came to recognize in this Yeshu a troublemaker of peculiar insidiousness. Let any Roman who would hope to govern a colony take note, especially any Roman who would help govern this intelligent but fanatical tribe, the Jews. Who, then, was Yeshu? Originally, a country preacher and healer, exorcist, and, if you like, miracle-worker, which was pretty much what all their "prophets" were, peasant demagogues too, and as such foes of their own Temple Authorities, their priestly hierarchy. My spies had kept me well informed about the man for some years before the Insurrection, and I'd have been well informed anyway, as Yeshu welcomed to all his demonstrations even the uniformed soldiers of Rome. His preaching was full of ideas, poetically expressed, mostly quotations, my experts advised me, from a Jewish sect called the Essenes, from Hebrew Psalms, and above all from earlier prophets, especially one Isaiah. It seems this Isaiah had depicted some sort of Golden Age in a Neverneverland, but when Yeshu recited him, the words had the force of an offer to the Jewish people, This is no Neverneverland, this is our Kingdom, here's your Golden Age, come and get it. *Yeshu is seen on a hillside at the peroration of a Biblical recital:*
"And behold! new skies above your heads and new ground beneath your feet, new heavens, new earth! The old Jerusalem gives place to the new! The chains of the captives break! The prison gates fly open! The Lord shall bind up their broken limbs! The Lord shall bind up their broken hearts! And they shall beat their swords into

plowshares, and their swords into pruning hooks! Nation shall not lift up sword against nation, neither shall they learn war any more! Each man shall live at peace beneath his own vine, beneath his own fig tree! The wolf shall dwell with the lamb! The leopard shall lie down with the kid! Calf and young lion and fatling—together! And a little child shall lead them!"

Pilate, *continues.* Inflammatory stuff, you will say. But we thought otherwise for a while since, though Yeshu did dangle this seductive fruit before the hungry faces of the poor, he also, or so we thought at first, forbade his followers to fight. It did not even seem that he discouraged payment of our taxes.

Yeshu is seen giving his own thoughts to his own people, the "am-haarets."
I address myself to you
The riff-raff, the rabble, the lost, the forgotten
My beloved am-haarets!
The lost shall be found
The remembered were never forgotten
He hath put down the mighty from their seat
And hath exalted the humble and the meek
The last shall be first
The scum of the earth are the salt of the earth
Those who have dwelt in darkness
Shall be the light of the world
Blessed are ye—the poor
Blessed the oppressed and the downtrodden
Blessed the weary and the heavily laden
Packhorses of the Lord!
Peace to you! Peace to all men!
Love your neighbor, as you have been taught
Love your enemy, as you may not have been taught
Great is harmlessness!
Harm no one and nothing, not even a fly.

Voice from the crowd. And if a man slap my face, what then?

Yeshu. If a man slap your face, what then? Turn the other cheek!

Another voice from the crowd. Should we pay taxes to Caesar?

Yeshu. Should we pay taxes to Caesar? *Pause.* Give Caesar what is Caesar's. *Pause.* Give God what is God's.

Pilate, *continues.* I issued a directive that second cheeks were to be struck only in real emergencies, and wrote the prophet down a collaborator. Had I been right he might really be alive to this day. I tried to keep him alive. But, of the many I have crucified in my time, this man was unique in that he himself chose the cross. As he put it, he "decided" to be crucified. This came about in several well-marked stages, which I shall reconstruct for my readers in dialogue form, so they may the better understand the perspective of Yeshu and his tribe. Try to imagine the background: a rebellion against the Roman army of occupation in Judaea—more precisely, against the Roman garrison in the Antonia Fortress at Jerusalem, the Judaean capital. Even before that, Sicarii—dagger-men—assassins—roamed the streets with weapons concealed in the folds of pious robes. Terrorists ran amok, and it was a terrorist named Barabbas who created their guerrilla organization, the Zealots, men all too full of zeal for their tribal god, Yahweh. Even at that, they would probably never have attempted Insurrection but for another sinister character named Judas. The name, being translated, simply means Jew. The man was a little hard to keep up with, even for my more intelligent spies. First, they reported him a follower or "disciple" of Yeshu. Second, they said he was a Zealot, and close to Barabbas. They were right both times: He had left Yeshu for Barabbas. Then again, they were wrong, as it was Judas who brought Yeshu and Barabbas together—how closely together we shall now see. Dialogue One: Conspiracy.

The place—all through the Dialogues—is just a room, though sometimes, as now, split up to make two rooms. The location of the room in Dialogue One is the northern province of Galilee. A young Jew is alone there, undressed, bathing. At a casual glance you might not be able to pick him out from a hundred other young Jews. What might be discernible to a less casual glance, the reader had better gather from the story that follows. For now, there is just a young man there, and a boy, evidently a helper of his, coming in to announce visitors.

Boy. People to see you, Yeshu.

Yeshu, *who has finished drying himself, putting on some clothes.* Who are they?

Boy. Didn't you hear? All the hugger-mugger?

Yeshu. Jews checking if there are Romans around?

Boy, *nodding.* Must be big shots. And they won't uncover their faces in front of me. Do I let them right in?

Yeshu. Certainly.

The boy leaves Yeshu's room, and then crosses the other room to the house door, letting in two Jews with covered faces.

Boy. You are to come right in.

One of them. My friend will wait here.

And the other one sits, not uncovering his face.

Yeshu, *as the guest appears in the doorway.* That voice. That voice has not been heard here—heard by me anywhere—for two whole years.

The man uncovers his face.

Judas, *for it is he.* Yeshu!

Though Judas is not in a uniform and carries no visible weapons, he would seem to be an army officer: He takes charge, he takes the stage, and his eyes gleam with something more than confidence—patriotic enthusiasm? Religious zeal? Both, no doubt, for in Palestine the two are one.

Yeshu. You are crying, Judas.

Judas, *wiping his eyes.* Two years—to the day!

Yeshu. Really? Was that deliberate?

Judas, *smiling.* Perhaps.

Yeshu. Well, sit down. Drink. Eat.

Judas, *sitting.* The fatted calf? Am I your prodigal son?

Yeshu. I'm sure not—

Judas. And yet? And yet? You have heard bad things about me.

Yeshu. No. It's just that you left—two years ago—without a word. And then, later, you were reported with Barabbas.

Judas. Was *that* bad?

Yeshu. It was upsetting.

Judas. How did you take it?

Yeshu. You were joining the Zealots. You were leaving me.

Judas. I never left you. I took you with me: in my head.

Yeshu. When you were here, you had Barabbas with you—in your head. Can a man serve two masters?

Judas. He can serve *with* two brothers.

Yeshu. Not if he's left one for the other.

Judas. Only, as I said, I hadn't.

Yeshu. Jacob and Esau were brothers. Sometimes brotherhood is a kind of . . . bifurcation. I am a man of peace. Barabbas is a man of war. We are opposites. We mix like oil and water.

Judas. It's true. There is truth *to* it. Compare these two lives. Barabbas, the soldier, building an army—not a visible one, to be sure, in shining helmet and armor, an invisible one, armed with only short sword or dagger, and housed in the hovels of the people. Yeshu, teacher, preacher, traveling exorcist, amateur physician, miracle worker—is it true you raised that fellow from the dead?

Yeshu. Lazarus? He *would* have died. I healed him. Healing is always a miracle.

Judas. Your training is rabbinical, you know your Bible, and you know the unwritten lore just as well, including the modern teachings, the Essene doctrine, the sayings of Rabbi Hillel, and you pass your wisdom among the commonest of the commonfolk, the so-called *am-haarets*—whom the Romans call the rabble but whom we accept as just ordinary Jews.

Yeshu. Them I love.

Judas. And because you love them, they love you, and your Word passes from mouth to mouth. Greeks call you the Logos, the Word, God's Word. If I had to put that Word into a word—a single word—I think it would be harmlessness. You teach your people to harm no one and nothing, not even a fly. Perhaps not even a Roman?

Yeshu. And so you left me.

Judas. Not before having many an argument with you, remember?

Yeshu. About turning the other cheek?

Judas. And about paying taxes.

Yeshu. And about terrorism.

Judas. And about . . . Insurrection.

Pause.

Yeshu. You always disagreed with me.

Judas. Is that your memory of it?

Yeshu. Yes.

Judas. It isn't mine. How did you explicate "Give Caesar what is Caesar's, give God what is God's"?

Yeshu. "To a good Jew, nothing in Palestine is Caesar's. The saying means: Give Caesar absolutely nothing."

Judas. And I disagree with that? And about that other cheek. Did you advocate turning the other cheek to Caesar?

Yeshu. No. "Resist not evil" applies only within our own ranks. "Brother does not resist the evil in brother," I said, "He turns the other cheek and promotes the brotherhood."

Judas. And I disagree with that?

Yeshu. Ah no, you objected to what you called my . . . ambiguity.

Judas. Of course, You left it open for people to think the opposite in each case: that they *should* pay taxes to Caesar, that they *should* turn the other cheek to him. As a result, you gained the reputation of a collaborator.

Yeshu. And you left me for the more logical Barabbas?

Judas. For the more courageous Barabbas.

Yeshu. Hm? I am a coward?

Judas. Let's say you had not yet found your courage.

Yeshu. Had not found myself.

Judas. It is the same.

Yeshu. Barabbas told men to refuse to pay taxes, and what happened to them?

Judas. They were forced to pay. The Romans just came and grabbed the money. Tax refusers were marked men afterwards. Few died in bed.

Yeshu. The same with your terrorism. A few Romans were assassinated—or killed in minor skirmishes—and Pilate would then execute double the number of Jews.

Judas. But you didn't condemn *all* force, *all* violence.

Yeshu. No. I said the time was not yet ripe.

Judas. And when *would* the time be ripe?

Yeshu. When we could win. When we could drive the Romans out.

Judas. And when would that be? You are blushing now, Yeshu. When *will* the time be ripe—the time to stop paying taxes, to stop turning other cheeks to enemies? When will it be time to take the Kingdom of God by storm—by fire and sword?

Yeshu. You think I am afraid of that question. I am not. All Israel knows the answer, for all of us Jews await that day: the day when the Messiah will come.

Judas. I must now take the bit between the teeth. *Swallowing.* Three years ago, when I joined your movement, you believed *you* were the Messiah.

Yeshu, *startled.* I never said that.

Judas. But you believed that. Your whole being radiated that belief.

Yeshu, *trying to smile.* I had been, as politicians say, groomed for the job. My mother, the rabbis, selected me well in advance.

Judas. Some claim your father Joseph is descended from King David.

Yeshu. Others, for that matter, claim that Joseph was not my father.

Judas. Many of *them* assign you another royal heritage. They have it that your father was eldest son of Herod the Great. In which case his title would now be yours.

Yeshu. King of the Jews! Surely *that* is legend.

Judas. "Where there is the smoke of divine legend, there is the fire of divine truth"—Yeshu of Nazareth. And your encounter with Yochanan the Baptizer was no legend.

Yeshu. But what was Yochanan, after all?

Judas. A would-be Messiah, originally. Proclaiming that *he* would bring in the Kingdom. "Change your hearts! Change your minds! The Kingdom of God is at hand!"

Yeshu. And it wasn't: Yochanan lost a head, Herod kept one.

Judas. Before losing that head, Yochanan made an announcement you can hardly have forgotten.

Yeshu. That the Messiah wasn't him but me.

Judas. That the Messiah wasn't him but you. *With heavy stress:* And you believed him.

Yeshu, *in a whisper.* He was God's voice.

Judas. Then how—why—when did you lose that belief?

Yeshu. Consider. The word Messiah has been in my ears since childhood. Whispered by every passing breeze. Mouthed by every would-be soothsayer. Palestine is a land of dreams but, oh, Judas, I have cause to wish fewer of the dreams were about me. Not thirty and already folklore! Those fairy tales about my mother, my birth, my childhood and youth! If Yochanan was God's voice, remember how many other voices compete with His in this our Palestine!

One voice even imitates his. Satan's voice. Of the fairy tales about me, the one I have most to learn from is the tale of the Devil flying me to the pinnacle of the Temple to offer me all Israel because, says Satan himself, "After all you are the Messiah!" I longed to be the Messiah, Judas, but I also feared I was deluded. So, about two years ago, yes, when a new star rose—that of Barabbas—I was happy to withdraw to Galilee to redeem the time peacefully. To preach peace. To live peace. The Messiah is a conquerer after all. Barabbas was a likelier candidate than I had ever been.

Judas. And that is where things stand now? Barabbas is Messiah, and when the day comes you will support him?

Yeshu. Yes.

Judas. Suppose—suppose one day Barabbas is not there?

Yeshu. How's that?

Judas. Judas Maccabeus, after all, was killed in battle.

Yeshu. He was not the Messiah.

Judas. Then let me ask this. Did you ever conclude *you* were not the Messiah?

Yeshu. I awaited the call. God's signal. I never got it. Barabbas got it.

Judas. One last question. Had you received the signal and the call, would you have had the strength, the confidence, the courage to *be* the Messiah?

Yeshu. A terrifying question. Who welcomes a confrontation with his deepest self? Who knows what he will find in the depths of his heart? I know only that God did place a strength in me that has not yet been used. He must be holding it in reserve for something.

Judas. For what? For what? No, no, that is one question too many. The rest must be said by Barabbas.

Yeshu. By—? When? Where is he?

Judas. On the other side of that thin partition, a silent witness to our talk.

Yeshu. What? *He goes to the door and sees the other visitor, who is of course Barabbas. Once he has uncovered his face, Barabbas appears before us as, so to speak, an older brother of Judas: a little taller, heavier and more muscular perhaps but with the same burning eyes which, as with Judas, can be seen as either saintly or diabolical, according to the point of view.* The lion of Judah! The second Judas Maccabeus!

Barabbas, *uncovering his face, rising, extending his arms.* And you, Yeshu! Of *your* titles I shall speak very soon.

The partition is removed, and the two rooms become one. Yeshu is now between Barabbas and Judas.

Yeshu. I must offer you both the hospitality of the house: wash you, feed you.

Barabbas. *smiling.* Just water, Yeshu, water to drink. And you needn't turn it into wine. *The boy pours water during this passage, then leaves.* I have listened carefully to your words. They are well. Including your differences with us. The time was *not* ripe, and we *did* waste lives. Your work has indeed served a purpose in preparing the brethren for a better time. Helping to build a New Jerusalem.

Yeshu. Thank you.

Barabbas. I have come here today to announce that, now at least, the time *is* ripe.

Yeshu, *an intake of breath.* Ah!

Barabbas. For a national uprising to expel the Romans . . . provided only . . .

Yeshu. Yes? Yes?

Barabbas. Tell him, Judas.

Judas. Barabbas proposes that you and he join forces.

Yeshu. Ha? My people are worth that much?

Barabbas. Who are *our* people? The fanatics and daredevils. Good. But yours are better, and yours are more numerous: They are the common people as a whole.

Yeshu. They are not soldiers, however.

Barabbas. Well, listen. Passover is approaching, and Jews will be converging on Jerusalem from all points of the compass. That is your cue. Galilee and Judaea resound already with your Good Tidings: "Change your hearts! Change your minds! The Kingdom of God is at hand!" Muster your followers and add thereto all the newcomers you can win to our cause. Move to Jerusalem with the rest and, at the head of an enormous throng—with the whole population looking on—present to Tetrarch Herod and High Priest Caiaphas a petition, demanding that they, in the name of the Temple Authorities, join the Insurrection. Tell them the truth: that the country is swept with an ecstasy of faith—faith in the original tenet—the land promised to us! "No Ruler But God! The Roman must go!" Hearing this, seeing the people massed in the courtyard below, Herod and Caiaphas, if only to avoid being torn to pieces by the crowd, will join the Insurrection. At that point, the

Roman garrison will lay down its arms.

Judas. It is well to have the support of the Jerusalem Establishment. But the alliance of Yeshu and Barabbas is unbeatable in any case. The Zealot guerillas are in readiness East of Jordan. If Herod and Caiaphas do not cooperate, we will cross the river, march on the Holy City, and lay siege to the Roman garrison in the Antonia Fortress.

Barabbas. So what do you think, Yeshu? How does it strike you?

Yeshu. It is splendid. Inspiring.

Barabbas. But? But?

Yeshu. Have you received the call, the signal? Has the Lord sent his angel?

Barabbas, *to Judas.* We can go right to the point. *To Yeshu:* Angel, Yeshu, means messenger. A messenger bears a message. I have received a message. It is this: I am not the Messiah.

Yeshu. Ha?

Barabbas. No. My terrorism has not been enough. My guerrilla warfare has not been enough. Sometimes facts speak louder than angels.

Yeshu. Then . . . ?

Judas. Who will step into Barabbas's place? You and I have already discussed that.

Yeshu. God would issue a call. Give the signal.

Barabbas. Indeed! And has given it. Is still giving it. *Pointing to Judas.* It is our presence here. Judas and I are His messengers. *Very slowly.* We have come here to hail you as the Messiah.

Judas. After your triumph in Jerusalem, the Insurrection will spread throughout Palestine. The entire country will be liberated.

Yeshu. All minds changed, and hearts? The Kingdom of God at hand?

Judas. The Kingdom of Palestine—God's. The King of the Jews—you. *Pause.*

Yeshu, *a hand to his head.* Have all my dreams suddenly come true? Pray for me.

Barabbas. By all means.

All three kneel.

We thank Thee, God, that Thou hast sent us our long-awaited Messiah!

Judas. The Liberator, the Lord's Anointed, the King of the Jews!

Yeshu. Grant me the strength! The confidence! The courage!

186

All. Amen.

Judas kisses Yeshu's feet. They rise.

Judas, *ecstatic.* All hail, Yeshu, Yeshua, our second Joshua! If our merely human plans should go awry, God today will part the waters of the Jordan to get our men across!

Barabbas, *ecstatic.* The second Judas Maccabeus addresses the second Joshua: for you the Lord will fell the walls of Jerusalem with his celestial axe! We shall meet in liberated Jerusalem. Till then, Yeshu.

He starts to go.

Yeshu. Barabbas!

Barabbas. Yes?

Yeshu. If we should fail?

Judas, *furious.* Fail?!

Barabbas. Quiet, Judas. You know how Rome punishes political offenders, Yeshu.

Yeshu. With crucifixion. Think of the pain of that!

Barabbas. And for us Jews it places the victim under the Lord's curse, for it is written: "He who hangs from the wood of a tree shall be accurst."

Yeshu. The Lord's Anointed under the Lord's curse?

Judas. Being crucified would prove you were not the Lord's Anointed.

Yeshu. Just one more false Messiah. Like poor Yochanan.

Barabbas. But now Yochanan smiles from the other shore on your success.

Yeshu. Yes. Yes. I can see his smile.

Barabbas. The angels themselves are smiling.

Yeshu. And you are my angels, you two. I love you both. Your coming here is truly a miracle, your news, your plans, your touching faith in me.

Judas and Barabbas. You are the Messiah.

Yeshu. Yes. Yes. Let me hear myself say it: I am the Messiah.

Judas and Barabbas, *turning, from the doorway.* No Ruler But God!

Yeshu. May He never forsake me!

Pilate, *reading.* The Messiah. The Lord's Anointed. The Liberator. The King of the Jews. The notion that Yeshu was this bizarre Semitic superman spread like wildfire through the land, and as he undertook the long trek from Galilee to Jerusalem, his following of a couple of dozen grew—first to hundreds, then to several thousand, armed with kitchen knives, carpenter hammers, butcher hooks, every ugly gadget that home or farm or workshop could provide. It was at the head of this motley crew that he made a kind of triumphal entry into the Holy City and demanded an audience with Herod and Caiaphas. What happened next I would like my readers to hear as Yeshu heard it where he awaited their answer— in a little hideaway just outside Jerusalem belonging to a follower of his who had nothing to do with the Insurrection, who indeed was considered so unfriendly to it that he was told nothing of it till now. The name is Stephen. Dialogue Two: Insurrection.

The Room now is Stephen's, and Yeshu is in it, alone. But almost at once someone else enters, an eighteen-year-old boy with the face of an angel—a somewhat Greek angel one would judge by the features, though his race and religion could be Jewish, as it will prove they are. The eyes are the clue to a state of being, and these are eyes that betoken a person for whom the material world hardly exists, except possibly as a snare and a delusion. They also betoken the fervor which, in one who ignores the material world, can be all the more singleminded. When Stephen looks at Yeshu, however, one notes that he does not dwell wholly in the abstract, for there is also love in his eyes.

Yeshu, *as the youth enters.* I can tell you now, Stephen. *For he it is.* Why I am hiding out here. What has happened, what is happening and will happen, why my strange silence.

Stephen. Yes?

Yeshu. The great Day is upon us. The Day for which Israel has yearned and striven ever since the Holy City fell into Roman hands.

Stephen, *without relish.* The day of liberation?

Yeshu. Are you so terrified?

Stephen. It is not terror.

Yeshu. I know what you think, what you have thought, Stephen, and have begged you not to turn either my head or your own with wild hopes of some Apocalypse! But now you have no excuse. For I have acknowledged who and what I am and have announced my mission. Stephen, either I am possessed of devils, or—stand still while I say this—I am not used to saying it yet, even to myself—I am indeed the Messiah.

Stephen, *lets out a strange cry, not joyful, yet with a note of recognition in it.*

Yeshu. Ah! You receive the tidings? You can receive *me* now!

Stephen. Speak on.

Yeshu. An angel of God came to hail me: Barabbas, Lion of Judah. Since then he and I have marched side by side, brothers in the Lord. Even you, who are almost a hermit, must have felt the stirrings.

Stephen. Stirrings of strife. Undertones of war. I catch them from everyone I meet: the farmer who brings the milk, the pilgrim that passes the door.

Yeshu. And two days ago the climax: I petitioned Herod and Caiaphas in the name of God to come out against Rome.

Stephen. You? You did that?

Yeshu. On the steps of the Temple at the head of a throng of thousands.

Stephen. And they?

Yeshu. Refused to see me. The puppet king shuns the people's leader. The bought priest shuns the penniless prophet. But when the crowd bade fair to set fire to the Temple, they sent a major domo to accept the petition. Restive, murmuring, the crowd awaited an answer. The major domo came out again on the steps. "Greetings from tetrarch and high priest! We request forty-eight hours to prepare the official reply, but let this be said forthwith: People and prophet are welcome! The day of conciliation is near! Shalom!" A sound of rejoicing then went up from the people such as Israel has not heard in generations!

Stephen. Have forty-eight hours passed?

Yeshu. More. The messenger is overdue.

Stephen. And when the conciliation is official?

Yeshu. The Roman garrison here will surrender, and Jews throughout Palestine will rise to expel the legions! At long last our people will change their minds and hearts, and as King of the Jews I shall proclaim that the Kingdom of God *is* at hand!

Stephen. Messiah—in the old sense!

Yeshu. Old sense! Are you still offering your new wine for the old wineskins? The old sense is the true sense: The Lord's Anointed who frees the Lord's people and reconquers the Promised Land! *A heavy knocking at the door.* Here comes the news.

He lets in a young man whose clothes are torn and muddy and whose face is in that state of shock that carries a person somewhere far beyond excitement and agitation.

Stephen. Judas!

Yeshu. The message of messages was entrusted to Judas—who else?

Stephen, *looking at Judas.* Something is wrong. Sit down, Judas.

Judas, *ignoring the invitation.* All is lost.

Yeshu. All is—?

Judas. It is you, *to both,* who should sit. Let me tell my tale. *He remains standing.* You handed your petition to the Major Domo. He handed it to Herod and Caiaphas. And what did they do? They read it once quickly through and sent it over to Pilate in the Antonia Fortress.

Yeshu. No! No! *Screaming.* Traitors!

Judas. Wait. Four hours later, east of Jordan, Barabbas got a message purporting to come from you: "Herod, Caiaphas refuse: attack at once." His men were massed on the east bank. Five pontoons had been constructed across the river to serve as bridges for the guerrillas. The west bank is heavily wooded, thick undergrowth down to the water's edge. Barabbas's Zealots moved onto the pontoons a few at a time and crossed the river. Hiding in the undergrowth on the other side were Pilate's men. Every Jew, as he set foot on shore, was killed by a single thrust in the belly with a Roman short sword until the pile of corpses rose so high it was visible above the bushes. Then what was left of Barabbas's gallant band panicked. Pilate was ready for that too. For now Roman horsemen rode out from among the higher trees and into the water, smashing the pontoons, killing or maiming the men. Only a handful, who had still not left the east bank, made a getaway.

Stephen. And Barabbas?

Judas. That great hero led all the heroes. Crossed the center pontoon ahead of his whole army repeating the watchword in his big bass voice: No Ruler But God! Pilate's order to seek him out was hardly needed. More valuable alive than dead, he was tied to a horse and rushed to the Antonia Fortress.

Stephen. How did you escape? Are you followed?

Judas. I have known these streets since childhood. I gave them the slip. I was one of three advance scouts on the west bank. The other two are guarding that door now. *He points to Stephen's door.*

Stephen. Woe, woe, for Israel!

Judas. Woe, woe!

Yeshu. Woe! *All three wail together. Then:* Silence! *There is silence.* My God! *No answer.* Adonai! *No answer.* Yahweh! *No answer. Why* hast Thou forsaken me?

Pilate, *reading.* The Insurrection, as I said, never had a chance. There was no chance that Herod and Caiaphas would defect. Barabbas, fine guerrilla fighter that he was, overvalued both his own army and Yeshu, whom he regarded as the Messiah. As to Yahweh's role in his Promised Land, it would seem to be that of an absentee landlord. The only interest the Insurrection holds for us here is that it marked a second stage on Yeshu's path to the cross. The next stage was reached a little later on in the same conversation of Yeshu with Stephen and Judas. Dialogue Three: The Voice of an Informer.

Judas is lying down, but with open eyes. Stephen is comforting Yeshu.

Yeshu, *in a quiet, dead voice, in contrast to the loud wailing Woes! of the previous scene.* The sound has gone out: I am *not* the Messiah.
Stephen. No. Not in that sense.
Yeshu. "That sense!" "That sense!"
Stephen. I shall not choose this moment to plague you with what *I* think.
Yeshu. The Messiah is the Messiah. He wins. I have lost. He saves his people. I have led them to their death.
Stephen. You could not have known.
Yeshu. Had I been the Messiah I would have known I was the Messiah. But when Barabbas said I was, I only knew I wanted to agree with him. Knew I did not agree with him. Knew I was not the Messiah. I misled Barabbas and murdered his men!
Judas stirs uneasily.
Stephen. You must not reproach yourself this way, Yeshu. You did *not* know you were not the Messiah. Look, I said I would not plague you with *my* view of things. But it isn't just *my* view. And it isn't just a view. It is a faith, already held by many—
Yeshu, *preoccupied with his suffering, hands clasped together.* Woe, woe, woe!
Stephen, *gazing at him intently.* Such, we believe, are the birth pangs of the *real* Messiah, the one that loses only to win, the one that dies to live again, the one that—
Yeshu. That dies. You want me to die.
Stephen. To rise again in glory!
Yeshu. To be another kind of Messiah. People all want me to be these great big things. If not one sort of Messiah, then another, even bigger. I listened so eagerly to Barabbas. And now I'm tempted to listen to you. I mustn't. *Suddenly.* I don't want to be someone else's superman! *Pause. Dully:* Or do I? I don't know *what* I want any more. Or if I want. *Pause. To Stephen:* Get thee behind me, Satan.
Stephen. I'm sorry I spoke.
Yeshu. I know what I *don't* want: I don't want to die. Maybe what I *should* want is to get away. Leave behind these grandiosities, one and all. Go back where I came from. Teach what I *was* teaching. The Kingdom in your own backyard. The blue bird of heavenly bliss perched all the time on the roof you left behind you. I should just have stayed in Nazareth, performing my conjuring tricks, my

exorcisms, and preaching harmlessness like Rabbi Hillel—what a beautiful thing *that* is—how beautiful when I myself would harm neither a Roman nor a fly . . . Are you listening, Judas?

Judas. Yes.

Yeshu. Help me get out. Help me on the road to the North.

Judas, *who has got up.* Leave the room, Stephen.

Stephen, *edgily.* I'm in the way?

Judas. Yes.

Yeshu, *to Stephen.* Let him have his will.

Stephen leaves, moodily.

Judas. The topic is betrayal.

Yeshu. Betrayal by whom?

Judas. You have heard.

Yeshu. Stephen?!

Judas, *vehemently.* Certainly, Stephen! Well you know Stephen never believed in the cause. Betraying it himself, he would gladly lure you into betraying it. The gall of the boy! Taking such gross advantage of the moment of defeat!

Yeshu. But what is his betrayal to mine? Good, simple souls followed me to death because I had promised them life.

Judas. Neither Barabbas nor you promised life. Rather: sweat, tears, blood, mutilation, death in agony. What you promised was liberation.

Yeshu. We did not provide it. Today Jerusalem is less free than ever. Pilate will be more watchful. Tiberius will send more legions.

Judas. And you conclude? *Silence.* Do you realize what your retreat to Galilee would mean? Again: betrayal. Betrayal of Barabbas. Betrayal of the Zealots. Betrayal of God.

Yeshu, *quickly.* Didn't he betray me?

Judas. What? *What* are you saying?

Yeshu, *guiltily.* I betrayed myself. You are right. Where is Barabbas?

Judas. In the Antonia Fortress.

Yeshu. Why haven't they killed him?

Judas. They will. Before that point is reached the game the Romans play is cat and mouse.

Yeshu. Then what could I do anyway?

Judas. A Barabbas dies. A brother steps into his shoes. That brother dies? Another brother steps in. To infinity. The people are infinite, since there are always more.

Yeshu. All I know is that I sent Barabbas to his death. Many others would be alive now but for me.

Judas. You do not trust God. You don't believe we shall win.

Yeshu. I blundered. Others are suffering for it. I would like to save still others from such a fate.

Judas. How?

Yeshu. How do I know? I am not coming to you with a policy. I am crying out with pain—my own—and that of others whose pain I caused!

Judas. Any general that loses a battle could talk that way.

Yeshu. Maybe they all should.

Judas. Are you telling God we have to win the war in the first battle lest your loss of confidence open the door to unbelief?

Yeshu. I was never a Zealot, Judas!

Judas. So much the worse for you. You joined hands with the Zealots—

Yeshu. Disastrously—

Judas. Inextricably. How can you withdraw when the going gets rough?

Yeshu, *quickly.* God withdrew from me!

Judas. Again, blasphemy!

Yeshu, *sullen.* Jerusalem withdrew from me. If I now withdraw from Jerusalem, what does Jerusalem lose? A nonentity of a country preacher who belongs in Galilee anyway.

Judas. You are the Messiah!

Yeshu. Do you still avow that?

Judas. To let you withdraw is to *dis*avow that. We will not let you withdraw.

Yeshu. In other words, you don't believe it, you just won't concede you don't believe it.

Judas. If someday you conquer, you are the Messiah. The imperative is to fight on till someday you conquer.

Yeshu. I am to offer myself up as a burnt offering to our Jewish logic?

Judas. Barabbas is a Zealot. I am a Zealot. You joined us. Your leaving us at such a juncture, given your immense magic, will have an immense effect!

Yeshu. What immense magic? My departure for Galilee might have some *small* effect—of healing, of peacemaking!

Judas. An immense effect. Of disruption. Debilitation. Demoralization. We shall not permit it.

Yeshu. You keep saying "We."

Judas. The men of the insurrection. All the insurrections. Every effort of the Jewish people to get the oppressor off its back. We *cannot* permit it.

Yeshu. What *can* you do?

Judas. Order you to fight on. Whenever. Wherever.

Yeshu. Order the Messiah?

Judas. The Messiah is not God.

Yeshu. You are?

Judas. Barabbas came to you as God's messenger. So do I.

Yeshu. Another angel!

Judas. To your mind, an evil angel.

Yeshu. Evil—from God?

Judas. Willing to dirty my hands for God.

Yeshu. You have lost me.

Judas. Do not lose yourself. Do not lose us. Oh yes, you can remain in hiding. In fact, you must. We shall try to keep you alive. Since today you occupy Barabbas's shoes. What matters is the master strategy: to tell the people you are alive and undaunted and that the struggle continues unabated till final victory. Defiance to Herod and Caiaphas! Defiance to Pilate and Caesar! You are the Messiah! You are the King of the Jews! *Silence.* Have me carry this message to the Temple right now. *Silence.* In token of agreement, place your hand there, on mine, in the name of the brotherhood. *Silence.* You are asking for time. There is no time.

Yeshu. I am not asking for time.

Judas. Then say the word. Make the gesture.

Yeshu. I cannot.

Judas. Cannot? Cannot? Do you know the consequences of that "cannot?"

Yeshu. I go back to Galilee.

Judas. We cannot afford to let you.

Yeshu, *dully.* What can *you* do about it?

Judas. Your evil angel can betray you.

Yeshu, *weakly.* My . . .

Judas. I can betray you. To the Romans.

Yeshu. Become an informer? You would never!

Judas. No?

Yeshu. You'd never be able to look yourself in the face again.

Judas. I don't have to look myself in the face again. I have to stop you going to Galilee.

Yeshu. What will this do to you?

Judas. Who am I? A zero in the service of the infinite.

Yeshu. Would you make me your murderer? I love you, Judas.

Judas. *He kisses him on the lips.* I love *you,* Yeshu. And you have an alternative: to continue the resistance.

A long silence.

Yeshu. I cannot.

Judas. So be it. *He claps his hands. His two companions enter and take up positions on either side of the doorway. Stephen, also responding to the claps, reenters, quickly takes in the scene.*

Stephen. What is happening?

Judas, *savagely.* Yeshu and I are killing each other.

Stephen, *wondering if he has taken leave of his senses.* What? What?

Judas, *more coolly.* I am turning Yeshu over to Pilate. Why do you ask? Would you like to save his life?

Stephen. I must! *But then taking thought:* No, no, Judas: On this we agree. Yeshu must not return to Galilee. *Declaiming:* "For it is written . . ."

Judas, *interrupting.* Fuck what is "written." *To his two companions.* To the Antonia Fortress. I will lead the way. *He hurries out. Behind him, the two bring Yeshu with them.*

Pilate, *reading.* Was Judas going to kill himself? There was a legend later that he did so, a legend I encouraged for a while, since I stood accused of excessive harshness and chose to reply: "Not at all, these Jews kill each other, they even kill themselves." But now that the episode is, as it were, ancient history, and Rome perforce is taking a very hard line with the Jews, let me report that Judas did not kill himself, never being offered the opportunity. Given his interest in the ironies of betrayal, he himself must at some time have ruefully realized that he could not betray his Messiah into our hands without betraying himself into our hands. I now had Barabbas, Yeshu, and Judas behind bars in the Antonia Fortress, and crucifixion was indicated for all three members of that unholy trinity. At the time, however, I had other plans for Yeshu and dispatched Herod and Caiaphas to talk with him in the death cell. Dialogue Four: Collaboration.

*The Room is now the death cell at Roman Headquarters in Jerusalem, namely, the
Antonia Fortress, so called after Mark Antony. Yeshu is alone and flat on his back in
the cell until two visitors are admitted. He then rises with a start.*

First Visitor. Caiaphas.

*This man, as William Blake would one day write, "was in his own mind/A
benefactor to mankind." Otherwise he would not have paid this visit now. On the
other hand, it would be vain to seek in this cold masklike face, beneath the oiled
ringlets and overdone priestly regalia, even a last vestige of benevolence or
humanity. Whereas one can truthfully say of some that it doesn't matter what
clothes they wear, in the case of others clothes are the man, and Caiaphas would
seem to be one of these. His clothes, and his self-presentation generally, express
love of pomp, prestige, and power. Since his style of dress is so hieratic—he is
after all high priest—one will not be surprised to find his style of speech and
thought unctuous and evasive.*

Second Visitor. Herod Antipas.

*Although Herod's clothes were designed nearly 2000 years ago some things are
always the same and his appearance will suggest to modern Americans a black
pimp in funky clothes with a white Cadillac, much oil in his hair, big jewels on
his fingers. If you will, he is "every inch a king," and that is too many inches on a
man of Herod's broad girth. Hearing his heavy jibes, and noting his sudden
spurts of bitchy hostility, the American reader may be reminded of another
sinister black type: the black overseer in an antebellum Southern plantation. Such
overseers saw themselves as friends to their fellow blacks since they could procure
small favors for them from the slave owners. This implies, however, that what
counted most was their own friendliness with these owners, to whom they made
themselves necessary, and from whom the large favors were for themselves.*

Yeshu, *staring.* I do not understand.

Herod. It is true we do not normally visit the prisons.

Caiaphas. You will appreciate how important we conceived *this* visit to
be.

Yeshu. Pilate must have ordered you to come.

Herod. *Suggested* it. I'm not sure it was a good suggestion.

Caiaphas. Oh, come, brother, we shall bend every effort to prove it
was a good suggestion.

Herod. Oh, very well.

Yeshu. I hate you, with your ridiculous clothes. Pilate paid the tailor's
bill, we can assume? I hate you.

Herod, *starting to leave, to Caiaphas.* I told you how it would be.

Yeshu. You murdered my teacher, Yochanan the Baptizer. Served his head up on a platter. Am I supposed to forgive and forget?

Herod. You little nothing, you less than nothing—

Caiaphas. Peace, brother. Be seated. *Herod does so, huffily.* Be seated, Yeshu. *Yeshu does not.*

Yeshu, *to Caiaphas.* And you. You betrayed your brothers to the oppressor. Every Jew in the pile of corpses beside the Jordan was murdered by you, high priest of Israel.

Caiaphas, *unruffled.* I know the logic by which you arrive at that conclusion. Judas, however, has stated that you held *yourself* responsible for the massacre.

Yeshu. Yes. I share the guilt of the guiltiest—of the Roman wolf and the little Jewish jackals at his tail.

Herod. You insolent—

Caiaphas, *cutting Herod off.* We, however, are willing to drop all recriminations—

Herod. Since we've won and you've lost!

Caiaphas, *to Herod.* I am sure Yeshu fully realizes what his position now is.

Herod. Hopeless.

Caiaphas. And what the penalty is?

Herod, *cheerfully.* Crucifixion! There's a lot of exaggerated talk about its horrors. Like they nail your hands and feet to the cross. Not true. They just tie you to it with ropes. For real torture the Romans aren't in it with my father. Or even me. They've got a compulsive sense of order, that's all. They take a hundred subversives and crucify them in neat rows of ten just to make a perfect square. That's the Romans for you.

Caiaphas. From the theological standpoint, the worst thing is the stigma. "Accurst of God." Need I remind you of Leviticus?

Yeshu. No, you needn't. Look, rats, why are you here? You "don't usually visit the prisons"! When I requested an audience from you two at the head of thousands of fellow Jews, you wouldn't receive me. Here I am, a discredited Messiah, and as you see it, am about to become a discredited human being. Yet now *you* come to *me.* And do not scuttle off when I call a rat a rat. Why?

Herod. I'm not staying indefinitely, I can tell you.

Caiaphas. You can be rather difficult, Yeshu, but I shall emulate the patience of Job, and stay.

Yeshu. What are you plotting?

Herod. Look, Yeshu, you're gonna be crucified. How can we make things any worse?

Yeshu. The power rests with Pilate. How can *you* affect things one way or the other? And since you are my enemies, why would you want to *help* me?

Herod, *to Caiaphas.* Let's go. I'll *enjoy* seeing this one crucified!

Caiaphas. Stay where you are: More than your enjoyment is at stake. Yeshu, do you want to die?

Yeshu. Oh? Do I have to answer questions?

Caiaphas. No.

    Silence.

Yeshu. I don't want to die.

Caiaphas. Then we have a basis for negotiation. Point One.

Yeshu. How so? I will break it off any time I smell a rat, and rat is what I have been smelling ever since you two arrived.

    Herod again starts to bluster, but Caiaphas, with raised hand, cuts him off.

Caiaphas. You do want to die.

Yeshu. No.

Caiaphas. Then I proceed to Point Two: It is conceivable—to Herod and me—that Pilate will pardon you.

Yeshu. He sent you with this message. Which will now be followed by some corrupt proposition.

Caiaphas. Point Three: We know you will not accept a corrupt proposition. We have come with a proposition you will not consider corrupt.

Yeshu. How would *you* know?

Caiaphas. Because it is of your authorship. What did you propose to do if Judas had not turned you in?

Yeshu. Do I have to tell you? *Silence.* Well, I have nothing to hide. I proposed to return to Galilee and my old way of life as preacher and healer.

Herod. No subversion. No rabble-rousing. Right?

Yeshu. Huh?

Caiaphas. Your work as it was before the Insurrection?

Yeshu. How would you know what it was?

Caiaphas. We had abundant reports.

Yeshu. From whom?

Caiaphas. Oh, priests.

Yeshu. Stool pigeons.

Caiaphas. Calm yourself, Yeshu. Your answers have been entirely satisfactory so far.

Herod. And by the way, this wasn't really Pilate's idea, it was mine!

Caiaphas. Ours! We habitually advise Pilate on Jewish affairs.

Yeshu. But he agreed. And *sent* you here.

Herod. Asked us if we would care to come over.

Yeshu. As I said.

Herod. Look, punk, you have a Herod and a high priest to mediate for you with the Roman governor! Not bad going for a hick preacher from a hick town. Where is Nazareth, by the way? As tetrarch of Galilee I own it. But I can't even find it on the map.

Yeshu. To Pilate the only good Zealot is a dead Zealot.

Herod. Which is why he needs our advice—on special cases.

Yeshu. I am special?

Herod. A Zealot with a non-Zealot record.

Yeshu. Ah? A likely traitor?

Caiaphas. Herod, be quiet. Yeshu, if your former way of life, your former teaching, is now again acceptable to you for your own reasons, surely you can permit Pilate to accept them for *his* own reasons? In politics, if we expect the other fellow to share not only our conclusions but our motives we shall never get anywhere!

Yeshu. I don't expect to get anywhere. Except on a cross.

Herod. You idiot, don't you know a break when you see one? We can get you off that wretched cross!

Yeshu. Then what's in it for *you?* Either of you? Maybe that's the only question for me to ask.

Herod. Do you really not know, or do you just want to hear me say it? Caiaphas isn't gonna say it: He doesn't want God to know he knows. But the Herods have always stuck their necks out, so here goes. What's in it for us? The answer is this, friend Yeshu: our absolute dependence on Rome. Our frank acknowledgment of that dependence.

Caiaphas. Herod!

Herod, *mimicking.* "Herod!" First of all, it's plain as the nose on your face. Second of all, I'm proud of it. Proud that the Herod family was the first around here to know the score and act accordingly. People have been calling you King of the Jews, have they, Yeshu? Why? Because of a rumor that you are the bastard son of my elder brother and therefore the grandson and heir of Herod the Great?

Oh yes, I know the legends about your paternity that circulate among our peasants and fisherfolk. Well and good. Even suppose you had the right to the title King of the Jews, where does it come from, eh? From Herod the Great. And how did he get it? By siding with the Romans. As a present from the raunchy Cleopatra's Roman bedfellow, Mark Antony.

Caiaphas. Herod!

Herod, *ignoring the interruption.* Praise Rome from whom all blessings flow! Such is the motto of any King of the Jews. *All* blessings. Want water from a well? The well belongs to the Romans. If you want non-Roman water you can die of thirst. Want to raise an arm against Rome? You can raise your arm. The Romans will cut it off, that's all. As you are about to learn, King of the Jews. Unless, that is, you care to accept Herod and Caiaphas as mediators.

Yeshu. What's in it for you?

Herod. This. We have to make ourselves necessary to Rome, we big Herods and Caiaphases, just like every little Herod and Caiaphas around the country—and throughout the Empire, which is to say the whole world. We want Pilate to need us.

Yeshu. Go on.

Herod. Well, he does need us to, um, help you make the final break with the Zealots. To get you back—is this right, Caiaphas?—into, um, the mainstream of Judaism.

Yeshu. Pah! You are an Arab.

Herod. Idumaean, my dear fellow. Of devout Jewish faith.

Yeshu, *to Caiaphas, contemptuously.* You swallow this?

Caiaphas, *nervously.* I dissociate myself from Herod's tone. A tone which, so far from "frankly" revealing the truth, as he claims, only serves to distort it.

Yeshu. But *you* want Pilate to need you?

Caiaphas. Pilate does need me, Yeshu. How can any colonial governor govern without very considerable support from, well, um—

Herod. Priests, Native priests. Preferably very high priests. You may call it back scratching; Caiaphas calls it mutual aid. *To Caiaphas:* Does Leviticus have something on that?

Yeshu. It makes a picture. I don't want to die. Have nothing to die *for* right now. I want to live. Could live—maybe almost happily—back home in Galilee. The Roman governor, it turns out, has no objection. Sends you over to check the situation out. You have no objection. Acting as mediators gives you a function. Builds you into the system. Gentlemen, we have here a most miraculous unity! The Romans, the Temple authorities, the priests, the client kings and tetrarchs, and, last if also least, the provincial prophets, the would-be rebels, all reconciled, all united, all content!

Herod. Can it be you finally got the message?

Caiaphas. He is being ironical, you fool. Yeshu, let me make one last appeal. Granted we are enemies, yet still and all—

Yeshu. This conference has lasted long enough. *There* is the door.

Herod. God damn you!

He strides out. Caiaphas, one last time, tries to speak but Yeshu speaks first.

Yeshu. Ah, yes, the man who hangs from the wood of a tree *is* damned of God.

Pilate, *reading.* Luckily, I didn't trust those two clowns further than I could throw them, and had my man at the cell door writing down every word. That way they could not persuade me that their visit to Yeshu had been other than a setback. They had not only failed to persuade, they had aroused new suspicions. What to do next? "When in doubt, try torture." That had been Tiberius's advice when he gave me this job. I was now in doubt.

Guards bring Yeshu in. They are numbered here 1, 2, 3, 4, but the lines could be redistributed for a smaller number of actors.

1. Triumphal entry.
2. Into the Holy City.
3. And on and on—to the steps of the Temple.
4. At the head of a throng of thousands.
1. I hereby petition you—
2. Herod and Caiaphas—
3. In the name of God—
4. To come out against Rome!

They torture Yeshu in silence for a while. Then:

1. That's just for starters.
2. Not for enders.
3. Unless you talk.
4. Until you talk.
1. Say it. Say: "I'll go to Galilee."
2. We doan *like* work.
3. We're lazy.

4. Wanna avoid unnecessary exertion.

   No answer from Yeshu.

1. Hear that?

2. Hear what?

3. The silence.

4. He's famous for his silences.

   Silence.

1. Goddamn! We're gonna be doin' overtime.

   They resume the torture. Yeshu now, though, seems to be signaling to them.

Yeshu, *weakly yet calmly.* I have a request to make.

1. To us?

Yeshu. To Pilate?

2. That's a new one.

1. What is it?

Yeshu. Tell him I want to see my young friend Stephen.

Pilate, *continues reading.* It *was* a new one. Those about to be crucified don't make requests, and, if they did, we wouldn't even consider them. But the idea must have appealed to my—was it my sense of humor? I granted the request, and will reproduce here the dialogue which my man at the keyhole wrote down. Dialogue Five: The Face of an Angel.

The death cell. Yeshu. Stephen enters. The two confront each other for a moment in silence, then:

Stephen. You sent for me.

Yeshu. I did, yes.

Stephen. I have hurt you. Very much.

Yeshu. That is true.

Stephen. Then why have you sent for me?

Yeshu. Maybe I am going insane in here. That happens in the death cell.

Stephen. Yeshu!

Yeshu. Anyhow I never thought Pilate would agree to it.

Stephen. Why did he?

Yeshu. Do you care?

Stephen. Not if you don't.

Yeshu. I have nothing more to lose.

Stephen. And new worlds to win.

Yeshu. What's that? Oh yes, that was what *I* was venturing to think. Maybe I *am* going insane.

Stephen. There is no such a thing as going sane.

Yeshu. I figured you'd say that.

Stephen. Do you resent me—for what I did?

Yeshu. Not any more.

Stephen. Why did you send for me?

Yeshu. Maybe I'm beginning to understand what you did. Oh, I'm sure you guessed why I'd sent for you.

Stephen. Because there could only be one reason. Now. With you in the death cell.

Yeshu. Death cell. Death knell. Death does change everything. Stephen, I'm scared. I can say it calmly, but I'm not calm. I could panic at any moment. I'm afraid to die.

Stephen. Fear of death is universal.

Yeshu. Young people don't feel it, though. I've always felt I'd live forever!

Stephen. Ah!

Yeshu. I didn't mean that your way.

Stephen. But isn't that how young people are led to what you call "my" answer?

Yeshu. Immortality? Well, the Pharisees believe in it.

Stephen. As do many Greeks. As did the Egyptians long ago.

Yeshu. I'm a Sadducee in this respect: We deny immortality altogether. Following the Psalmist: "Ye are all gods; ye are all the children of the Most High; but ye die as men."

Stephen. Then, once more: Why am I here?

Yeshu. Not just to sell me the immortality of the soul. More. In the death cell, one plumbs the depths, one reaches for the heights.

Stephen. Pilate offered you your life?

Yeshu. I declined the offer.

Stephen. Praise be to God!

Yeshu. You want me dead! That was why you joined Judas when—

Stephen. Joined Judas! The betrayal which punished you for not being his kind of Messiah . . . *He breaks off. Pause.*

Yeshu. Made me your kind of Messiah?

Stephen. There is only one kind. There is only one Messiah.

Yeshu. But it is still me?

Silence.

Stephen. It was always you.

Silence.

Yeshu. So the voices said. But I never quite believed them. Even what Barabbas proposed seemed too much. Was too much. Has turned to dust and ashes.

Stephen. And yet?

Yeshu. A death cell is a death cell. Unlike anything else. Up to then one has lived in a life cell.

Stephen. And so?

Yeshu. There, one will believe . . . anything.

Stephen. However absurd?

Yeshu. This is not absurd.

Stephen. Ah!

Yeshu. What?

Stephen. Progress! If you no longer find it absurd.

Yeshu. But if I were the Messiah, I would always have known it.

Stephen. And didn't you?

Silence.

Yeshu. What hard questions you ask, Stephen. Know I was the Messiah? Of course not. Never. Not even when I told Barabbas I did. And acted out that charade as people's leader in Jerusalem.

Stephen. And yet?

Yeshu. There was always . . . something. There were always the legends. The voices. And even the military catastrophe . . . *He breaks off. Silence.*

Stephen. Has not entirely . . . ?

Yeshu. Eliminated that . . . something implanted in me—was it from the beginning?—that tells me, Yes, you are the . . . *He stops.*

Stephen. Messiah?

Yeshu. Maybe this is just death house talk! Fear of death will make a man think anything!

Stephen. Even the truth at the very bottom of the pile. Covered with the debris of a lifetime.

Yeshu. Anyhow, I brought you here, thinking—perhaps for the first time, deep down, that I might really be the Messiah.

Stephen. God's name be praised!

Yeshu. But I know nothing about it. Less than nothing. As a false Messiah of the old sort. You will have to educate me.

Stephen. Which is why you sent for me.

Yeshu. Of course.

Stephen. You will more than "educate" me. Put your questions.

Yeshu. What *is* the Messiah?

Stephen. A beautiful question! With how beautiful an answer! Would that I could do it justice! God will help me. Lie down, Yeshu. *Yeshu obeys.* Close your eyes and open your ears. Open your heart and your soul, and I shall unfold to you the history of the world! In two miracles. First, the creation of Man. Adam fell into sin, and man would have been lost eternally had not the Father wrought a second miracle, and created a second Adam: his only begotten son. And the Father sent him to earth, a ransom for many, indeed for all who believed. God's Word became flesh and dwelt among us.

Yeshu. It *is* a beautiful answer.

Stephen. And tragic. For to effect that universal redemption, the Son had to die in agony. That sinners might live eternally, He who was without sin must suffer and must die.

Yeshu, *with mounting ecstasy.* What joy to die in such a cause! And what joy was to follow when the Son returned to the bosom of the Father!

Stephen. He suffers. He falls. He descends into hell. Rises again. Ascends into heaven. And after a thousand years returns from the sky on a great white horse with legions of angels at his back to destroy the Scarlet Whore of Rome forever and make of this whole

206

earth one New Jerusalem! Oh, the beauty of it all, Yeshu! For what is it that men really need? Not what Caiaphas offers, not even what the Prophets and Patriarchs offered! Much, much more! A god who is visible! A man who is a god!

Yeshu. And resurrection?

Stephen. How does one face death? By removing it! By conquering it! Death—greatest of man's defeats—is swallowed up in victory, the victory of the man who is God!

Yeshu. Who is God?

Stephen. The Messiah is the Son of God. The Son of God is himself a god.

Yeshu. It makes me dizzy. It is intoxicating. But how can a *man* know he's a *god*?

Stephen. An angel hails him as the Messiah.

Yeshu. Barabbas claimed to be an angel. So did Judas. How does one know the actual angel?

Stephen. By his face.

Yeshu. Your face is angelic, Stephen. Everyone always said so.

Stephen. Look into my face. Thus speaks the angel. The Advent of the Son of God is announced by Signs. Who is your mother?

Yeshu. Mary.

Stephen. Did Mary receive Signs?

Yeshu. It was said she did. From the Archangel Gabriel.

Stephen. Did he plant in her the semen of God himself?

Yeshu. It was said he did.

Stephen. And when the child was born?

Yeshu. Much was made of that. Of a star guiding astrologers to the birthplace. Of the sky opening. Of a host of angels singing.

Stephen. And when the child was grown?

Yeshu. Miracles.

Stephen. God's chiefest Sign. And what was the final miracle?

Yeshu. Final?

Stephen. We shall return to it. What of the baptism?

Yeshu. Some said they heard a voice from on high.

Stephen. From the All Highest. Saying?

Yeshu. This is hard—

Stephen. To remember?

Yeshu. To say.

Stephen. Try.

Yeshu. "This is my beloved Son . . . in Whom I am well pleased."

Stephen. Yes. Yes. We can now return to the final miracle. What was it?

Yeshu. I don't know.

Stephen. In which the beloved Son showed the power of the Father and prefigured his own death and resurrection—proving in advance its possibility, its actuality!

Yeshu, *moving tormentedly.* No, no, don't ask that.

Stephen. Then you know the answer. Give it.

Yeshu. No! No!

Stephen. Then I will give it. Six months ago, Lazarus of Bethany was raised from the dead. By the Father through the Son. The beloved Son in Whom the Father is well pleased.

Yeshu, *gives a loud cry and falls to the ground, his head in his hands.*

Stephen. And this too is a reply: your agony. It is the agony in the garden preceding the great decision. Do you see where we are now, Yeshu? It is the garden of Gethsemane, and I, God's deputy, am holding out to you a cup. The cup of death. The cup of the cross. What is it you're saying? I can hear it though no sound has passed your lips. "Remove this cup from me." The final trial. Which you must face alone. Alone with the Father. *He starts to move to the door.* Slowly, gradually, the emptiness in your heart will be filled with Him, as was the womb of your mother years ago, and behold! You are no longer Yeshu the frightened Jewish boy, son of Mary, you are Jesus the Christ, Only-Begotten of the Most High! *Stephen moves to the door, then turns toward Yeshu:* My Savior! My Lord! My God! *He turns again to leave the cell.*

Yeshu, *raising from the ground a devastated, tear-stained face.* Stephen, stop it. Stop it, Stephen. The cross. Crucifixion. Oh yes, I have thought about it. And, Stephen, I wouldn't be able to bear it! *A shriek, an animal in pain:* I'm afraid!

Stephen, *continuing in this vein.* This *is* the agony, this—

Yeshu, *getting a partial grip on himself, able to hold down the sobbing and think one thought straight, in a low, steady voice.* I *was* insane to bring you here. I am *not* your Christ. I never claimed to have brought Lazarus back to life. Never. It's the legends again, the folklore, spreading like a forest fire. *Stephen turns pale.* I *am* the frightened Jewish boy. "Ye are all gods, ye are all the children of the Most High, but ye die as men."

208

Pilate, *reading:* What a fox Stephen was! Pretending to some sort of personal revelation when actually he took it from us! For all the puffing and blowing, Stephen had simply taken a leaf out of the Roman book. For, as every schoolboy knows, it was our poet Virgil who predicted the miraculous birth of the baby boy who would bring peace to the whole world. The child was of course Augustus Caesar, who also bears the title of Savior, and ascended into heaven, and is now worshipped as a god. Luckily for me, Stephen overplayed a strong hand, and Yeshu quailed before the prospect of being not only King of the Jews but Emperor of this world and the next. He would now, I thought, listen more readily to the argument for staying alive—if only I could get it presented by someone more acceptable to him than Herod and Caiaphas. Among the names proposed by my advisers, the one I chose was Annas, a former high priest who had been removed from office for being insufficiently cooperative with Rome. That should endear him to Yeshu, and my calculation was that he would now cooperate with Rome without knowing it. Dialogue Six: Capitulation.

The death cell. Yeshu. While Herod and Caiaphas had seemed to wish to overwhelm Yeshu with the grandeur of their dress, toilet, and deportment, the man who now enters might seem any old Jew one would encounter in the marketplace until one notes the fire of whatever old battle still in his eye and a certain patriarchal dignity in his gait. He holds himself very straight and does not immediately seek a seat. His long cloak is so simple, drab, and downright sad one could take it for a penitential robe.

Yeshu. Who are you?

The Man. My name is Annas.

Yeshu. Not . . . *the* Annas?

Annas. The former Annas. The late Annas. The days of my glory are past. The days of my life are almost past.

Yeshu. Once a great spirit, always a great spirit.

Annas. May I sit?

Yeshu. I am honored.

(They sit and look at each other.)

Annas. And *dis*honored. For it is not High Priest Annas that speaks today. It is the father-in-law of High Priest Caiaphas.

Yeshu. Caiaphas?

Annas. I come before you with Caiaphas's proposal, Herod's proposal, in definitive form: Pilate authorizes me to state that you may have a complete pardon on the sole condition that you resume your former life in Galilee. *Yeshu strides over to Annas and spits in his face. Annas wipes off the spittle and continues.* The differences between me and my son-in-law, not to mention those between me and Herod, are many, but the chief one today is that I am not going to take "No" for an answer. Spit on me again. Pace the room. Scream. Gnash your teeth. Raise your fists against me. Those are trivia that old Jews are accustomed to. They cannot by one jot or tittle affect the outcome. You are going to accept Pilate's offer.

Yeshu. Get out!

Annas. You are strong enough to *throw* me out, young man. Rather than let that happen, however, I would summon the Roman guards and have them hold you down while I talk. You are going to listen.

Yeshu. Why not carry me to Galilee in chains?

Annas. When you have heard me out you will go of your own free will.*Silence. To which Annas responds:* Thank you. I thought it best to state at the outset what, for better or worse, I have in common with Herod and Caiaphas. We could then proceed to what I do not have in common with them: Unlike them I have nothing to gain by this visit.

Yeshu. How do I know that? Pilate—

Annas. Removed me from power as an uncooperative Jew.

Yeshu. But perhaps now—?

Annas. Has offered me some bribe? Money? Services? Yeshu, I have but one thing to say about that. Do you believe it?

Silence.

Yeshu. Not if you say "no."

Annas. I have prided myself on incorruptibility. It is too late for me to change. I shall talk treason here today, and Pilate's spy at that door will take it down. What then? Would Pilate care to take my life? I have had my life. In any event, it would be a privilege to give it in such a cause.

Yeshu. If you have nothing to gain, what is it you wish?

Annas. To save you. I ask nothing but that, as you yourself wish, you lead your normal life again.

Yeshu. It makes no sense. You don't even know me.

Annas. Not as these young men have known you, Judas, Stephen, who have been close, sometimes too close, to you. But I have my ear to the ground—Israel's youth is Israel's future—I follow what the young are doing. I have known you from afar.

Yeshu. Well, it's visitors' day in the death house! If I can let Stephen talk me into being a god, I can let you talk me into being the country preacher I actually am.

Annas. Thank you. You are a good Jew.

Yeshu, *bitterly.* What may *that* be?

Annas. What indeed? That is my theme today.

Yeshu. And your answer is treason?

Annas. To be a good Jew is to live a good life within the confines God provides, within the iron ring of necessity, the actual course of history. To be a good Jew is to live with the Jewish fate.

Yeshu. Defeat? Persecution? Bondage? Exile?

Annas. Defeat, persecution, bondage, exile. What is new about Pilate? Or the Emperor Tiberius either? Before Rome did we not know Persia, Babylon, Egypt?

Yeshu. We had our moments of glory, of deliverance: the Red Sea, Jericho . . .

Annas. Moments—in centuries of oppression.

Yeshu, *savagely.* Then your son-in-law is right. All we can do is lick the oppressor's boots.

Annas. Repeat those words.

Yeshu is silent.

Annas. You cannot repeat those words. Good. Can your mind break through to the right conclusion?

Yeshu. No.

Annas. Then I will spell it out. Our religion is prophetic, and what is it the prophets tell us? That the waters will divide at our approach, the walls of Jericho fall down at our bidding? On the contrary, the prophets tell us that, in our sinfulness, we have incurred God's displeasure and that He therefore has not only permitted us to be conquered, massacred, enslaved, deported, He has arranged all this to teach us a lesson—*the* lesson—to live with our fate, the fate of slaves. Just there lies the challenge. Caiaphas fails to meet it and says: if a slave, why not also a whore? Caiaphas is a lost Jew. You have met with betrayal. Caiaphas is the ultimate traitor. God's challenge is, in bad times, to be a good Jew. This is what you will be in Galilee. And this is why I want to send you there.

Silence.

Yeshu. Is there no larger hope? No grander vision? *Silence.* Find the words for me.

Annas, *quietly.* There is no reason to believe that the future will be any different from the past. Let me too play the prophet and predict that the Jews will be conquered again, massacred, enslaved, deported again and again, through centuries to come, by empires yet unborn!

Yeshu. Woe! Alas!

Annas. Is it not true, my child, that you have already accepted guilty responsibility for Jewish lives lost in the Insurrection?

Yeshu. It is true.

Annas. Accept now, equally, guilty responsibility for the enormous despair of the survivors. For, each time that false hopes are raised in the people, the people sink into an impious and soul-destroying desperation.

Yeshu. All is dark, and there is no way out!

Annas. That is not so, either, my child. Living with all this most bitter wisdom, we shall yet, with God's help, work our modest miracle.

Yeshu. A miracle?

Annas. Yes. For, when the Roman Empire has gone the way of Babylon, and when other empires, still without a name, have gone that way, the Jewish people—dispersed through the world perhaps—will still be there, will still hold together.

Yeshu. That is the miracle?

Annas. Yes.

Yeshu. And that is your "treason"?

Annas. Yes.

Yeshu, *after a silence.* It is not enough.

Silence.

Annas. I have failed then after all. You are refusing even me.

Yeshu, *coming out of the painful meditation.* What? Oh. Oh, yes, you want me in Galilee, don't you? And you wish me well. So why not? Why not? What does it matter where I am now? Tell Pilate I will go to Galilee.

Pilate, *reading.* It is seldom far from the death cell where rebellious natives are held to the working quarters of the colonial governor. Yeshu and I were in the same building: the Antonia Fortress. I had him brought in with all speed, and so for the first, and almost the last, time we two, Roman governor and Jewish prophet, stood face to face. Dialogue Seven: Crucifixion.

The room is still in the Antonia Fortress but in a section as far removed as possible, literally and stylistically, from the death cell. It is Pilate's work room. Whereas the Pilate we have seen up to now is a retired civil, or rather military, servant of some sixty years of age, the Pilate we now see before us is several decades younger, very much the Roman soldier and by the same token an efficient administrator. To us of today, his appearance is bound to suggest a Roman statue. His clean-shaven face, and short-cropped hair, make a very bold contrast with all the other heads in the story, which are Jewish. Even Stephen has a feathery, blond beard and long locks . . . Yet on one point Pilate differs from the statues. They are idealized and usually suggest unalloyed dignity. Though Pilate has the hauteur of a ruling class, he is the man Tiberius chose for drastic military and police action of the kind our story abundantly illustrates. The harshness, the sheer savagery, required for such action is not entirely hidden by the sophistication and poise of his speech and habitual carriage. However, as the following Dialogue opens, he is at his gentlest and most relaxed, and glances almost casually up from his desk as Yeshu is ushered in.

Pilate. "Tell Pilate I will go to Galilee." *To the guards:* Leave us. *The guards leave the room. Silence.* Yes, I'm Pilate. Am I what you expected? I am what I am. *Silence.* Annas told me all. *Silence.* Not that he needed to. He himself, as he said, was covered by my spy at the door. So I know more than Annas told me: I know how little you sympathize with Annas. *Silence.* But, to be practical, you *will* go to Galilee? *Yeshu is impassive before this question as before all the previous remarks.* No, this time, Yeshu, I have to have an answer. Will you go to Galilee?
Yeshu, *dully.* I will go to Galilee.
Pilate. Returning to your former work? *Silence.* Answer please.
Yeshu. Returning to my former work.
Pilate. Which was preaching and healing? *Silence.* Hm?
Yeshu. Which was preaching and healing.
Pilate. Preaching peace. Goodwill. Harmlessness.
Yeshu. Peace. Goodwill. Harmlessness.
Pilate. Which would represent a decisive break with the Zealots?
Yeshu. A decisive break with the Zealots.
Pilate. Thank you. You can relax now. Sit down. I want to talk to you.
　　Yeshu might not be inclined to relax in a chair—is not used to chairs anyhow—but sinks down on one in sheer exhaustion.
　　It is strange to study someone so intently at a remove, to spy on them so long, and after all that meet them. Would we ever

understand each other, we two? Let me hear the voice that has been reported to me so often by others. Say something.

Yeshu. I have nothing to say.

Pilate. He has made a career out of speech-making and he is speechless. He found a million words to rouse multitudes to fight Pilate; for Pilate himself he cannot find one word? *Silence.* If you will not harangue me, Jew, then satisfy my curiosity by answering a few natural questions. What, for instance, made you think your insurrection could succeed?

Yeshu. Must I answer?

Pilate. Why not?

Silence.

Yeshu. We have a saying, If God is for us, who is against us?

Pilate. It didn't stand you in very good stead. We were against you and we won.

Yeshu. God was not for us.

Pilate. Why put up with a god like that? We have many gods but would never tolerate a turncoat.

Yeshu. I spoke of the One God.

Pilate. Brilliant idea. Like one Caesar. Who is, or can become, a god, and anyway is king of kings and lord of lords. Can your god be defeated by mere men?

Yeshu. Never.

Pilate. It would take another god to defeat him. And since he has just been defeated, that proves there *is* another god. Self-evidently his name is Caesar.

Yeshu. I did not wish to speak. Should not have spoken.

Pilate. You will not dispute the fact that Caesar exists. I will dispute the contention that Yahweh exists. And it does seem to me a distinct advantage, especially for a god, to exist, hm? *Silence.* Blessed are the peacemakers!—Your line, but I'll fill in for you. Any actual peace is a peace that our god, Caesar, made by winning a war. Your nonexistent god offers—I must speak your lines again—a peace that passeth understanding. The merit of Caesar's peace is that everyone can understand it.

Yeshu. "He makes a desert and calls it peace."

Pilate. A misplaced quotation indeed! Caesar irrigates the desert, and it *is* peace. And plenty. And men smile for a change. Cities rise up and prosper where formerly there were only the tents of nomads

215

and the huts of tribesmen. Such is the peace all men understand. *Silence.* No comment?

Yeshu. What can I say?

Pilate. At least say it.

Yeshu, *swallowing.* Caesar kills Jews.

Pilate. No more than non-Jews. After the Spartacus revolt we crucified six thousand Italians. Caesar is absolutely without racial prejudice. Hm? Can Yahweh say as much? *Silence.* Yahweh cannot say as much. Romans kill Jews because Jews kill Romans, and you know it. You also know that the Romans will stop killing Jews just as soon as Jews have stopped killing Romans.

Yeshu, *quickly.* Rome was the aggressor. Rome broke the peace.

Pilate. Now you're talking. Thank you. Permit me simply to observe that you are mistaken. Provably. On matters of fact. While our peace, founded on war, is a fact, yours, founded on nothing, is mere legend. I have made it my business to study your country and its history. Every page stained with blood. Internecine strife and nothing else from time immemorial. Can you deny it? *Silence.* You cannot deny it. Primitive tribes forever at each other's throats exactly as in Italy, Germany, and distant Britain. And what ended this strife?

Yeshu. Nothing. You continued it on an ever grander scale!

Pilate. Now you're arguing—and well. Yes, we make war on a somewhat grander scale, moving ever closer to a grander, and somewhat contrary goal: a peace that is enduring. Pax Romana!

Yeshu. Peace on earth—

Pilate. Peace on earth! The phrase is yours. The fact, however, is all ours. The Pax Romana is the only pax this earth has known, the only peace that is destined to spread over the *whole* earth . . . Give or take a little of my rhetoric, can't you see a measure of truth in all this, Jew?

Yeshu. "No Ruler But God!"

Pilate. Zealot rhetoric! This is an odd moment for you to resort to Zealot rhetoric.

Yeshu. Could *you* accept foreign rule?

Pilate. Continue.

Yeshu. Where you see peace, my people see usurpation, theft, enslavement, and ask what business Romans have in Israel?

Pilate. Fair enough. Then let me ask what business your Moses had

there and your Joshua and the rest? Didn't they move in uninvited
like any Roman general, usurping authority, stealing the land,
offering the inhabitants a choice of slavery or death?

Yeshu. They were *not* uninvited.

Pilate. No?

Yeshu. The Lord Himself invited them!

Pilate. Over the dead bodies of the native population, however. No
ruler but Yahweh! And what kind of ruler does Yahweh make? By
their fruits ye shall know them! Does that saying of yours apply to
him?

Yeshu. Above all to Him.

Pilate. He talks to you, doesn't he?

Yeshu. He spoke to the patriarchs.

Pilate. He talks *too much*, your god. Talks a peace that he could never
deliver. Never. For how would a tribal deity—and that is all
Yahweh is, god of the Jews—deliver peace between tribes? For
that you need an imperial deity: Caesar, who imposes peace upon
all the tribes. By their fruits ye shall know them, eh? *Silence.* Your
silence tells me *I* too talk too much, hm?

Yeshu. You talk of peace. I think of—crucifixion.

Pilate. And what is crucifixion? Simply the Roman way with a rebel:
placing him in plain view and saying to potential rebels, Pray think
twice! Cruel? That is the point. But unlike your terrorists we
Romans are not in love with violence.

Yeshu. Six thousand crosses, and multiply that by—

Pilate. By many. What can justify that? What is worth such a price? I
will answer that, and we shall see if you can answer my answer.
Your Yahweh talks ideals but never impresses them on the actual
world. Caesar, to the contrary, brings to the conquered this pearl
beyond all price: civilization. You stare. The word means nothing
to you? That is your loss. Your ignorance. What is civilization? If
only you had seen these places, Britain, Gaul, yes, and Israel before
the Romans came! If then you had witnessed the building of our
cities, roads, bridges, the creation of cultural and commercial
intercourse between nations—we have even set up a postal
system—if you had witnessed, above all, the substitution of
Roman law for the law of—I have to say it, the law of the jungle,
you would think differently, even of crucifixion. Now civilization
presupposes law and order; while law and order presuppose the

Pax Romana. It follows that a threat to Rome is a threat to peace, to order, to law, to civilization. Rome is the one hope for this world, since this world's one alternative to Rome is barbarism. Or? *Silence.* You agree? *Silence.* You disagree so deeply you aren't talking? *Silence.* I ask you to talk and end up lecturing you on civilization. By all means, let's return to the practicalities. *He is handling scrolls on his desk now.* Here are my spies' reports. I will not claim to have grasped all the subjective nuances and Semitic supersubtleties, but anyway. Tiberius has ordered me to release one of the two leaders of the revolt. To demonstrate Roman magnanimity. Barabbas being an intransigent Zealot, it is quite logical to release you. You accept this? *Pause. Then Yeshu nods.* And you will let us escort you back to Galilee?

Yeshu, *nods slowly, then raises his hand to his brow, as if dizzy.* Can we end this interview?

Pilate. Just as soon as I have outlined the formalities. *Yeshu stirs uneasily at this word. Pilate notices this.* Our clemency to be valid, must be as rational as our cruelty. *Yeshu is now apprehensive.* No, Yeshu, we do not intend to push you beyond the position you have taken. We must, however, take reasonable advantage of that position.

Yeshu, *muttering.* What?

Pilate. My lecture was not all that academic. Civilization means law; law entails procedure. The procedure we now propose, *im*pose, is recantation. You joined a conspiracy, Yeshu. You must now *re*nounce it and *de*nounce any fellow conspirators who have not recanted.

Yeshu. Barabbas . . .

Pilate. Judas your betrayer and so on down to the rank and file: We have drawn up a list . . . Your release will not only demonstrate our magnanimity. Better even than a crucifixion, it will serve to discourage potential rebels.

Yeshu. What are you asking of me?

Pilate. A public recantation, thrice repeated. First you will read it before the common people in the Temple courtyard; second before the captive rebels in the nearby jail; and third you will read it before the cross on which by then Barabbas will be hanging. That may not come easy but it will soon be over, and—What's the matter, Yeshu? *Lifting both hands to his head in an overpowering attack of vertigo, Yeshu has fallen unconscious to the floor.*

Pilate, *reads.* I had him carried to his cell. "Bring him back when he comes to," I said. My doctor reported he could not return that day at all: He was in a coma. The same the second day. It was on the third day that he rose again from his bed, saying: Take me to Pilate. The final Dialogue, Number Eight, with apologies to brother Stephen, I entitle Resurrection.

Pilate. Well, Yeshu! We were worried about you. You're now ready to go through with the recantation?

Yeshu. I left without answering your question.

Pilate. The time for debate is over.

Yeshu. But not the time for answers. If I left a three-day pause it was not for dramatic effect.

Pilate. And after being three days unconscious?

Yeshu. Rather, becoming conscious.

Pilate. Conscious of what?

Yeshu. You spread out before me the panorama of civilization. Rome is all splendid institutions and even more splendid principles. One need not study the archives, or journey to Italy, to learn the truth about Rome. Rome is the Abomination of Desolation! Its statecraft is murder, corruption, and intrigue! Its god-emperors are slavering halfwits and rampaging maniacs!

Pilate. That is quite an answer.

Yeshu. And you yourself with your talk of peace, law, order, et cetera, what is *your* record here in Israel? You have desecrated our temples! You have massacred our people!

Pilate. Have you become a Zealot again in these three days?

Yeshu. I have become myself. For the first time.

Pilate. And that self is a Zealot?

Yeshu. Is a barbarian. It is not in Rome that we Jews will find the answers. We shall reach into our own hearts and find there—

Pilate. Old Annas said it: acceptance of oppression as your fate.

Yeshu. God bless Annas! Wise and good about so many things, missing out on the one thing.

Pilate. Namely?

Yeshu. The Messiah.

Pilate. Him again! Tiberius told me when I left Rome, Bear in mind that the Jews, though very spiritual and all that, are completely crazy.

Yeshu. You think I'm going mad?

Pilate. Wouldn't you call a village preacher mad if he claimed to be Julius Caesar? How about a village preacher who claimed to be God's undefeatable Messiah?

Yeshu. I *was* mad.

Pilate. Your God forsook you, as you put it.

Yeshu. As I wrongly put it. I don't blame Barabbas. I could have told him "no." But I was so deluded I nearly did it again: invited

Stephen to repeat the Barabbas experience on a grander scale and on an invisible battlefield where my defeat could never be proved. It was bad enough to let someone else believe I am a god but when I started to entertain that possibility myself . . . You are right, Pilate, I have consorted with madness.

Pilate. But, in the person of old Annas, you consorted with sanity.

Yeshu. Annas is sane the way the Roman Empire is sane. For the oppressor it is sane to oppress; for the oppressed, it is sane to *be* oppressed.

Pilate. You choose the insanity of Messiahship?

Yeshu. I am not the Messiah. That *was* insane.

Pilate. Then the Messiah is Barabbas? Judas?

Yeshu. Not Barabbas either. Not Judas. Not today. Not tomorrow. The Kingdom of God is *not* at hand!

Pilate. Ah! So you were wrong, all of you—?

Yeshu. Yochanan and Yeshu were wrong. Barabbas and Judas will continue to be wrong.

Pilate. And Annas was right.

Yeshu. Annas was even wronger! He said "never" when he should just have said: The Kingdom will be *a long time* coming. The blood spilt now in its name will be as a drop in the ocean beside the blood my people will shed before Messiah comes. But where there is no vision, the people perish.

Pilate. Let me get this straight now. Your people, being visionaries, are going to await a Xerxes, an Alexander, a Julius Caesar?

Yeshu. Must the Messiah be an individual? Might he not be Israel, God's suffering servant among nations? Might not every Israelite be an atom, a spark, of the Messiah? For me, at any rate, to say the Messiah will come is to say we Jews will *never* accept oppression as our fate. *Pilate starts to speak.* Annas lost that faith, and when the Insurrection failed, I lost it too, lost it because I could not be the Messiah. Such was my arrogance. Wondrous are the ways of the Lord: Your arrogance has brought me to my senses. *Silence.* Have I answered your question?

Pilate. You have made my head swim. We were arranging a little deal, and you have taken me on a speculative journey like some Greek philosopher.

Yeshu. Some Jewish philosopher.

Pilate. Can we get this recantation over with?

Yeshu. So you haven't understood.

Pilate. Civilization? The Messiah?

Yeshu. Or even this little deal.

Pilate. This is your devious, sacerdotal way of telling me the deal is unacceptable. You don't want to go to Galilee after all.

Yeshu. You *have* understood.

Pilate. Have *you* understood your situation?

Yeshu. It is clear. I have decided to die.

Pilate. *What?* What's the catch?

Yeshu. Do you never look at people when you talk to them?
Pilate looks at him closely.

Pilate, *grunting.* You're trying to show me the face of one who has "decided to die." To me, it looks pretty much like the face of someone desperately ill who suddenly decided to live.

Yeshu. You do look at people. You've noticed I'm a new man. I was dead but am alive again.

Pilate. What?

Yeshu. Died when the Insurrection failed. Came alive again only this morning.

Pilate. And coming alive again, only this morning, decided to die this very evening?

Yeshu. Yes, that's right. Tiberius has ordered you to release one of us and to execute the other. You will execute me. You will release Barabbas.

Pilate. But you are no longer a Zealot!

Yeshu. A war has two sides, not three. Choosing between the Zealots and you, I cannot but choose the Zealots.

Pilate. So now we have it. The whole story. I am to release Barabbas.

Yeshu. You will have to. I am refusing to recant.

Pilate. I will have to. Hm. Well, Yeshu, my friend, we are moving now from your field, which is that of dreams, to mine which is that of action. Only Caesar tells Pilate what he *has* to do.

Yeshu. And Caesar says you have to release someone.

Pilate. Check. But not checkmate, brother Yeshu. Very well. I kill you. I release Barabbas. That will mean precisely nothing. He is far too important a rebel to be left at large. Confident of my emperor's full approval, I would kill him too. Have him mysteriously disappear.

Yeshu. You would do that? *Silence.* Of course you would do that.

Pilate. So where are we now? You wish to die for absolutely nothing?

Yeshu. I will not denounce my brothers. I love them. Yes: including Judas. Nor will I insult the suffering body of Barabbas on his cross.

Pilate. Then you leave me no alternative.

Yeshu. No alternative at all. *He prepares to leave the room.*

Pilate. One moment, though. A thought. Suppose we were to withdraw the demand for a recantation?

Yeshu. All three recantations? All the denunciations?

Pilate. I have reached you now. Yes. All the recantations. All the denunciations. Hm? Rome is not known for flexibility perhaps, but we change course when we have to. I'll make it definite. We do withdraw our demand.

Yeshu, *with an intake of breath something like relief.* Ah, then, so I need not—

Pilate. Need not go through all that after all. No. You may withdraw to Galilee and your old life *without* any obligation to us here in Jerusalem.

Yeshu. I would really enjoy Galilee.

Pilate. Then you shall.

Yeshu. And the deal is concluded. Except I am not interested in deals.

Pilate. Not . . . ? Look, Yeshu, think clear, think fast. We have just waived all our demands on you. We ask nothing. If you die now, it *will* be for absolutely nothing.

Yeshu. You want me in Galilee for a reason: "Better even than a crucifixion, it will serve to discourage potential rebels."

Pilate. And, since you are no longer a Zealot, what's wrong with that? Peace on earth, good will to men, a quiet harmless life, that was and will be your Galilean creed.

Yeshu. The Zealots taught me this much: Who acquiesces in your oppression is not harmless, he has betrayed my kingdom to your empire.

Pilate. You will die a Zealot?

Yeshu. I shall die a Jew.

Pilate. To hang from a cross is to be accurst of God. That's what Jews believe. You yourself said it.

Yeshu. I also said God had forsaken me, and He hadn't. Who accepts His curse for the good of Israel shall be blessed.

Pilate. Hm. Well, listen. You have everything figured. Except the actual, material cost: We have made the penalty a death—a dying— so hideous that no man, no man could willingly embrace it, least of all a man like yourself, far from the toughest, oozing timidity and panic a matter of hours ago. You have never thought what being crucified is like.

Yeshu. It hurts.

Pilate, *deliberately.* Being suspended from the crossbeam of the so-called cross—it is actually just a "T"—imposes an unbearable strain on the heart. The waste which the heart cannot eliminate poisons the muscles, which go into convulsions. The victim is suffocated—to the point of the unendurable. Screams for someone to put him out of his agony. No one does. No one is allowed to. And death will not come for forty hours. Forty hours. During which the unendurable is endured.

Yeshu. And this is what Barabbas and Judas are about to go through! Take me to them!

Pilate, *at a loss momentarily, then:* It's only *their* sufferings you feel? You bother me, Jew. We must get you on that cross fast. *He strides to the door to call the guards.*

Yeshu. Oh, the pain! The pain of the Jews! *Pilate stops and looks at him.* At the same time, Pontius Pilate, this is the happiest day of my life.

Pilate, *reading.* It was soon to be the happiest day in Stephen's life. Less than a week after Yeshu died on the cross Stephen announced he was still alive and popping up all over Palestine as a ghost, a "holy ghost." The legend that we nail men to crosses played a role here: For the ghost of Yeshu invited doubters to stick their fingers in the nailholes. Since which time, the friends of Stephen have become a cult, with Yeshu as their god. And the record has been touched up. The crucifixion is blamed on Caiaphas and the Jewish Establishment. We Romans had nothing to do with it. In this way Stephen's people seek to appease us. According to one legend, as I mentioned, Judas killed himself. Another has it that Barabbas was set free after all. What is truth? What is legend? I know the truth on one point. Yeshu was crucified alongside two other men, and these were not nameless bandits as the touched-up record would have it but the two leading Zealots—Barabbas and Judas. There is a story that, while on the cross, Yeshu said: "This night you will be with me in paradise." That too could be a legend, but, if he did say it, he said it to his seducer and his betrayer, respectively. Knowing Yeshu, I wouldn't put it past him. For when I tried to make him feel the pain of crucifixion he felt only *their* pain. "Love driveth out fear." Is that one of his sayings? It is something he demonstrated in action. It unsettled me. Yet what did I have to fear? Although from childhood on, Yeshu had been encouraged to believe he was so extraordinary, might well be the Messiah, he had in fact proved rather ordinary. Neither his teaching nor his poetry were original. Inept in politics, nonexistent as a soldier, outclassed by Barabbas as a leader, and now, it seems, by Stephen as an organizer, he was hardly what we Romans would consider a great man—only a victim of great delusions who in consequence let himself be pushed around by Barabbas, by Annas, even up to a point, by the unspeakable Stephen. And of course by me. Till that final meeting when he declared himself an ordinary Jew and thereupon proved extraordinary. I don't just mean he died gamely, though he did. I mean that when he told me he was a new man, he *was* a new man or, better, the ordinary man who must always have been there behind the extraordinary masks. But then it is really the wild masks of delusion and dream that are humanly ordinary, and authenticity that is extraordinary. I tried to undermine him, and couldn't touch him. No one should be *that* authentic. An ordinary Jew, powerless, about to die, a little man from a little people, who yet could scare the Roman governor! His defeat *was* a victory, too. The news was soon around that Yeshu had died rather than cooperate, and this was a blow to the constituency not only of Caiaphas but of Annas. A boost to the constituency of Barabbas and Judas. Whatever his failures, Yeshu did help keep alive the spirit of resistance. Since his death, others have fanned the flame. And today we stand on the verge of a full-scale war between Rome and this incorrigible tribe. We shall win. We shall win if we have to take Jerusalem apart stone by stone. But let no one think I am changing the subject when I recall crying out to Yeshu that he was a madman, yet feeling in the pit of my stomach that *I* had gone mad. Had always been mad in a mad world. The point I am trying to make is that such men are a threat to empire. Study him, Romans, to know your enemy.

APPENDIX

In performance Pilate's final reading may prove overlong, in which case the following shorter version should be substituted:

Pilate, *reading.* "Love driveth out fear." Is that one of his sayings? When I tried to make him feel the pain of crucifixion he only felt the pain of Barabbas and Judas. It unsettled me. I tried to undermine all his defenses one by one. But there was some defense or other that I couldn't undermine. No one should be *that* authentic. "The weak shall be strong." Is that him again or has he got me to thinking his way? A little man from a little people who could scare the Roman governor! His defeat *was* a victory too. He kept alive the spirit of resistance. Since his death, those he influenced fanned the flame, and today we stand on the verge of a full-scale war between Rome and this incorrigible tribe. We shall win if we have to take Jerusalem apart stone by stone, but let no one imagine I am changing the subject when I recall crying out to Yeshu that he was a madman yet feeling in the pit of my stomach that *I* had gone mad, had always been mad in a mad world. Such men are a threat to Empire! Study him, Romans, to know your enemy.

Afterword

S hould I be embarrassed to discover that at least four plays of mine that, on the surface, had been entirely separate projects turned out to be, at bottom, the same project, even, in certain essentials, the same play? The titles of the four are: *A Time to Die, A Time to Live, From the Memoirs of Pontius Pilate, The Recantation of Galileo Galilei.* Two of them depict a younger person deciding to die, the other two an older person deciding to live. What all four have in common is a situation and a development out of it—a common dramatic action with its beginning, middle, and end.

Outwardly, the "situation" is a social conflict, a war between two groups of people. Thus far we have straight political theatre, even melodrama, good guys versus bad. But the leader of the good guys— my protagonist—is a divided person, a person of uncertain identity, a self-deceiver who cannot be him- or herself because he or she does not know him- or herself. A series of shocks forces the protagonist, in each case, to be himself or perish in more than the physical sense. Indeed, he (or she in the case of Antigone) may decide to perish in the physical sense. That is what "deciding to die" comes to mean. "Deciding to live" is deciding to live *on,* when letting oneself die would be the easy way out.

I didn't plan any of this—even for one play, let alone a series of plays. It was something I was impelled, *com*pelled, to write as part of my own struggle to live—and to accept the idea of one day not living. As to "understanding" it, the act of writing the plays gave the best help in that regard, and my understanding, such as it is, can better be handed along to others in the words of the plays than in explanations thought up later for essays like this one.

Still, I cannot resist telling the reader of my joy in finding, after I had written the plays, that the experience I had tried to embody therein had been described very circumstantially before I came along in the works of a writer I revere, Martin Buber. In Buber's terms what I had been trying to describe was Decision and Return. Defining sin as decisionlessness (indecision, indecisiveness), Buber speaks of Jewish religion as the religion of decision, as against Indian religion which is that of insight. Under certain circumstances, the will to decide awakens, primal forces break through, the divided person becomes one again, becomes himself, and with his whole, newly recovered self, decides. Such is his Return.

Which is the story I have tried to tell at least four times. Buber describes,further, how we all live by deceiving ourselves and others:

> By our contradiction, our lie, we foster conflict situations and give them power over us till they enslave us. From here there is no way out but by the crucial realization, "Everything depends on myself," and the crucial decision, "I will straighten myself out." But in order that a man may be capable of this great feat he must find . . . his own self . . . the deeper self of a person living in a relationship to the world.

I have said that, in my plays, I start from social situations and generally from war—the extreme social situation par excellence. The passage just quoted from Buber indicates how we get back again *from* the individual and his inner plight *to* the social situation and its challenge. The "deeper self," seen this way, is not found by introspection but in human relations, by encounter, through enmity and through brotherhood.

George Moore, in his book *The Brook Kerith*, has presented the classic portrait of a mystical, introspective, "Indian," Buddhistic Jesus. For this Jesus, the militancy of the whip in the Temple was a temporary aberration rooted in a veritable megalomania of activism. He finds himself by withdrawal from the world.

Buber says Jesus was "a Jew to the core," and this would mean that "corporeal reality is divine," and religiousness is "doing in this world." In my play, written without benefit of Buber, I made "Galilee" something of a symbol of withdrawal from society and struggle, the place where my Jesus "finds himself" being Jerusalem, heart of the Holy Land, as to which there could be just one aim for any Jew: to liberate it.

As to whether the events of my story are history or legend, these are matters to deal with in works of historical scholarship, not in novels, poems, and plays. My play is not more fictitious than the New Testament, but that admittedly is saying little. My emphasis is elsewhere. Repudiating the god-man, and the superman, I am left with—no, I choose—a Jesus who is Everyman. A nonentity? A mediocrity? This is a Jesus who *could* prove a nonentity, a mediocrity. Believing that one might be the Messiah when in fact one isn't is no sign of unusual insight. The drama lies precisely in the chance of total fiasco. Have you not felt it, reader, in *your* life? The image of the Messiah is this Jesus's Walter Mitty fantasy. And which of us males was not a Messiah to his mother? Losing that fantasy *without at the same time losing all hope* becomes one's task in life.

"I only want to be a genuine person," we all repeat ad nauseam. Buber completes the phrase thus: ". . . a genuine person *whose transformation helps toward the transformation of the world."*

The Jesus I have presented is not only not god or superman. I don't even mean him to have the best of the argument with Pilate. I don't intend his answers to Pilate's defense of imperialism to be satisfactory. This is not one of those stage debates in which one person is always right, the other wrong. Dilemmas are involved, predicaments, and questions that I myself am far from thinking I know the answers to. Still, Pilate, too, has his vulnerabilities. All is not as he has described it in the Roman Empire. He is covering up not only the blunders but the crimes. Because Roman rule brings many material benefits he is asking us to overlook, as he does, that what came first was always the establishing of domination, of enslavement.

In what sense does the Jesus I present offer a transformation of the world? On the surface, it would seem that he will be a less transforming force now at his crucifixion than he was formerly as a saintly Quietist preparing the world for ways of peace. And this to be sure is the truth for those who can find only a pacifist in Jesus. They have a case. His nonpacifism has as its aim the liberation of Jerusalem, and Jerusalem was not liberated; not long afterwards it would be removed from the map.

At this one point, perhaps, my viewpoint might be called religious, its truth, if any, being in a sense transcendant. Let me try to explain. At his death Jesus *failed* to transform the world. Pilate held the world in place. Yet had Jesus refused to die he would have stifled growth in the many folk who knew of him. Pilate saw this, and speaks of this stifling in political terms: A repentant Jesus would have rendered followers and admirers politically docile. Politics was only part of it, though. These people would have been discouraged not merely as rebels against Rome but as human beings trying to keep living. And right there is the universality that successfully or not I have assayed in a Jesus stripped of the official and ritualistic glory. For me that glory is unreal. But a real glory is in the story somewhere. I hope I have been able to find it and pass it on like a torch.

All four plays—and this is what makes them political theatre—deal with a power structure. All four dramatize an individual's struggle with it. Of the four protagonists, Jesus (Yeshu) is the only one who does not belong to the ruling caste: They are trying to "coopt" him. The drama I found in the other three protagonists was that of a child of what we now call the Establishment who turns against his own when he discovers their (as well as his) nature. Galileo is the fair-haired boy, the spoiled darling of powers both temporal and spiritual, and all he wants is acceptance. He owes his awakening to the enemy. Had they been otherwise, he would have remained—politically, socially speaking—happily conservative and conformist to the end.

Still, to discover them was, finally, to discover himself. For to learn, so late, that they were enemies—that their interests conflicted with his, and that they knew it—was to learn how naive he had been: The man of intelligence had been stupid. There was drama in this, I thought, and I realize now that the self-deception of all four of these protagonists is that of very great naivete. This is clearest in the case of Antigone who is "permitted" to be naive because she is (a) female and (b) adolescent. Peleus (in *A Time to Die*) is male and old but just as naive, having led a sheltered life governed by the "old" (pristine) values. Yeshu is naive is misjudging every element of the power struggle with Rome. Most naive of all is Galileo, the most brilliant, who cannot believe that truth might be unacceptable—for reasons, a central reason, dramatically, being that they could not accept him, the truth-bearer. They could not let him replace the pope as God's press secretary. Nor did his personal qualities help. While he wished them to take his arrogance for charm, they exercised their right, at times, to take his charm for arrogance.

I hope my plays are not didactic, but, if something *is* being taught, it is perhaps that certain people of whom one might expect more fail to understand power and then compound their problem by making a virtue of their failure to understand. The "didactic" point I might like to get across is: Failure is failure, and stupidity is only the more devastating in a person of intelligence and high purpose. I hope I have presented the encounter of the pope with Galileo so as to put the former in the right, the latter in the wrong, on at least one large issue: not astronomy and scientific theory but history and everyday human affairs. This pope really is concerned with human welfare, a subject Galileo Galilei *has never really concerned himself with at all.*

The problem for Galileo could be stated this way: that he has to apply this vast intelligence to an area it has always turned away from—it has been the means by which he *could* turn away from it. His intelligence has to be turned upon his masters and their mastery—and therefore, at long last, upon himself and his slavery. Then the worm, recognizing itself as worm, can turn. The primal forces can break through, the vanities and half-deliberate blindnesses can be dropped. A decision is preparing itself. "If they are my enemies, I am *their* enemy." And hostile is as hostile does.

Is this play a sermon in favor of cheating? At the end, Galileo is resigned to the task of deceiving the Church authorities and thus acting as the self-appointed agent of their foreign foes. As I see matters, though, he remains a good Catholic and has in no way become a friend of Protestantism, let alone of unbelief. As far as the cheating goes, what was more of a cheat than the recantation itself? Yet it cheated no one: It was a transparent bit of play-acting—Italian opera.

Some students have thought Galileo was indeed a shady character. Arthur Koestler has represented him as such. Brecht assumed all along he was a shady character but changed his mind as to whether this was a bad thing or a good. I think he was just Italian and not really shady at all. But it was appropriate that, at a certain point, he get his hands a little dirty, since for so long he had made a rather false and ignorant virtue of keeping them clean. The recantation was not really a shady deal. But it was symbolically appropriate that it had an air of shadiness about it. Even the great Galileo does not stand outside "original sin."

Then again, the final "sequence" of my play is not about a man learning to cheat, it is about a man learning to live. A partially spurious person, through long travail, has become a genuine person and his transformation, no less than Yeshu's, "helps toward the transformation of the world." Isolated from what earlier he took to be society, he is now for the first time being "socialized," as he enters into a "conspiracy"—that being the enemy's word for any brotherhood.

It could be said that, "objectively" speaking, Yeshu finally joined the Zealots and Galileo finally joined the Protestants. Aid and comfort was certainly afforded; solidarity, affirmed. Still, Yeshu was not a Zealot, and the "brotherhood" that Galileo joined is not that of Luther and Calvin, Henry VIII and Cromwell, but that of Antigone, Peleus, and Yeshu. "Two of whom never even existed!" you exclaim. "Yeshu may not have, either," I concede. Yet there are many names from "real" life that could be cited. The ones I have in mind are too numerous to cite. Nor would my list necessarily say much to you, dear reader. You have your own.

The theatre can present only a few figures. Stories tend to center on one figure. There might seem an "elitism" in this. But the mythic figures mean what we want them to mean. An Antigone need not signify that only princesses matter and that the fate of the chorus matters nothing. It is historical figures whose meaning is fixed or at least restricted. A Napoleon, a Caesar, presented on stage, cannot represent the plain man, only the superman. (Generally, this has been assumed to be true of Jesus too. I am challenging that assumption.) As for the admittedly mythic figures, they are "heroes," yes, but heroism is not the work of supermen only, or perhaps of supermen at all: You don't need courage if you have omnipotence. Nor is the "little man" by definition unheroic. For him, heroism is a distinct possibility and has often proved an achieved fact.

My Yeshu is a little man like you and me. Like him, you and I might prove to be heroes.

Galileo—mine or anyone else's—is no little man. Rather, a giant of the Renaissance. Yet the paradox that my play dramatizes is that this giant proved a veritable pigmy. After which he grew back to at least normal size—by heroic action.

I have been silent about *Are You Now* in this afterword because in many ways it is a different kind of work from the others. Not, however, in what I myself regard as its main thrust. As *Are You Now* unfolds before an audience, they may for a while be muttering, "Muckraker!" or even: "Character assassin!" yet the play culminates in resistance—the resistance of Hellman, Stander, Miller, and Robeson.

"But they are celebrities," some critics have said, "and as such not typical. Pretending to attack Hollywood, you are really sprinkling stardust and hoping to cash in on it."

Now I am not above being willing to mention Gary Cooper if that will make an audience quiet down and listen, but more is involved. Consider, for example, Larry Parks's statement that he became a Committee target *only because* he was a star. Here stardom crops up as the source of the trouble in a dramatic plot that is very "troublesome" indeed. In *Are You Now*, stardom is a key subject—legitimate, interesting, and significant. (My prize for the most significant title in recent theatre goes to *Jesus Christ Superstar*.) Seen as a star, a celebrity—a big man—by the Committee, Larry Parks comes to be seen by my audience as a little man. In this "coming to be seen"—this shrinkage— lies the whole* drama of the Parks episode and, in miniature form, of the Robbins and Kazan episodes later. (Abe Burrows starts little and gets littler.)

As I saw it, the drama of the resisters—Hellman, Stander, Miller, Robeson—had a double twist to it—moved in one direction and then, suddenly, dramatically, in the other. While the resisters are celebrities, they are being stripped of their celebrity. The Committee counted on that other aspect of our American VIP-worship, our resentment of VIPs, our wish to discover that our celebrities are wicked or worthless, our eagerness to shoot them down. This is clearest in HUAC's attempt to make a little nigger out of the very big Paul Robeson by quoting other blacks against him. Then comes the reversal. Robeson was a witness who, having been destroyed as a VIP (celebrity, star, headliner), then, by an act of resistance—on stage, the *enactment* of resistance—recreates himself before our very eyes as a full-size human being.

It is better, after all, to be a real hero than a "hero," honorifically, of the celluloid dream factories. And it is possible. Not, surely because one *is* a "hero" of the dream factories! No! That bigness is illusory, and in the day of need simply not there. The possible heroism is possible for the little person that the big celebrity has become. And for other little persons.

---

*Except for the 1953 letter, which shows Parks reconstructed like Brecht's Galy Gay as a human fighting machine and Frankenstein's monster.

Composed in Palatino by New Republic Books, Washington, D.C.

Printed and bound by The Maple Press, York, Pennsylvania

Designed by Gerard Valerio.